CHRISTIAN DIOR

DESIGNER OF DREAMS

CHRISTIAN DIOR

DESIGNER OF DREAMS

Photographs *by* Nicholas Alan Cope

Thames & Hudson

CONTENTS

CHRISTIAN DIOR,
THE RETROSPECTIVE

1987–2017. It is almost thirty years since the last retrospective of Christian Dior's work was held in Paris, in the Pavillon de Marsan of the Musée des Arts Décoratifs where the Haute Couture creations on display looked out on an eminently Parisian cityscape: the Tuileries Gardens and Rue de Rivoli, a timeless, classical view in terms of design and architecture—terms that were so important to Christian Dior.

1947–1957–2017. Artistic life is nourished by its anniversaries, inspirational moments that recur like the seasons. A museum such as the Musée des Arts Décoratifs, which holds one of France's key fashion collections, plays a part in the writing of fashion history through its presentations of major cultural phenomena, pivotal social and technical developments and the distinguished designers who embody them. When Christian Dior presented the New Look collection in February 1947, couture recovered its prestige and Paris its preeminence. The devastation caused by the war was far-reaching and everything needed to be rebuilt—including women's perception of their bodies, their femininity, their role in the new society. In a short time and with considerable éclat, Dior introduced a fashion language founded on discretion but sprinkled with his famous "coups de Trafalgar"—sensational dresses whose impact always seemed to confirm his intuition for what would make a splash. This new language allowed for endless variations on themes that were dear to him: the flower-woman, the silhouette, femininity, images inspired by his travels and his natural curiosity. In the space of ten years, Christian Dior added a whole new chapter to the heritage of France, establishing a view of Haute Couture that lives on today. His sudden death in Italy on October 24, 1957 plunged France into mourning and sent waves of sadness around the world. But the story of his fashion house continued.

2017. The Musée des Arts Décoratifs is holding a historical retrospective on Christian Dior, enriched by the research and discoveries of the last thirty years. An exhibition space of some 3,000 square meters in the fashion galleries and central nave presents over 400 Haute Couture designs by Dior—and by his successors, who have interpreted and transformed the imagination and aesthetics of a man with an encyclopedic grasp of culture and an eclectic artistic repertoire. Resonating with the fashion items on display, art objects from every period and continent reflect the universal nature of Dior's vision. The couturier's close links with the history and collections of the Musée des Arts Décoratifs and with key players in its life made our museum the ideal place for this exhibition. My warmest thanks go to the two exhibition curators—the great fashion historian and Dior specialist Florence Müller, Avenir Foundation Curator of Textile Art and Curator of Fashion at the Denver Art Museum, and Olivier Gabet, Director of the Musée des Arts Décoratifs—and to all those who contributed to the success of this ambitious project.

In his memoirs, *Dior by Dior*, the couturier spoke frankly of his alter ego, referring to "the two Christian Diors – Christian Dior the public figure, and Christian Dior the private individual," the latter saying of the former, "'I *am* he'. For whether I like the thought or not, my inmost hopes and dreams are expressed in *his* creations." This exhibition is intended as a tribute to Dior, the designer and the man.

PIERRE-ALEXIS DUMAS
PRESIDENT OF LES ARTS DÉCORATIFS

FOREVER DIOR

The House of Dior was founded in 1947, achieving an international acclaim that has never diminished—a sure indication of its excellence. The vision of feminine elegance proposed from the outset by the company founder, Christian Dior, was stronger, bolder, purer, more varied—in short, more inspired than the prevailing fashions of the time. By constantly exploring and developing this extraordinary formula, seventy years after its creation the House of Dior is still reinventing its collections. I never tire of admiring the effects of this miracle of harmony and expression of grace, and strive to ensure their continuation.

In the euphoria of the Liberation, Christian Dior gave a silhouette to elegance and a form to freedom. The New Look was pertinent to its time, with jackets that hugged the waist and highlighted the bust, and knee-length dresses that flattered the wearer's movements—complementary to women's emancipation and a freer kind of femininity.

Dior's inspiration came from myriad sources: he was a collector, a gardener, a friend of the greatest painters and a flower enthusiast with a passion for Versailles, the Surrealists, the cliffs of Granville, the headlands of the Esterel Massif in southern France, colors, perfumes, the bright light of day and the shadows of evening. And above all, he had a passion for the skills of the human hand: the hand that draws on paper, the hand that uses a sewing needle to transfer an idea onto fabric. Dior was the inspiration for the level of excellence achieved by the atelier at 30 Avenue Montaigne—a level that is maintained today. Christian Dior could easily have been just a fashion aesthete; instead, he "constructed" his business and "crafted" his couture house with as much taste and care as each of his dresses. As inheritors of this legacy, our aim is to impart its spirit to our dressmakers, our clients and all those who work to keep this great heritage alive.

Held to celebrate the seventieth anniversary of the founding of the House of Dior, *Christian Dior, Designer of Dreams* is a historic exhibition. The Musée des Arts Décoratifs has never before dedicated its exhibition spaces to such a large-scale retrospective. Over four hundred designs by Christian Dior and by the talented artistic directors who succeeded him are displayed alongside artworks on loan from the world's finest museums, displaying all the charm of the Dior spirit and inspiring dreams of its future.

BERNARD ARNAULT
CHAIRMAN AND CHIEF EXECUTIVE OFFICER OF LVMH /
MOËT HENNESSY-LOUIS VUITTON

CHRISTIAN DIOR and US

Olivier Gabet
Florence Müller

Christian Dior, the visionary creator of the New Look that reshaped the post-war fashion world, saw himself as a reactionary. This accidental revolutionary looked to the future, while nourishing his work with the history of art and of costumes. The films and plays that he liked in his youth clearly reflect the personality of a romantic and nostalgic poet. After World War II shattered everyone's lives and hopes, the couturier understood that people needed to dream of a better world, one of elegance and beauty, metaphors for a happiness recaptured. From an ode to nature sprang the luminous and universal concept of the flower-woman. His vision had an immediate and worldwide impact, an unprecedented event in the history of fashion. After a period of war dominated by masculine energy, the Dior hourglass silhouette was a like a hymn to life and fertility, pointing to an era of reconstruction and a new future. From 1947 to 1957, Christian Dior reinvented the pleasure of being appealing and reestablished the couturier as an arbiter of an elegance that defined fashion, in sync with the spirit of the times. After his sudden and unexpected death in 1957, and even to this day, his successors have all translated into Haute Couture the zeitgeist, the changing moods, the trends and lifestyles of each era. Every new art director took a direction defined by their own personality, while following the well-defined path of the founder. Yves Saint Laurent, Marc Bohan, Gianfranco Ferré, John Galliano, Raf Simons and Maria Grazia Chiuri: each heir to Christian Dior was part of a genealogy of a multifaceted style, perpetuating and reviving—as well as shaking up—a legacy that was created in just ten years; they all rose to this unique challenge, midway between respect for tradition and bold innovation.

Seventy years after the creation of the New Look, the *Christian Dior, Designer of Dreams* exhibition presents an overview of the multiple aspects of a creative process that has become synonymous with Haute Couture everywhere. The spirit that made Dior a universal and quintessential French asset arose from powerful choices, including the idea of clothing as an idealized reconstruction of nature, with fabric as the building material for the architecture of the body, and art and culture as the essential inspiration for design. Over seven decades, the collections, rooted in the legacy of Christian Dior, have embodied a delicate balance between dazzling dramatic effects and the simplicity of timeless, authentic, unwavering Parisian elegance. Fashion, according to Dior, is a harmonious ensemble consisting of basic shapes and essential details, innovation and wisdom, seduction and restraint—and generally speaking, a strong desire to celebrate the beauty of women.

The last exhibition dedicated to Christian Dior was held in the spring of 1987, at the Musée des Arts Décoratifs, in the Pavillon de Marsan that housed the first Musée des Arts de la Mode, which had opened the previous year. For many people, *Homage to Christian Dior 1947–1957* left a profound, long-lasting impression. It was a momentous event that brought together many famous dresses from the most remarkable museum collections around the world and from the wardrobes of women who had supported Dior's magnificent adventure from the very start. They were a testament to the enduring appeal of the women who had known the New Look, including Olivia de Havilland, Patricia López-Willshaw and Francine Weisweiller, not to mention the loans and support from people who remained loyal to the memory of their friend, the couturier: Henri Sauguet, Alexander Liberman, Suzanne Luling, Boris Kochno and Roger Vivier.

Fashion became a de facto part of art history when it entered the museum, at the same time adopting its principles and cycles. In painting, it had become a matter of course to present a solo exhibition of the great masters every twenty years. And so today, in fashion, there was a clear need to organize a major historical retrospective—one

that Christian Dior and the house he founded deserved more than ever, as successive art directors and managers have kept alive and perpetuated its rich and fascinating story. Our knowledge of Christian Dior has grown considerably over the past thirty years, through multiple research efforts, as well as via the patient and delightful hunt for Dior treasures conducted by Dior Héritage, but also by an ambitious and comprehensive campaign to archive and conserve the masterpieces produced since. We should also note that the 1987 exhibition created an awareness of a heritage—which the 2017 show has drawn upon and further developed.

To celebrate seventy years of creative activity, we had to think big: for the first time in the history of the Musée des Arts Décoratifs, an exhibition is occupying the iconic rooms of the nave and the fashion galleries. It is an unprecedented display, covering nearly 3,000 square meters, including hundreds of Haute Couture designs, archives, documents and photographs from the collections of the house of Christian Dior, as well as from the Musée des Arts Décoratifs, the Union Française des Arts du Costume and multiple other institutions such as the Palais Galliera, the Victoria and Albert Museum in London, the Costume Institute at the Metropolitan Museum in New York, the de Young Museum in San Francisco, the Fondation Pierre Bergé–Yves Saint Laurent, the Museum of London and the Musée Christian Dior in Granville. We would like to express our gratitude to all the directors and curators for their support and their keen sense of the exceptional nature of this project. This exhibition is also meant to be a unique artistic and visual experience, presenting a clear and intelligible view to the public of the close dialogue that the house of Christian Dior maintained from the start with art and history, objects and literature. The entire exhibition presents an interplay of Baudelairean connections between fashion and art—a Boldini or a Gainsborough suggests a silhouette by Christian Dior; Egyptian sculptures echo the imaginary world of John Galliano; a canvas by Sterling Ruby reflects the poetry of silk by Raf Simons; and the grace of Romaine Brooks' *Spring* recalls the committed femininity of Maria Grazia Chiuri. This collection of artwork is also unique, consisting of remarkable pieces from private and public collections, notably the Musée des Arts Décoratifs, the Musée du Louvre, the Musée d'Orsay, the Centre Pompidou, the Petit Palais and the Château de Versailles. Here again, our colleagues agreed to loan us first-class works, to suit the circumstances, for which we are grateful. Bringing together so many remarkable works also required an exhibition design that could set off each piece in a relevant way; Nathalie Crinière, after designing a show at Moscow's Pushkin Museum, found that the museum's architecture offered the perfect showcase that such an exhibition requires.

Like every major exhibition, this one was designed to meet multiple goals: to create dreams, teach, learn and share, stir emotions and overwhelm. Thanks to the trust and goodwill of Bernard Arnault, Chairman and CEO of LVMH / Moët Hennessy-Louis Vuitton, and Sidney Toledano, President and CEO of Christian Dior Couture, as well as the generosity of Nadja Swarovski and the Swarovski company, *Christian Dior, Designer of Dreams* will unquestionably be the standard by which exhibitions of this type are measured, and for many years to come, as it explores the traditions, expertise and unending revolutions that came directly from Christian Dior. "Our era is seeking a face just as every previous era has done. The mirror that will reveal it can only be that of truth. Natural and genuine, revolutions occur without having to go look for them. […] In tumultuous times like these, we must maintain these traditions, which represent our luxury and the very best of our civilization."

THE ESSENCE
OF COUTURE

FLORENCE MÜLLER

The beginning of the Dior saga paved the way for the most extraordinary epic in the history of Haute Couture. Bearing the promise of a bright new fashion future, Christian Dior was perceived by the world as a hero of the postwar period, a Frenchman of even greater renown than General de Gaulle. Invited to tour the United States in 1947, he was fervently welcomed by the Americans who saw in him the "product of three centuries of elegance that run back to the reign of Louis XVI."[1]

At a time of rationing and shortages, the fashion world was languishing, no longer sparking desire or inspiring change. Christian Dior brought a breath of fresh air, the hope of a better world where women would be free to make themselves beautiful and attractive. Louis XIV had raised elegance to the rank of a courtly art; good looks, good health and elegance were essential aspects of the power play conducted on a daily basis at Versailles. Fine clothes suggested wealth—whether actual or hoped for—and were a means of social elevation. The *bourgeois gentilhomme* with his frills and flounces, satirized in Molière's eponymous comedy, represented a grotesque but revealing facet of a changing society. In the eighteenth century, the ladder to dignity was shaken by a whirlwind of novelty. To escape the outmoded pomp and ceremony of court life, Marie Antoinette sought refuge at the Petit Trianon, dressed as a shepherdess. The subtle simplicity of printed cotton replaced the heaviness of embroidered silk, heralding the French Revolution's rejection of flaunted distinction. Haute Couture was invented in the mid-nineteenth century in response to the democratization of appearance engendered by the Revolution. The artisan of this movement was Charles Frederick Worth, whose lavish swathes of fabric and sumptuous adornments of silk, braid and embroidery gave a largely reconstructed social order the keys to an appearance of distinction. Fashion design was declared a new art form; feminine allure was envisioned like painting. Bespoke garments, specific to Haute Couture, underscored the client's individuality. Worth added a new dimension to the beautification of women, opposing an "artistic" Haute Couture to a fashion "industry" founded on the possibility of duplication. This creativity, expressed by constantly changing fabrics, seemed heaven-sent to the suppliers of the fashion world, from the textile producers of Lyon to the lace makers of Alençon.

Christian Dior gave a similar boost to French Haute Couture in 1947. His vision of elegance found expression in a profusion of new forms, materials and adornments. He called a successful design "a veritable painting!" Neiman Marcus, who awarded his fashion "Oscar" to Dior, knew that the industry as a whole stood to benefit from the New Look, whose full skirts had hems measuring from nine to over forty yards (from sports to day wear). Before long, the House of Dior alone accounted for over half of France's Haute Couture exports; internationally, it was seen as the quintessence of French taste and style. The rooms of his couture house evoked images of the court of Louis XVI, with a gray and white décor featuring medallion chairs and frames with Fontanges bows alongside evocations of the Second Empire and the Belle Époque. Crinolines, corseted silhouettes and bustles reappeared in appealing new versions that introduced a fresh enchantment to the world.

Previous double page: Dominique Issermann, *Anne Rohart*, July 1985. This photograph was used in 1987 for Dior's fortieth anniversary celebrations.

Richard Avedon, *Renée, Place de la Concorde*, August 1947. *Palais de Glace* ensemble, Fall-Winter 1947 Haute Couture collection (*Corolle* line). Young Parisians take a second look at the model Renée, as she twirls her corolla skirt, the iconic symbol of the New Look.

Irving Penn, ensemble from
the Fall-Winter 1950 Haute
Couture collection (*Oblique* line).

Paradoxically for a man with a taste for the celebration of splendor, Christian Dior was desperately modest and discreet. His loyal friend Pierre Gaxotte, a historian and columnist for *Le Figaro* newspaper, saw him as "a good, calm and generous man of exquisite simplicity who almost never talked about himself, never about his success, never about his fame." According to Gaxotte, Dior once told him, "I should really be grateful for my parents' ruin. It impelled me to act."[2] The cherished son of his mother Madeleine, Christian Dior was raised with a love of art and beauty. With World War I behind them, the young man and his artist friends relished the carefree atmosphere of the Roaring Twenties. Dior took a keen interest in the avant-garde movements of the day, opening a gallery that promoted both up-and-coming and established painters. But the economic crisis of 1929 plunged his family into bankruptcy and left him destitute. His salvation lay in work. His friends, the fashion designers Jean Ozenne and Max Kenna, gave him the keys to earning a living in the fashion world: a thorough knowledge of art history and an ability to draw. Dior followed this advice and, after honing his natural drawing skills, found work as a magazine illustrator. He joined the Robert Piguet couture house, then that of Lucien Lelong and then, from 1938 onward, designed many film and theater costumes. This rich artistic experience constantly inspired his couture collections.

Dior's couture style is cultivated, measured and artistic—classical in spirit but with touches of the boldness of French baroque. The shirtwaists, suits and afternoon dresses of periods of calm were followed by stunning cocktail dresses, heralding what came to be known as the "coup de Trafalgar" effect, with dresses as dangerous and sensational as the battle of the same name. Five or six "coups de Trafalgar" made a splash in each collection. The friction between nature and artifice sparked a synergy: "My prime inspiration is the shape of the female body," said Dior, "for it is the duty of the couturier to adopt the female form as his point of departure and use the materials at his disposal so as to enhance its natural beauty."[3] The concept of the line arose from this exercise in structure. With his announcements concerning the lines that represented each season's new styles, Dior invented a new form of dialogue with the press; a sense of drama was orchestrated by press releases promoting the key "concepts" of the season, strikingly associated with stylized geometric figures such as the *H*, *A*, *Y* and *Zig-Zag* lines. In the dictatorial manner of Charles Frederick Worth, Dior swept away his previous creations with each passing season, remaining unruffled in the face of protest. The *Corolle* and *En 8* lines—and the length of the New Look skirts in particular—met with vehement opposition from women who formed the "Little Below the Knee Club" and marched with placards saying "Dior go home" to protest such extravagance. In a surprising volte-face, Dior's winter collection of 1953 brought the return of the short skirt. The *H* line in winter 1954, nicknamed the "String Bean" line and criticized for flattening the bosom, unleashed a new wave of protests.

But Dior knew how to temper his taste for the sensational with expressions of gentleness and simplicity. The New Look created a "flower-woman" silhouette; the swing of the corolla skirt gave its wearer all the charm of a ballerina. "After woman, flowers are the most lovely things God has given the world," said the couturier, whose view of femininity was inspired by his passion for gardens and rose beds.[4] To achieve grace, Dior liked to get down to basics; he knew when something needed "clipping"—a key to Haute Couture elegance. His spectacular but measured vision brought the House of Dior an instant success that was exceptional in fashion history—but the spotlight that came with each season's new collection eventually took its toll, draining the couturier's imagination. The constant traveling and stress occasioned by his company's meteoric expansion ultimately weakened Dior, who died of a heart attack in Montecatini in October 1957. His backer, Marcel Boussac, and his business director, Jacques Rouët, could not allow the extinction of a fashion house that had become the international symbol of Haute Couture; they resolved to pass on the legacy of "Dior"—a magical name which, in the words of Jean Cocteau, combines "*Dieu* [God] and *Or* [gold]."

Horst P. Horst, *Ciseaux* and *Camaïeu*
dresses, Fall-Winter 1949 Haute Couture
collection (*Milieu du siècle* line).

Dior's heirs stood by his desire to "make women happier and more beautiful." The perpetuation of the Dior spirit—a harmony of elegance, splendor and simplicity— found expression in the ever-changing designs of successive creative directors. Each new appointment represented a radical break, but each respected the fashion house's founding principle. The risky choice of the young Saint Laurent was followed by a rational response with the appointment of Marc Bohan. Then came the flamboyance of Gianfranco Ferré, the sensationalism of fashion punk John Galliano, the "minimalism" of Raf Simons, and the unexpected recent choice of Maria Grazia Chiuri, a woman designer with a commitment to Girl Power.

Marcel Boussac appointed Yves Saint Laurent in 1957 after checking the sales figures for the young man's designs, which represented a quarter of Christian Dior's last collection. Journalist Lucien François imagined how the late Christian Dior would have described the young prodigy to Boussac: "He's a born couturier, just as Mozart was a born musician. He's sensitive to the poetry of fashion. He never imagines dressing Mrs X or Y. He dresses his childhood girl-next-door, the one he saw passing every morning on her way to school. He dresses the cousin he used to play with on vacation, or the sisters he admires. He dresses his mother the way he would have liked her to be dressed when she kissed him goodnight before leaving for the theater. He dresses heroines from fiction and history—*Le Grand Meaulnes*, Mahaut d'Orgel, Mme de Lafayette. Not in the clothes they would probably have worn, but in those they would be wearing if they were to cross our paths today or tomorrow."[5] Saint Laurent, who had been Dior's assistant, created his own interpretation of "an unaffected splendor that refrains from shocking the insensitive, the strong-minded or the vulgar, but finds its audience, [...] expresses itself with noble ease through nymphs and goddesses."[6] The "little-girl" look of his debut line *Trapèze* in 1958 was a triumph.[7] Saint Laurent's arrival marked the end of the corseted silhouette established by his master. Heralding the 1960s, the loose waists of the collection liberated the body; idolized for his talent and youthful charm, Yves Saint Laurent was crowned "the little prince of fashion." True to Dior in terms of structured couture, the high waists of his *Courbe* line in the winter of 1958 were inspired by Venetian painting of the Renaissance and the semicircular arches of architect Andrea Palladio. Saint Laurent did not forget the famous Dior "coup de Trafalgar"; the one that made the biggest splash came with the *Beatnik* collection. Eugenia Sheppard, formidable fashion columnist for the *New York Herald Tribune*, said of the model sporting the famous black leather *Chicago* ensemble, "she looks as if a gold-plated motorcycle were waiting for her at the door." In view of clients' consternation at a collection that seemed better suited to the rockers and boisterous teens of Saint-Germain-des-Prés, the directors were induced to entrust the Dior legacy to someone else.

Richard Avedon, *Dovima with Elephants*, Cirque d'Hiver, August 1955. *Soirée de Paris* dress, Fall-Winter 1955 Haute Couture collection (*Y* line). Avedon considered this one of his most important photographs. It was taken under the glass roof of the Cirque d'Hiver menagerie, with elephants Frida and Marie, trained by Sampion Bouglione, surrounding Dovima, who holds a calm pose despite the danger.

Melvin Sokolsky, dress from the Spring-Summer 1965 Haute Couture collection, published in *Harper's Bazaar*, March 1965. For this famous series, the photographer suspended Dorothy McGowan from cables linked to a crane, a special effect he erased from the print.

Marc Bohan took a completely different approach from that of Saint Laurent, declaring, "I don't like provocation for its own sake, or aggressivity."[8] He described his fashion as "fire under ice," aware that his clients "refused to appear 'over the top' but wanted that extra 'something' without being obvious." For him, the Dior style meant "not getting it wrong."[9] Bohan put his creativity at the service of women's beauty. The *Slim Look*, from his debut Spring-Summer 1961 collection, was as good as its word, literally slimming the figure with bias-cut *Flèche* skirts, loose blouses and slightly dropped waistlines. The collection, a non-nostalgic throwback to the Roaring Twenties, brought a youthful touch that was greeted enthusiastically—notably by Elizabeth Taylor, who ordered twelve dresses. Like Christian Dior, Bohan had come to Haute Couture through his work as a magazine illustrator. After first working for Jean Patou, he became assistant designer to Robert Piguet, whom he considered his master. Bohan put Piguet's advice into practice at Dior: "What counts is the reality of the dress on the model, not on paper."[10] Appointed creative director at Christian Dior London in 1957, he succeeded Yves Saint Laurent in 1960. Marc Bohan was a friend of Austrian conductor Herbert von Karajan and a frequent visitor to Salzburg and Bayreuth who painted for relaxation at weekends in the country. A fan of Strauss, Mahler, Wagner and Mozart, other favorite sources of inspiration included painters Caspar David Friedrich, Egon Schiele and Goya, and German-language authors Robert Musil, Max Herrmann-Neisse and Thomas Mann. The embroideries in Bohan's 1984 summer collection recalled the paintings of Gustav Klimt and the luminosity of the Vienna Secession movement, and until the early 1980s he remained influenced by Gigi, the fictional heroine of French author Colette. Throughout his twenty-nine year stint at Dior, Bohan's collections remained true to his ideals: adapting feminine seduction to the spirit of the times, without excess, and using craftsmanship to create a harmony of fabrics and colors.

Lord Snowdon, Fall-Winter 1985 Haute
Couture collection, model Isabelle Pasco.

Following double page: Patrick Demarchelier,
Natalia Vodianova poses with Dior's
craftspeople in front of 30 Avenue Montaigne,
Fall-Winter 2008 Haute Couture collection.

Juergen Teller. *Ailée* dress, Fall-Winter 1994 Haute Couture collection (*Hiver dans une forêt extraordinaire*). model Kristen McMenamy.

Gianfranco Ferré's appointment as the head of Dior in 1989 was met with outrage by the fashion press. An Italian as creative director of France's most iconic couture house? Despite the indignation, there was considerable rejoicing that thirty years of a "preppy French flavor" on Avenue Montaigne had been succeeded by "Italian *stravaganza*."[11] The Milanese designer sought forgiveness for his "Italianness," reminding his host country that Catherine de Medici had "imported Italian elegance to the court of France." According to Ferré, Dior was "the Watteau of couturiers, full of nuances, delicate and chic."[12] His appointment at Dior represented a watershed in the history of Haute Couture, coinciding as it did with the latter's return to the forefront after a period of reduced visibility, accompanied by a sense of outdatedness that was exacerbated by the rise of ready-to-wear. "Haute Couture has become fashionable," observed the press; "it has become a source of inspiration: a top designer's details, pleats and peculiarities are being 'adapted' by mass-produced ready-to-wear."[13] With his postmodern view of fashion, Gianfranco Ferré was a key contributor to this revival. From a conservative bourgeois background, he symbolized Italian sophistication, inherited from his industrialist father and highly elegant mother. Having trained as an architect, he shared Dior's sense of the seriousness of fashion and the need for well-constructed clothes. He admired Frank Lloyd Wright and Aldo Rossi, and regarded the architects Ernesto Rogers and Franco Albini as his masters. Gianfranco Ferré, who liked to relax and recover his energy in his luxury villa on Lake Maggiore, drew inspiration from the work of Picasso, Miró, Braque, Lucio Fontana, Giorgio Morandi and Fernand Léger (painters collected by his parents). His taste encompassed the art of Gustave Eiffel, the films of Kurosawa, Godard and Fellini and the music of Vivaldi and Bach. For his 1992 summer collection, *Au Vent Léger de l'Été*, he sought inspiration in the gardens of the Impressionists and in classical Greece, creating evening gowns with bodices resembling Corinthian capitals and high-waisted skirts pleated like Doric columns.

Ferré represented the baroque aspect of Dior, with a profusion of sumptuous fabrics, an extravagance of folds, scatterings of flowers on trains, fur trims and voluptuous décolletages. He claimed to share Dior's ability to "use simple forms to great effect."[14] Fashion journalist Suzy Menkes noted his ability to always create "something transparent, fluid, so that as a woman walks, she leaves a sign behind her."[15]

The arrival of John Galliano in 1997 was a bombshell. The Gibraltar-born British designer had the reputation of an eccentric punk creator who defied every fashion convention; he was deemed to have no business working for a prestigious couture house. Punk visionary Malcolm McLaren, manager of the Sex Pistols, saw Galliano's appointment as perfectly logical, however, considering that his "New New Look" introduced a touch of nightclub fashion into a couture house for which Dior had "inadvertently created the first real rock'n'roll look based, ironically, on the Belle Époque dresses of his mother." According to McLaren, Galliano "appropriated and modernized the look, transforming an austere 19th century architectural folly into a sexually primitive Masai warrior."[16] McLaren called this a "mix-and-match" approach, based on an unlikely combination of elements from cultures distant in time and space. The first example of mix-and-match from Galliano was the gown he designed for Lady Diana, for the Met Ball in 1996: a boudoir-inspired silk sheath that dressed/undressed her.

Each collection required a "period of research" during which the couturier took his teams to explore the world, gaining entrance to inaccessible museums, discovering picturesque landscapes, learning about age-old customs. He returned with a wealth of artifacts and Polaroid snapshots that he glued into his "bibles"—a treasure trove of inspiration. Dior's muses—Alla, Victoire, Mitzah Bricard—were succeeded by the Marchesa Luisa Casati, Madame Butterfly, Empress Sissi, Tibetan princesses, Botticelli, Pocahontas… His shows were orchestrated like major Hollywood productions, staged with an enthralling sense of the dramatic. Excitement backstage reached fever pitch, galvanizing the models whom Galliano taught to walk and pose to match the character they represented. The success of the collection's fantasy world hinged on the show.

Galliano's Fall-Winter 1999 collection, *Matrix*, took everyone by surprise. But, beginning with the "Hobo" collection, Galliano's shock version of the Dior "coup de Trafalgar" became a daily occurrence at 30 Avenue Montaigne. At a time when six million people were unemployed in France, the press condemned a collection that appeared to be making light of the homeless issue. Of the forty journalists invited to the post-presentation lunch, only ten turned up. Galliano denounced the hypocrisy of his critics. "Like many people, I was brought up with Charlie Chaplin films," he said. "My inspiration for this collection was the banks of the Seine and all the amazingly dignified people who hang around there, call them hobos if you will."[17] In Bernard Arnault's view, "a breath of genius swept over the room" during the show, which he considered "the most forceful since John's arrival at Dior."[18]

From that time on, Galliano let his imagination run riot, fueled by art, life and the street world around him. "The other day, I saw hundreds of metro tickets and cigarette butts on the ground. It was a work of art! It was the 'modern art moment' of the day!"[19] enthused the designer. His fantasy world was inspired by cinema, history, pop culture and figures such as performance and body artist Leigh Bowery. In response to critics of his taste for excess, he said, "It's better to have no preconceived tastes than to be limited by good or bad taste. I'm afraid of nothing when it comes to style."[20] He had the backing of Christian Dior Couture chief executive Sidney Toledano, who stated, "John Galliano is an artist who mustn't be curbed or checked when it comes to his shows […]; he's also a great professional who's fully involved in the commercial rollout of his catwalk designs."[21] Dior's turnover tripled to reach €523 million in 2003. But the scandal surrounding Galliano's departure from Dior was even greater than that of his arrival.

The extraordinary backdrop to Raf Simons's debut show in July 2011 caused quite a stir: a mansion whose walls were covered with hundreds of thousands of fresh flowers, a symphony of mimosa, orchids, peonies, roses, narcissi… In the gloomy economic climate of the time, this lavish, romantic approach recalled Christian Dior's ode to luxury in 1947. "I grew up surrounded by nature. I'm obsessed by flowers, just as Christian Dior was," said the designer.[22] Raf Simons made his name as an anti-star of fashion, spurning celebrity status and the supremacy of the image: "I don't have a story of the day or a concept to propose. I believe in a modern aesthetic. Women aren't interested in clothes that restrict their movements. [My work] is less theatrical. I don't design styles for fashion magazines or red carpet moments."[23] From his debut collection onward, the curves of the Dior flower-woman morphed into structured silhouettes suggesting the freedom of the body. A woman should be able to "wear an evening gown the way she'd wear a pair of jeans, lightheartedly and without any fuss, as if she were walking on a country lane."[24] The *Bar* jacket was updated to a tuxedo version, heralding the return of the pantsuit. Raf Simons considered himself a designer for real women; he rejected the conceptual approach to fashion, preferring to focus on the essence of Dior: emotion, joy and beauty. A former industrial designer, he let the structure of a garment speak for itself, with his signature color blocks as finishing touches, dotted with fine embroidery. He explored Impressionism (Monet, Seurat, Turner), abstract art and the Mid-Century design movement,[25] and collaborated with American artist Sterling Ruby. He traveled the world for his 2013 Fall-Winter collection, beginning by observing "the Haute Couture clients from different continents and different cultures, and their own personal style."[26] For Spring-Summer 2014, Simons chose a spaceship setting to present a biomorphic collection inspired by the 1950s, 1960s and Pol Chambost ceramics. The delicacy of his couture mirrored the personality of this hypersensitive, self-effacing creator. The announcement

Peter Lindbergh, *Isadora Duncan* dress, Fall-Winter 1997 Haute Couture collection, model Trish Goff.

Following double page: Willy Vanderperre, dress from the Fall-Winter 2013 Haute Couture collection, model Élise Crombez. This dress is a contemporary take on the *Soirée* dress worn by Rita Hayworth at the gala for the film *Gilda* in Paris, 1947.

of his departure in 2016 came as a surprise. According to Simons, Haute Couture is "a mechanism entirely fabricated to trigger the buying impulse […], it's fulfilling when you're on the business and figures side, far less so when you're creative."[27]

The choice of Maria Grazia Chiuri to succeed Raf Simons disconcerted the fashion press once again. Following his appointment of a woman as the head of a fashion house founded by a man, Sidney Toledano explained, "When you listen to a woman talk about a woman, whether it is her body or her lifestyle—her work, the way she travels, what she needs—it is not conceptual. It is practical."[28] Drawing on her own experience as a woman who successfully balances family life and a demanding career, Maria Grazia Chiuri wants "the new Dior woman to be desirable, fragile but self-confident, with a true inner strength."[29] For her debut ready-to-wear and couture collections, she took an unexpected approach, with allusions to all Dior's creative directors from 1947 onward. The Haute Couture collection—a modern fairy tale, staged in an enchanted labyrinthine garden—evoked the passing of the seasons and the flower-woman metaphor. Maria Grazia sees the House of Dior as "a series of stories and designers."[30] In the designer's view, "Dior, Saint Laurent and Gianfranco Ferré took a traditional, truly wearable approach to couture. John Galliano was very theatrical with a penchant for scenography, and Raf Simons contributed a modernist touch. To bring my own identity to Dior, I worked with the atelier on the idea of timelessness, I wanted Dior's initial idea, that couture should be wearable. It's important for me to have a dream, but remain realistic."[31]

Chiuri sees the challenge of Dior's seven decades of history the way "a curator might when they see a large collection of historic paintings."[32] Modernizing the interaction between the origins of a style and a contemporary view of fashion, associating the concepts of evolution and revolution, the Italian designer is rising to the challenge of maintaining the extraordinary legend of the House of Dior.

Above: Michal Pudelka, *Baiser rouge* dress, Spring-Summer 2017 Haute Couture collection, model Ruth Bell.

Left: Paolo Roversi, *Esprit de changement* trouser suit, Spring-Summer 2017 Haute Couture collection, model Jean Campbell. With curved peplums and roomy pleated culottes, this ensemble is a tribute to Christian Dior's New Look.

Following double page:
Peter Lindbergh, *Séduction d'esprit* suit, Spring-Summer 2017 Haute Couture collection, model Mariacarla Boscono.

1. *Time*, March 4, 1957, p. 33.
2. Pierre Gaxotte, of the Académie Française, "Savez-vous qui était vraiment Christian Dior!," *Elle*, 1957.
3. Christian Dior, *Dior by Dior: The Autobiography of Christian Dior*, London, V&A Publishing, 2nd ed., p. 70.
4. *Christian Dior's Little Dictionary of Fashion: A Guide to Dress Sense for Every Woman*, London, Cassell and Company Ltd., 1954, p. 31.
5. Lucien François archives, typewritten text. Dior Héritage.
6. Ibid.
7. Alice Chavane, "Christian Dior: collection Trapèze," *France Soir*, February 1, 1958.
8. Marina Sturdza, "Behind the Dior Empire," *Edmonton Journal*, May 23, 1982.
9. "'La mode, l'élégance, le style Dior' vus par Marc Bohan," Dior press release, January 1974. Dior Héritage.
10. Marina Sturdza, "Behind the Dior Empire," *Edmonton Journal*, May 23, 1982.
11. Barbara Schwarm, "Dior à l'italienne," *Le Point*, July 24, 1989.
12. Dior press release. Dior Héritage.
13. Frédéric Mory, "Prêt-à-porter de luxe," *Madame Figaro*, January 26, 1991, no. 14439.
14. Press conference, May 11, 1989, Hôtel Crillon, transcription. Dior Héritage.
15. Suzy Menkes, "Ferré: Rigueur and Romance," *International Herald Tribune*, July 22 and 23, 1989.
16. Malcolm McLaren, "Dior gets hip!," *Telegraph Magazine*, March 1, 1997.
17. Sandrine Boury-Heyler and Farid Chenoune, "Galliano confidentiel," *Mixt(e)*, no. 14, June–July–August 2001.
18. "Tempête dans un dé à coudre," *Le Figaro*, January 17, 2000.
19. Loïc Prigent, "Diorifique," *Numéro*, August 2000.
20. Anne-Laure Quilleriet, "John Galliano, chic et sauvage," *Le Monde*, March 17, 2004.
21. "Le monde selon Dior," *Les Échos*, supplement to no. 19811, December 8, 2006.
22. "Éclosion d'une robe Dior," *Gala*, no. 1029, January 30, 2013, p. 46.
23. *Paris Match*, July 5, 2012, p. 76.
24. Isabelle Girard "L'art de créer," *Madame Figaro*, July 19, 2012, p. 50.
25. A modernist movement in architecture and design from the 1940s to the 1970s.
26. "Dior, le classique qui innove," *La Libre Belgique*, July 5, 2013, p. 2.
27. "Pourquoi Raf Simons a quitté Dior," *Challenges*, March 13, 2016.
28. Vanessa Friedman, "Maria Grazia Chiuri Now at Dior: How It Happened, What It Means," *New York Times*, July 8, 2016.
29. *Vogue Paris* website: Vogue.com, January 23, 2017.
30. Ibid.
31. Ibid.
32. Stefano Roncato, "Dior's Maria Grazia," *NowFashion*, November 1, 2016.

DIOR IN THE PRESS

JÉRÔME GAUTIER

Christian Dior was one of the four people "who garnered the most press coverage"[1] in the spring of 1947, along with Winston Churchill, Maurice Chevalier and Rita Hayworth. He earned this claim to fame for the spectacular New Look, which fashion magazines discussed, promoted and reproduced non-stop. "Christian Dior's launch has been a resounding success," noted *Vogue Paris.* "His first collection, highly anticipated for months in the fashion world, has confirmed […] the confident and perfect taste of a new couturier."[2] *Femina* agreed: "Christian Dior's first collection was eagerly awaited. It is in a class of its own."[3] "With his first collection he not only shot into fame, but retrieved the general situation by reviving interest in a somewhat uninspired season: a wit dubbed his collection 'the Battle of the Marne of the Couture.' […] His ideas were fresh and put over with great authority, his clothes were beautifully made, essentially Parisian, deeply feminine."[4]

There was a whiff of success already in the air when fashion week started, on February 5, 1947—an important date as it marked the return to a prewar approach, when couturiers showed their models to foreign buyers, to encourage them to return to Paris in large numbers. Two subjects monopolized the conversation: "the cold weather and Dior."[5] The temperature in late January had plummeted to −14°C in Paris. Electricity was rationed, there were coal shortages, people were freezing. But nothing was going to slow down Christian Dior. Lucien Lelong's former designer was feverishly putting the finishing touches to his collection amid the buzz that was spreading throughout the city. Just a few days before the show, his friends, all very well connected to high-society and intellectual circles, dropped a few hints about his collection. "He's making huge pleated skirts like those the Marseilles fishwives wear, long, like this, and with tiny bodices and tiny hats," said Christian Bérard to the fashion editor of the American edition of *Vogue,* Bettina Wilson (later Bettina Ballard), while sketching a few models on a restaurant tablecloth. "You will see, Christian Dior is going to change the whole fashion look when he opens tomorrow."[6] Bérard, Étienne de Beaumont, "Mapie" de Toulouse-Lautrec, Loli Larivière, Marie-Louise Bousquet (*Harper's Bazaar*), Michel de Brunhoff (*Vogue Paris*), Hélène Gordon-Lazareff (*Elle*), Lucien and Cosette Vogel (*Jardin des modes*), Paul Caldaguès and James de Coquet (*Le Figaro*) would keep everyone interested until D-day arrived.

The fashion world arrived in a supercharged mood to Dior's show on February 12, 1947—the last day of fashion week. They would not be disappointed. He sent out his *En 8* silhouettes, with "clean-cut rounded lines, prominent bust, tiny waist, accentuated hips," as described in press releases and repeated word for word in *L'Album du Figaro.*[7] Dior came up with the idea of giving guests at each show a press kit with all the details of the new line, the dominant aspects and the list of models, so that newspapers and magazines would publish his message loud and clear. The famous *Corolle* line then appeared, "swirling lines with very full skirts, close-fitting bodices and nipped-in waists." The mannequins twirled, and ashtrays went flying. "We were given a polished theatrical performance such as we had never seen in a couture house before,"[8] remembered Bettina Wilson, a view confirmed by Hélène Gordon-Lazareff: "I have attended countless shows, but I have never again felt the atmosphere that held sway at Dior that day. Fashion was no longer a show, but a unique moment of creativity. We were overwhelmed and awestruck. There were many artists present, including Jean Cocteau, Marie-Louise Bousquet. I thought to myself: they knew Diaghilev, and this moment that we were experiencing at Dior must be similar to what they had felt when they discovered the Ballets Russes."[9]

Serge Balkin, *Green* dress, Spring-Summer 1947 Haute Couture collection (*En 8* line). Christian Dior was inspired by the sober and elegant style of the eighteenth century for the interior design for his fashion house, which he felt best showcased his collections. Balkin chose it as the setting for this first article about Dior in the American issue of *Vogue,* April 1, 1947 and the British issue of April 1947.

Press coverage had never been so unanimous in its views of a collection. "It's such a New Look!" enthused Carmel Snow, the combative editor-in-chief of the American edition of *Harper's Bazaar*. "The 'New Look' had just been launched, and Paris was once again the world's capital of fashion," remembered Bettina Wilson.[10] Dior and the New Look indeed signaled a renaissance: that of Parisian Haute Couture, which had been looking seriously threadbare in the immediate postwar period. This was the context in which many glossy French magazines awoke from their lethargy. *Femina* returned in May of 1945, while *Jardin des modes* began to appear regularly in 1947, as did *Vogue Paris*. "Thanks to agreements signed with the Ministry of the National Economy, we have significantly increased our print runs for the year 1947,"[11] announced editor-in-chief Michel de Brunhoff, who, to compensate for the break in publication during the war, had launched *L'Album de la mode du Figaro*, renamed *L'Album du Figaro* and published as a quarterly magazine in 1947. And then, on November 21, 1945, came the auspicious launch of *Elle*, with an initial print run of 110,280 copies[12]—a staggering figure for the time. Hélène Gordon-Lazareff came up with the idea for this new type of weekly publication when she was working as a journalist in New York during the war. Her work with *Harper's Bazaar* and the *New York Times* helped define the format and content of her magazine; its target audience was active, modern women, for whom she wanted to make fashion accessible. *"For [Hélène Gordon-Lazareff], women have a single superior vocation: to seduce,"* recalled Françoise Giroud, who was editor-in-chief from 1945 to 1953. "She's a missionary for seduction. Her cause is Dior."[13] She and *Elle* were passionate about the New Look and about promoting Christian Dior; indeed, the magazine was the first to put one of his designs on the cover.[14]

Dior was also put on the cover of the special American edition of *Vogue* on the "Paris Spring Collections."[15] The illustration, which represents the *1947* model (a day dress in navy blue wool from the *Corolle* line), was by Dagmar Freuchen. *Vogue* had dispatched the Danish artist, based in New York since 1938, to Paris to capture the models of the season, along with Serge Balkin. Hired by the American magazine in 1941, the Russian photographer was covering the Haute Couture collections for the first time, and he contributed a series for the April issue that was unusual, to say the least. With his Rolleiflex, he took snapshots of the Dior models in broad daylight: in front of the couture house, in the staircase and in the salons. Of the twenty-one total images of Parisian couture, fourteen of them were of Dior's models, illustrating the importance given to him by the magazine. These fourteen images presented a vibrant vision of Haute Couture, a sharp contrast to the stylized studio shots that *Vogue* usually offered its readers. The same was true of *Harper's Bazaar*[16] and *L'Album*

Lila de Nobili, *Maxim's* dress,
Spring-Summer 1947
Haute Couture collection.
Corolle line, published in
Vogue Paris, May–June 1947.

du Figaro,[17] where the models were photographed by Jean Moral and Willy Maywald, respectively, in natural settings under daylight.

Fashion photography was changing. The range of possibilities was expanding, while improvements in high-volume printing, via half-tone engraving, meant that fashion illustration was somewhat sidelined—but illustrators could not yet be discounted. Some were so talented that they could transform a magazine page into a genuine work of art. Magazines therefore regularly employed them to render the most beautiful of the couturiers' creations, particularly those of Christian Dior. As previously mentioned, it was a drawing by Dagmar that was selected for the cover of the American *Vogue*, marking the arrival of the corolla shape. In the May issue, Italian artist Lila de Nobili, who moved to Paris in 1943 and had been working with the magazine for several months, made three watercolors for American readers, showing the Dior models at Les Halles, the flea market and the theater.[18] The British and French editions of *Vogue* published her illustration of the *Maxim's* cocktail dress worn at Maxim's[19] and the *Bar* outfit as depicted by Christian Bérard.[20] This model alone summed up the entire New Look aesthetic: "*Bar* holds the key to the new fashion,"[21] wrote *Harper's Bazaar* alongside a drawing by René Gruau. Bérard and Gruau were two of Christian Dior's friends, who created iconic images of the couturier's neo-romantic style. Dior had been introduced to the former by the composer Henri Sauguet nearly twenty-five years earlier; he met the latter in the mid-1930s, when they were both working for *Le Figaro illustré* and Christian Dior was just starting out in the fashion world.

It was in early 1934, during a stay in Font-Romeu, in the Pyrenees, where he was recovering from tuberculosis, that Christian Dior made his decision to work in fashion. "I wanted [...] to express myself in my own way, and so I started designing dresses."[22]

René Gruau, *Bar* suit, Spring-Summer 1947
Haute Couture collection. *Corolle* line,
published in *Harper's Bazaar*, May 1947.

Clifford Coffin, *Adélaïde* dress,
Spring-Summer 1948 Haute Couture
collection (*Envol* line) published in
British *Vogue*, April 1948, model
Wenda Parkinson (born Rogerson).
The grand staircase of the Opéra
Garnier in Paris was the ideal backdrop
for this photograph, showcasing an
evening ensemble with a full skirt,
inspired by Second Empire crinolines.

Encouraged by his pattern-cutter friends Jean Ozenne (one of Christian Bérard's cousins, whom he had also met through Sauguet) and his companion, Max Kenna, Christian Dior started to learn about illustration. He displayed a natural talent and sold his designs to couture houses like Schiaparelli, Molyneux, Balenciaga and Robert Piguet, as well as to *Le Figaro illustré, Jardin des modes* and *Harper's Bazaar*. He knew the Paris editor for *Bazaar*, Marie-Louise Bousquet, worked with the vibrant Paris correspondent, Louise Macy (known as Louie), and was close to the editor-in-chief, Carmel Snow. At *Jardin des modes*, he was encouraged by Lucien Vogel and his wife, Cosette, the sister of Michel de Brunhoff, editor-in-chief of *Vogue Paris*. Brunhoff did not select Dior's drawings for the pages of *Vogue*, but he did recommend them to Robert Piguet, who hired him as a pattern-cutter in 1938. Dior continued to expand his impressive network.

In 1939, after he had been mobilized then discharged, Christian Dior took refuge in Callian, in the Var, where he returned to his work as an illustrator, working from the south. Piguet offered him a job in his couture house, but Dior hesitated; when he finally returned to Paris to accept the offer, the job had been filled by someone else. His friend Paul Caldaguès, from *Le Figaro*, introduced him to Lucien Lelong, who in late 1941 hired him as a designer. In 1946 he launched his own couture house and in 1947 achieved worldwide fame. He was forty-two years old. "The youngest of our great couturiers"[23] was certainly no longer a beginner, and his experience as a pattern-maker and designer would prove to be highly beneficial: the newcomer was no novice. His talent and kindness would do the rest. The press would sing his praises for a full ten years. From 1947 to 1957, from the first to the final collection, the "Dior bombshells" set the tone.

A look back over those years at the glossy magazines reveals the overwhelming presence of Christian Dior. His creative power illuminates some of the most iconic images of this golden age of couture—the "Dior" age—with Paris, back on her feet again, forming a realistic yet utterly magical backdrop. While it is impossible to compile an exhaustive list, a few outfits deserve special mention: *Embuscade*, worn by Dovima and photographed atop the Eiffel Tower by Richard Avedon;[24] *Adélaïde*, with Wenda Parkinson on the main staircase of the Garnier Opera, captured by Clifford Coffin;[25] and Dovima once again, hiding under the large hat of the *Raout* model, in a bistro, shot by Henry Clarke.[26] These are eloquently elegant images—what Roland Barthes called "fashion's *bon ton*, which forbids it to offer anything aesthetically or morally displeasing."[27] Christian Dior's sudden death in 1957 was a turning point. This could have marked the end of Dior, but the couturier, a shrewd businessman, had chosen his heirs: Yves Saint Laurent and Marc Bohan for Haute Couture, and Frédéric Castet for Haute

Fourrure (fashion furs). In a world that was becoming increasingly fast-paced, Haute Couture was losing ground as ready-to-wear forged ahead; times were changing in fashion and in how it was represented. A few ambitious newcomers were overturning convention and inventing new types of images, subtly combining realism and fiction. "I yielded to the obligation to show clothes" said William Klein. "After that requirement, I could do just about whatever I wanted with the rest: décor, poses, settings."[28] His work with his models and poses imbued the photographs with unusual power. It resulted in Dorothy McGowan goofing around with her arms in the air opposite Klein;[29] Nicole de Lamargé in the "Éloge de la folie" series with Guy Bourdin;[30] a revealing Sylvia Kristel with Helmut Newton.[31] While the photographs were strong, presenting the Dior designs in a new light, the image of one of the prestigious names in the French luxury world had dulled somewhat, and in 1989, the Italian designer Gianfranco Ferré was hired to breathe new life into it. Ferré, who had a degree in architecture, reinvigorated the Dior cut, which was then celebrated by Steven Meisel, Mario Testino, Mario Sorrenti and David Sims. The new stars in fashion photography had studied their history and its references, the better to transgress and redefine them. Through their choices of models, hair and makeup, styling and staging, each one produced striking images imbued with a certain degree of tension: Farrah Summerford in the New York subway photographed by Meisel, and Phoebe O'Brien looking entirely natural by Testino. It was direct, efficient, modern and resolute.

In October 1994, John Galliano presented his own collection, and its delightfully New Look forms represented a clean break with the grunge aesthetic then in vogue.[32] "This was my vision of Monsieur Dior," he acknowledged. "At this time, of course,

Above: William Klein, *Moderato Cantabile* dress, Fall-Winter 1960 Haute Couture collection (*Souplesse, légèreté, vie* line), published in the American edition of *Vogue*, September 15, 1960, models Dorothy McGowan and Little Bara.

Following double page, left: Guy Bourdin, dress from the Spring-Summer 1966 Haute Couture collection, published in *Vogue Paris*, March–April 1966, model Nicole de Lamargé. Right: Helmut Newton, fur from the Fall-Winter 1976 collection, published in *Vogue Paris*, November 1976, model Sylvia Kristel.

Previous double page, left: Craig
McDean, Spring-Summer 2003
Ready-to-Wear collection, published
in *Vogue Paris*, March 2003, models
Frankie Rayder and Diana Dondoe.
Right: Brigitte Lacombe, *Sidera* dress,
Spring-Summer 2017 Haute Couture
collection, model Ruth Bell.

Opposite: Steven Meisel, *Helitre* dress,
Spring-Summer 1995 Haute Couture
collection (*Extrême...*), model Farrah
Summerford, published in *Vogue Italia*,
Haute Couture special issue, March 1995.

no one, starting with myself, had any idea how the future would play out."[33] The rest is history: Galliano brought the magic back to Dior. There were his designs and the images of his designs; those seen in magazines and in advertising campaigns. This fashion rabble-rouser was part of a new class of all-powerful designers, called "artistic directors," who controlled everything, from the design of the collections to displays in stores, along with the development of the advertising campaigns. From the start, the English designer worked with a compatriot, the photographer Nick Knight. Together, they redefined Dior's image as romantic and eccentric, whimsical and magical, incandescent and scandalous: this was "porno-chic," which would have a long-lasting impact. Galliano also worked with his favorite photographers for magazine shoots.[34] The designer, a chameleon whose spectacular catwalk bows were always eagerly awaited, posed in front of Peter Lindbergh and Paolo Roversi. Galliano fully embodied the superstar designer, a path paved for him by Dior. By posing on the cover of *Paris Match*[35] and *Time*,[36] answering interviews and giving advice to magazine readers, "Monsieur Dior" had a savvy grasp of the use of media in his era, and was able to shift his image from that of a couturier to one of a public figure.

The arrival of a new artistic director required an official portrait. When Raf Simons joined Dior in 2012, he naturally asked an old friend, Willy Vanderperre, to take his photo. He also hired him for his ready-to-wear campaigns. After the Galliano years, Simons clearly wanted to create a new Dior woman, symbolized by Vanderperre's images. "His photographs are steeped in a nostalgia of childhood, of memories,"[37] said Raf Simons. The Belgian photographer, a graduate of the Antwerp fine-arts school, drew inspiration from the Flemish masters to produce sensitive and somber portraits of young floral-bedecked girls, the ultimate metaphor for the New Look.

The Dior saga has been in the hands of a woman, Maria Grazia Chiuri, since 2016. When she arrived, she started exploring the Dior archives, "like an exhibition curator,"[38] not only looking into the legacy of Christian Dior, but also that of his successors; indeed, she adopted some of their identifying elements for her inaugural collection (Spring-Summer 2017 ready-to-wear). For her first Haute Couture collection, however (Spring-Summer 2017), the Italian designer chose to focus on the Christian Dior decade, particularly the couturier's extravagant, sumptuous evening gowns, which graced a number of memorable balls. Maria Grazia Chiuri revived *Junon* (Fall-Winter 1949), one of Christian Dior's most iconic gowns, photographed by Richard Avedon alongside the *Vénus* dress at the restaurant Le Pré Catelan one August evening in 1949. Today, looking at this famous image from *Harper's Bazaar*,[39] the two Dior creations captured by Avedon appear to be timeless, proof positive that this level of fashion photography far transcends any mere fashion shoot.

1. *Elle*, July 8, 1947, pp. 4–5.
2. *Vogue Paris*, March–April 1947, p. 54.
3. *Femina*, April 1947, p. 80.
4. *Vogue* (British edition), April 1947, p. 47.
5. *Vogue* (American edition), April 1, 1947, p. 135.
6. Bettina Ballard, *In My Fashion*, New York, David McKay Company, Inc., 1960, p. 236.
7. *Album du Figaro*, April 1947, last-hour supplement, p. 1.
8. Bettina Ballard, *In My Fashion*, op. cit., p. 237.
9. Denise Dubois-Jallais, *La Tzarine, Hélène Lazareff et l'aventure de "Elle,"* Paris, Robert Laffont, 1984, pp. 124–125.
10. Bettina Ballard, *In My Fashion*, op. cit., p. 336.
11. *Vogue Paris*, January–February 1947, p. 75.
12. *Elle*, November 14, 1955, p. 33.
13. *Elle, nos cinquante premières années*, Paris, Filipacchi, 1995.
14. *Elle*, March 18, 1947.
15. *Vogue* (American edition), April 1, 1947, cover.
16. *Harper's Bazaar US*, April 1947, pp. 188–189.
17. *L'Album du Figaro*, April 1947, p. 79.
18. *Vogue* (American edition), May 1947, pp. 152–153.
19. *Vogue* (British edition), April 1947, p. 46; *Vogue Paris*, May–June 1947, p. 90.
20. *Vogue* (British edition), April 1947, p. 50; *Vogue Paris*, May–June 1947, p. 96.
21. *Harper's Bazaar*, May 1947, p. 130.
22. *Elle*, September 14, 1948, p. 9.
23. *Femina*, April 1947, p. 76.
24. *Harper's Bazaar US*, September 1950, p. 197.
25. *Vogue* (English edition), April 1948, p. 56.
26. *Vogue* (American edition), April 1, 1956, p. 87.
27. Roland Barthes, *The Fashion System*, Berkeley, University of California Press, 1990, p. 261.
28. William Klein, *Mode In & Out*, Paris, Éditions du Seuil, 1994, p. 7.
29. *Vogue* (American edition), September 15, 1960, p. 150.
30. *Vogue Paris*, March 1966, p. 181.
31. Ibid., p. 126.
32. *Pin up* collection, Spring-Summer 1995.
33. *Vogue Paris*, May 2005, p. 221.
34. A number of series, including "État de grâce" with Nick Knight for *Vogue Paris* (December 2006– January 2007), "C'est magique!" with Craig McDean for *Vogue Paris* (March 2003) and "Celebration" with Solve Sundsbo for *L'Officiel* (February 2003).
35. *Paris Match*, August 8, 1953.
36. *Time*, March 4, 1957.
37. *System*, Spring-Summer 2014, p. 71.
38. *Vogue Paris*, February 2017, p. 163.
39. *Harper's Bazaar US*, October 1949, p. 133.

CHRISTIAN DIOR: HIS MUSÉE IMAGINAIRE

Olivier Gabet

"HE KNEW SO MUCH. HE'D VISITED SO MANY MUSEUMS!"

The place of Christian Dior within the museum world—and within that of art history itself—seems self-evident today. Various aspects of his multifaceted identity emerge from his autobiographical writings—among which his book *Dior by Dior* comes across as particularly sincere—and from texts by authors and biographers with access to the relevant archives: Dior the couturier; the inspired gallery owner; the brilliant writer and lecturer who captivated his audience at the Sorbonne;[1] the postwar fashion visionary; the lover of ornament; the discreet player on the dazzling, exuberant stage of Parisian café society. *Dior by Dior* seems to offer a relatively true reflection of his solid personal culture, which combined the contemporary taste and sensibility of his milieu with evocative references to painters or architects.

Christian Dior was a child of his times, with a traditional upbringing and a more adventurous sense of curiosity, the former providing a solid foundation for the latter. As a young man, he attended the fashionable events in 1920s Paris where modern art was bubbling to the surface, but he probably gleaned the major part of his visual and material culture from museums. The stylistic references in his work as a couturier were often painterly, with frequent allusions to Paul Helleu or Giovanni Boldini to describe the impression made by a dress or a silhouette. Christian Dior was a man of taste who had read, seen and studied; he was also a frequent museum visitor, as confirmed by his lifelong friend and collaborator Suzanne Luling. In one of her interviews with Stanley Garfinkel, conducted between 1983 and 1984 for the documentary *Completely Dior* (1987), this important, observant witness evokes Dior's sources of inspiration, referring to his interest in the ornamental and decorative resources of Persian carpets: "He asked me to find him some documentation. I remember some beautiful books with illustrations of carpets from all over the world on display in museums. I used to play a game with him. I'd put my hand on a photo and ask him, 'Where's this carpet?' and he'd answer, 'It's in Vienna' or 'That carpet's in such and such a museum, in London.' He knew so much. He'd visited so many museums!"[2] This game of "what goes where" necessarily included the Museum für Angewandte Kunst in Vienna and the Victoria and Albert Museum in London—both of which have large collections of carpets, like their Parisian alter ego the Musée des Arts Décoratifs, which often exhibited its Islamic carpets during that period.

Dior's work took him to many countries where he discovered new museums. During his trips to the United States, his museum visits included the Museum of Fine Arts in Boston and the Art Institute of Chicago, where he was deeply moved by the remarkable collection of Impressionist paintings and "sad to see them exiled […] from the land where they were painted."[3] A Parisian by adoption, he was probably a regular visitor to the French capital's museums, which were organized slightly differently in those days. The Musée du Louvre was his undisputed favorite, and he knew its collections by heart. With his love of painting, the Musée du Jeu de Paume, which contained masterpieces by Manet, Degas, Monet and Renoir, key figures in Dior's artistic pantheon, must also have been a favorite destination for his Baudelairean strolls through the capital.[4]

The footsteps of this "pedestrian of Paris" must also have taken him to the Musée des Arts Décoratifs, at the other end of the Tuileries near the Louvre palace. This museum, set up in 1905 in the Louvre's Pavillon de Marsan and the adjoining buildings,

The Musée des Arts Décoratifs in the 1930s.

displays impressive collections of furniture, art objects, textiles and costumes, in accordance with the mission entrusted to it by the manufacturers, artists, designers, collectors and art lovers who founded it in 1864: to support the French design and creative industries by showing their finest technical and artistic achievements and to uphold the ideal of "beauty in usefulness." Many of its exhibitions must have appealed to Christian Dior—as a promising young designer, and later as a prominent public figure—though he tended to relativize the significance of such influences: "An exhibition or a museum are important sources of inspiration, chiefly with regard to details."[5] But those details are highly revealing. Dior must have loved the Musée des Arts Décoratifs, judging by his discerning descriptions of the décor of his childhood home in Granville with its penchant for Japonisme, and of his subsequent Parisian homes and the architectural design of 30 Avenue Montaigne. With its non-profit status, the Musée des Arts Décoratifs had closer connections to Parisian high society than most national museums: its board members included both senior officials and representatives of the social elite where Dior the gallery-owner found his clients and Dior the couturier his admirers. Dior's mysterious muse Mitzah Bricard, for example, was the wife of Hubert Bricard, a relative of Gaston Bricard, the leader of the locksmith industry and an influential member of the museum board throughout the 1940s and 1950s. Members of the families who owned the Paris luxury industries—Louis Boucheron, Georges Fouquet, Jacques Guerlain and Tony Bouilhet—sat on the board alongside acquaintances of Dior—Baron Gourgaud, Baron Robert de Rothschild, Baron Fould-Springer, Viscount Charles de Noailles and Arturo López-Willshaw—who partied with him at the same dazzling events of the 1940s and 1950s, and designers whose tastes he admired, such as Jean-Charles Moreux and Serge Roche, the then president of the Syndicat des négociants en objets d'art, tableaux et curiosités (Association of Dealers in Art Objects, Paintings and Curios); many of these names featured in the yearbook of the Union Centrale des Arts Décoratifs in 1957, the year of the couturier's death. Other acquaintances of Dior joined over the years, including his friend the architect Emilio Terry, an advocate of the "Louis XVII style" of neoclassicism tinged with surrealist fantasy. Christian Dior exhibited a number of his drawings and models at the Galerie Bonjean in 1933, including the double-spiral house that Salvador Dalí featured in his painted portrait of Terry the following year. This now famous model, presented at the MoMA in New York in the 1936 exhibition "Fantastic Art, Dada and Surrealism," was donated by Terry to the Musée des Arts Décoratifs in 1965.[6]

Display case from the exhibition *Splendeur de l'art turc* at the Musée des Arts Décoratifs, 1953.

There are a surprising number of connections between works in the collections of the Musée des Arts Décoratifs and their presence—actual or alluded to—in Dior's home or professional world. The historical exhibition *Splendeur de l'art turc* (Splendor of Turkish Art) at the Musée des Arts Décoratifs in 1953 cannot have inspired the fabulous embroideries in the style of Iznik ceramics on the *Palmyre* evening gown of 1952, but it nonetheless presented the finest masterpieces created for the court of the sultans: carpets such as those mentioned by Suzanne Luling, and objects known in France since the mid-nineteenth century through the museum's collections and the publications of Adalbert de Beaumont—an ancestor of Comte Étienne de Beaumont, who hosted some magnificent costume balls at his Paris mansion, the Hôtel de Masseran, attended by Christian Dior. With its vast array of ornamental motifs, this 1953 exhibition was a source of inspiration for the couturier; surviving photographs of the exhibition layout afford a glimpse of the large display of textiles and costumes, caftans in particular, with some striking resemblances to floral motifs used by Dior at the time. Such parallels and similarities can also be found in the museum's collections of Haute Époque, eighteenth- and nineteenth-century objects; many of the decorative details in Dior's Paris interiors or in the Château de La Colle Noire, often featured in the more intimate photographs, have their equivalents in the museum's permanent galleries of the 1930s to the 1950s. They include items such as the *tisanière*, typical of Paris porcelain, that features in a portrait taken in his apartment on Rue Royale; neoclassical sphinxes and baroque ivory vanitas; antique ceramics and medieval tapestries; wallpapers from the romantic period decorated with classical scenes or with the more exotic panoramas that Dior seems to have particularly loved (the most famous examples of which are held in the museum); Louis XVI and Charles X furniture and pieces from the Second Empire, interest in which was revived by the museum's exhibitions of the 1930s; obelisks and architectural-themed objects that gave Dior inspiration for décors and accessories, and for his lipstick and perfume packaging. Dior is known to have had a number of "shadow portraits" or "silhouettes" made, so one can easily imagine his admiration for the coffee service pieces from the Meissen porcelain factory, exhibited in the museum at the time; dating from the 1780s and 1790s, they are decorated with silhouette profiles of members of Europe's reigning families. And the swing motif designed by Jean-Baptiste Huet for the Jouy factory (the original grisaille and graphite drawing for which, dated 1783–1789, is held in the Musée des Arts Décoratifs) appeared, in toile de Jouy, in the first tiny Dior boutique on Avenue Montaigne in 1947.[7] During the same period, the Musée des Arts Décoratifs was also the only one to display the subtlest, most emblematic Art Nouveau designs, although the style was almost completely outdated or, at worst, scorned by art historians. A photograph taken in Dior's house on Rue Royale shows him sitting near a table that holds a 1900-style female figurine, probably made by Georges de Feure, two similar examples of which are held in the museum. Dior shared this unusual fin-de-siècle taste with his friend Salvador Dalí—the first to pay tribute to Hector Guimard, who had fallen into oblivion at the time, with a famous article published in *Minotaure* magazine in 1933, "On the Terrifying and Edible Beauty of Art Nouveau Architecture."[8] The famous 1933 Surrealist exhibition organized by Christian Dior and Pierre Colle in their gallery featured a chair by Guimard, deliberately placed at a lopsided angle near Dalí's *Retrospective Bust of a Woman*. Years later, Dalí remembered the taste he had shared with Dior for outmoded Art Nouveau: "In order to defeat primitive objects, I launched the vogue for hyper-civilized objects of the '1900 style' which we used to collect with Dior and which were one day to come back into fashion with the 'New Look.'"[9] This audacious connection between Art Nouveau and the New Look inevitably brings to mind the flower-woman, a kind of femme fatale that closely links those two artistic and historic forms of expression.

The author of *Dior by Dior* defined the eclecticism of his taste as follows: "Good taste was much less important than my own taste, for after all, living in a house which does not suit you is like wearing someone else's clothes."[10] This statement underscores his spontaneous enthusiasm for areas of art history that were held to be of lesser importance or were contrary to accepted tastes: "A Matisse drawing was to hang side by side with a Gothic tapestry, a Renaissance bronze, a Jacob ornament."[11] This seems to echo the museum's approach to its collections and exhibitions on the art of furniture in the Middle Ages and the modern period, especially the eighteenth century, with the 1951 exhibition *Chefs-d'œuvre des grands ébénistes de Georges Jacob à Giroux* (Masterpieces by the Great Cabinetmakers from Georges Jacob to Giroux), but also, more surprisingly, with those devoted to art and archaeology in South America—*Les Arts anciens de l'Amérique* (The Ancient Arts of America) in 1928, *Chefs-d'œuvre du musée de l'Or de Bogota* (Masterpieces from the Gold Museum in Bogota), *Art ancien du Pérou* (Ancient Art of Peru) and *Costumes des Indiens du Guatemala* (Costumes of the Indians of Guatemala) in 1956, the year Dior's book was published.

Amid all the excitement of Parisian cultural life, some of the exhibitions at the Musée des Arts Décoratifs must have appealed more than others to Christian Dior. With his love of the Belle Époque, which he associated with his childhood and youth—"the picture of a time full of happiness, exuberance and peace, in which everything was directed towards the art of living"[12]—he must have relished the exhibition *Décor de la vie sous la IIIᵉ République* (Interior Design during the Third Republic) at the Pavillon de Marsan in 1933. The objects on display would have reminded him of his early years in Granville, the atmosphere of his family home, the *horror vacui* of interiors full of ornaments, his father's somewhat imposing neo-Renaissance taste and the gentle femininity of the many portraits by Renoir, Manet, Tissot, Degas, Eugène Carrière and his beloved Boldini and Helleu—rather unfashionable in the early 1930s. Room ten in the museum, presenting a bedroom suite by Louis Majorelle, features paintings by Maurice Denis, an artist from Granville, and a whole room behind glass presents creations by the Worth and Doucet fashion houses and hats by the French milliner Caroline Reboux—sources of inspiration for the future couturier, and reminders of his mother, Madeleine Dior.[13]

The museum held many noteworthy exhibitions devoted to successive periods. In 1922, *Décor de la vie sous le Second Empire* (Interior Design during the Second Empire) showcased a decorative style that Dior adapted to his own taste in the following decades; the décor of his house on Boulevard Jules-Sandeau was reminiscent of this prolific exhibition, epitomized by the watercolors of Pierre François Eugène Giraud and Jean-Baptiste Fortuné de Fournier representing the interior design of the homes of Princess Mathilde or Empress Eugénie, with its richly upholstered rooms and conservatory with lush green plants. In 1930, the exhibition *Décor de la vie à l'époque romantique* (Interior Design in the Romantic Period) once more dazzled the contemporaries of Art Deco and the Union des Artistes Modernes with the inspired artistic output of the nineteenth century. Two other exhibitions, following the same thematic principle, must have particularly impressed and touched the young Dior: in 1937, *Décor de la vie en 1900–1925* (Interior Design in 1900–1925) and in 1939, *Ballets russes de Diaghilev, 1909 à 1929* (Diaghilev's Ballets Russes, 1909–1929). These two exhibitions were greatly influenced by Paul Poiret, for whom Dior expressed his admiration in his memoirs with Flaubertian concision: "With the coming of Paul Poiret all this was altered."[14] Dior recognized the revolution in taste and perception brought about by the popularity of the Ballets Russes: "Iribe's new pink supplanted the Pompadour's pink, and lamé, showing strong Oriental influence, dethroned the eighteenth-century brocades."[15] The exhibition on the Ballets Russes in Spring 1939 was an extravaganza featuring several hundred drawings, paintings, objects and documents, and even the stage curtain for the ballet *Parade*, painted by Picasso; so many of Dior's friends were represented at this exhibition—an artistic highlight of the year—that he is certain to have visited it with the greatest attention. The *Décor de la vie en 1900–1925* exhibition was held in 1937 alongside the International Exhibition of Art and Technology in Modern Life, and though the nostalgic theme of the former might seem rather surprising within this context of modernity, it was like an homage to a golden age of French and European decorative arts that was particularly inspiring for Christian Dior; the content of the exhibition closely mirrored the couturier's evocation of this period almost twenty years later in *Dior by Dior*. Pieces in the exhibition included furniture by Paul Iribe, Guy Pierre Fauconnet, Maurice Dufrène and Pierre Chareau, period rooms with mannequins dressed in the finest creations by Paul Poiret, Jeanne Lanvin and Madeleine Vionnet, and the portrait of Ida Rubinstein by Léon Bakst, loaned by Lord Moyne.

Brassaï. Christian Dior in his apartment at 10 Rue Royale in Paris, late 1946 to early 1947. Granville, Musée Dior, Catherine Dior collection.

Room from the exhibition le *Décor de la vie en 1900–1925* at the Musée des Arts Décoratifs, 1937. The three evening gowns in this photograph, in the midst of other art objects, show that even in the prewar period, fashion was already well represented in the museum's exhibitions.

Room from the exhibition *Grands ébénistes et menuisiers parisiens du XVIIIᵉ siècle* at the Musée des Arts Décoratifs, 1955.

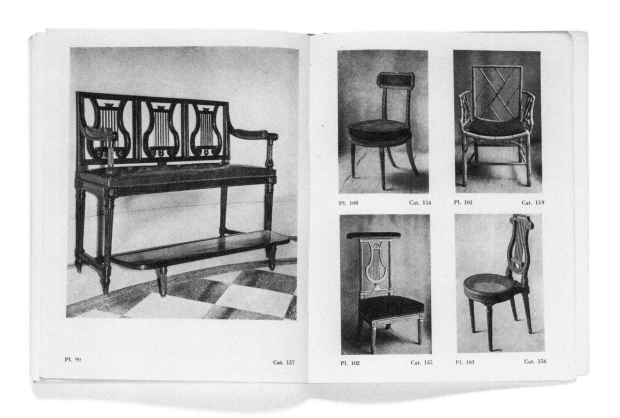

Pl. 99   Cat. 157
Pl. 100   Cat. 154   Pl. 101   Cat. 159
Pl. 102   Cat. 155   Pl. 103   Cat. 156

Catalog for the exhibition *Grands
ébénistes et menuisiers parisiens
du XVIIIe siècle* at the Musée des Arts
Décoratifs, 1955. Christian Dior loaned
the chairs numbered 154, 155 and 159.

EXPOSITION "LES GRANDS ÉBÉNISTES DU 18e SIÈCLE"
_____

Prêté par M. Christian D I O R
7, Bd Jules Sandeau, Paris, 16e

G. JACOB   -   Prie-Dieu   120.000 frs
reprise J.B. SENE - Banquette à 2 dossiers reprise 1.500.000 reprise
X I. LEBAS   -   Fauteuil cabriolet   150.000
G. JACOB   -   Petite chaise   150.000
G. JACOB   -   Fauteuil (simulant un treillage) 200.000
HEURTAUT   -   Boîte de régulateur   2.000.000

X N'a pas donné le bon fauteuil indiqué
          22.XI échange fait

List of objects loaned by Christian Dior for the exhibition
Grands ébénistes et menuisiers parisiens du XVIIIe siècle
at the Musée des Arts Décoratifs, 1955.

Dior's connection with the Musée des Arts Décoratifs was confirmed a few years later in 1955, with a now famous exhibition called *Grands ébénistes et menuisiers parisiens du XVIIIe siècle* (Great Parisian Cabinetmakers and Carpenters of the Eighteenth Century). The event reflected an enduring interest in the decorative art of the reigns of Louis XV and Louis XVI on the part of great collectors, art lovers (including many clients of the House of Dior) and the French art market, which was flourishing in that field at the time. Dior had often contributed to the recognition of this "moment of grace" in French art, particularly the Louis XVI style, so modern in many ways. The couturier had become a worldwide celebrity and an icon of French taste; having amassed a collection of furniture and artifacts worthy of featuring in such an exhibition, he was naturally solicited for loans. Many of the 336 works in the exhibition came from national museums or from the collections of Arturo López-Willshaw, Patino, Niarchos, Fould-Springer, David David-Weill, Fabius frères, Balsan, etc. Christian Dior lent no fewer than six major pieces: a Louis XV veneered grandfather clock case decorated with chased gilt bronze, stamped by Nicolas Heurtaut (no. 134); a gilt wood chair with cross-braced back supports, decorated with scrolls and interlacing (no. 154), a carved wood *voyeuse* chair, painted white, with an openwork lyre-shaped back (no. 155) and an unusual imitation bamboo armchair with a square seat and back, in carved and painted wood (no. 159), all stamped by Georges Jacob; a carved wood daybed with two scroll backrests, stamped by Séné (no. 302); and finally a Transition-period cabriolet armchair stamped by Jean-Baptiste Lebas (no. 177). Except for the last, all the pieces lent by Christian Dior were featured in illustrated plates; as this was not the case for all the objects included in the exhibition catalog, this attention on the part of the museum and the exhibition curators indicates the significance of the loans.

Careful study of the archives reveals a more elective affinity between the couturier and the museum: the press release, annotated in an unknown hand "sent to all the French and foreign press,"[16] explains the originality of a project presenting "furniture pieces […] almost completely unknown to the public [which come] from over fifty private collections, making the exhibition quite exceptional"; the curators spent a year choosing from 5,000 pieces. A more surprising detail is the note clearly displayed at the top of the release and addressed to "Messrs. the Editors-in-Chief and Photographers": "At the press cocktail party to be held at 11:00 on November 30, the exhibition settings will be brought to life by models wearing evening gowns by the House of Dior. They can be photographed within the framework of the exhibition." The exceptional nature of this event is confirmed by a beautifully printed card, also in the archives, with the stamp of the Musée des Arts Décoratifs on the front, and on the back the sentence "The gowns worn to present the exhibition are by Christian Dior." There are several surviving photographs of this rather unusual occasion when a fashion show was held among the works loaned for exhibition in the museum: a rather fierce and determined-looking model wearing the *Soirée brillante* gown from the 1955 Fall-Winter collection lays a gloved hand on the mantel clock that stands on a chest of drawers by Jean-Henri Riesener, near one of the chairs loaned by Christian Dior and a Louis XVI armchair from the Heine collection (no. 148); another, more seductive model seems about to open the light mahogany roll-top desk by David Roentgen, loaned by M. Touzain (no. 273), in front of a gilt wood folding stool (no. 306) from

Marie Antoinette's games room at Fontainebleau, while in another photograph an elegant model wearing the *Soirée fleurie* gown is seated on a sofa *à la turque*, most likely the bed with triple scrollwork backrests made by Jean-Baptiste Tilliard (no. 313); yet another places her right hand on the face of a floor clock decorated with diamond marquetry, stamped by Martin Carlin, and topped by a crowing cock—a quintessentially French scene, all in all.

Christian Dior had stepped out of his role as visitor to become a player in the museum world.

Soirée brillante, Soirée de Noël and *Soirée fleurie* dresses, Fall-Winter 1955 Haute Couture collection (*Y* line), presented at the Musée des Arts Décoratifs during the inauguration of the exhibition *Grands ébénistes et menuisiers parisiens du XVIIIᵉ siècle*, November 30, 1955.

1. On August 3, 1955, Christian Dior gave a lecture-dialogue with Jacqueline Menou, professor of French civilization, to over 4,000 students in the Grand Amphithéâtre of the Sorbonne. It was followed by a fashion show.
2. Suzanne Luling, *Mes années Dior: L'esprit d'une époque*, Paris, Le Cherche Midi, 2016, pp. 207–208.
3. Christian Dior, *Dior by Dior: the Autobiography of Christian Dior*, London, V&A Publishing, 2nd ed., 2007, p. 48.
4. Ibid., p. 4.
5. Ibid., p. 57.
6. Pierre Arizzoli-Clémentel, *Emilio Terry 1890–1969: Architecte et décorateur*, Paris, Gourcuff Gradenigo, 2013, pp. 28–31.
7. As evidenced by a photograph taken the day before the New Look show in February 1947.
8. Salvador Dalí, "De la beauté terrifiante et comestible de l'architecture modern'style," *Minotaure*, no. 3–4, pp. 69–76.
9. Salvador Dalí, *Diary of a Genius*, Creation Books, 1998, p. 24.
10. Christian Dior, op. cit., p. 191.
11. Ibid.
12. Ibid., p. 171.
13. Archives of the Musée des Arts Décoratifs.
14. Christian Dior, op. cit., p. 15.
15. Ibid.
16. Archives of the Musée des Arts Décoratifs. Grateful thanks to Éric Pujalet-Plaà for drawing our attention to this valuable find.

CHRISTIAN DIOR'S APARTMENT

PATRICK MAURIÈS

THE FRAGRANCE OF A WOMAN

What can we blame Marcel Proust for? Nothing, obviously—except for having unwillingly given us the adjective "Proustian": the cliché of all hacks, trotted out as needed to describe an interior with intense emotional meaning. Nostalgic, plush, sophisticated, with objects and images, furnished with discreetly bourgeois taste: there is not a single aesthete—from Luchino Visconti to Yves Saint Laurent or Madeleine Castaing—who has not got caught up in the cliché, blurring any sense of unique style.

Was Christian Dior "Proustian?" Probably, as he mentioned it himself when discussing his interiors, his *temps retrouvé*: "At that moment I experienced the famous sensation of *temps retrouvé*," he wrote, when he discovered that the apartment on Boulevard Jules-Sandeau brought him "within fifty yards of Rue Albéric-Magnard, the home of my youth."[1] But once again, this doesn't *tell* us anything, because his interiors were essentially, and substantially, a reflection of himself—even if he could relate, via his own story, his situation in time, to the world of the asthmatic novelist.

Once the young Dior—a fifteen-year-old Dior—left the peaceful, bourgeois atmosphere of his family home, he could indeed have encountered the "gentle, lazy life in the provinces," and, through his friendships, met the aging Proust in the salons of the faubourg Saint-Germain, in the apartment of Madame de Polignac or the Comtesse de Chevigné (Proust died in 1922; Dior was born in 1905).

Instead of this improbable encounter, Dior had the impalpable and far more profound exposure to the silhouettes of women with tightly cinched waists, trembling skirts, proud bearing and intoxicating fragrances that surrounded Proust, and which indelibly marked the imagination of this provincial young man from Granville—so much so that they resurfaced, in a transformed, embellished state, in the line he imposed on the entire world more than fifty years later.

This heady feminine fragrance—be it iris or heliotrope—this scent of an elegant women dressed for a ball, or stepping into a salon, her face hidden by a half-veil, wafts not only over his fashion but over all the places that Christian Dior loved so deeply—from Rue Royale to Boulevard Jules-Sandeau, from the Milly-la-Forêt mill to the Château de La Colle Noire. "What I remember most about the women from my childhood," he wrote, "is the memory of their perfumes, tenacious fragrances—much more than today—which enveloped elevators, long after they had left. Swaddled in fur, Boldini-like gestures, amber necklaces."

AN IMPRESSION

Dior made no secret of his passion for architecture and interior decoration; he claimed it as a leitmotiv in *Dior by Dior*; it was his "first and true vocation," an activity that had "fascinated me ever since I was a child." He wrote that he became a couturier almost by default, describing couture as "ephemeral architecture."

His perception of time came from a seismographic sensitivity to changing styles, not in terms of major historic sequences, but in the tiny shifts which from decade to decade mark the development of taste and changes in the way we view things.

Dior's memory was essentially one of shapes, colors, textures, spaces, furniture and objects. He discussed his own path through his memory of the rooms he lived in, and which in turn fashioned his approach to style. "Temperamentally, I am reactionary,"

Frank Scherschel. Christian Dior in his apartment at 10 Rue Royale in Paris. 1947.

The Dior family apartment at 9 Rue Louis-David in Paris, ca. 1925. The eighteenth-century spirit of this room reveals just how much Christian Dior drew on his childhood memories when he created an interior for his couture house based on a 1910 interpretation of the Louis Seize style.

Christian Dior as an adolescent
in the garden of the Villa Les
Rhumbs in Granville, ca. 1920.

he wrote, but "not to be confused with retrograde." He fully belonged to what the "moderns" of today have decided to call "anti-modern." For Dior, interior decoration was like the two faces of Janus: establishing a future life, the settings in which one is meant to live, the place where one's desires and actions are staged, while simultaneously looking towards the past, one's childhood.

A soft pink roughcast house eroded by brine, alongside gray gravel: Dior's entire world, his dominant colors, came from these ordinary details. Next came the interior of his first Parisian home, on Rue Albéric-Magnard: "It was there that I discovered and was conquered forever by 'Louis Seize-Passy.'" "From 1900 to 1914, decoration à la Louis Seize was all the rage in the 'new' houses in Passy: white woodwork, white enameled furniture, grey hangings, glass doors with square panes and bronze light brackets with small lampshades." This made such a strong impression that Dior wrote about it again in virtually identical terms at the start and end of his memoirs. Harmonies and colors "thought to be 'Pompadour' but which were in fact already 'Vuillard,'" which had been "truly cursed throughout the long period that followed their fleeting triumph," recalled Dior with his characteristic sensitivity.

DÉCORS WITHIN DÉCORS

Other luxurious, secret décors are quietly nestled within the house: those of childhood books that seem to have grown into the griffons and chimera carved on the buffets and sideboards in the family dining room. And subjects from bedside table books appear in two paintings: the view of the opulent great room of the Nautilus, from *Twenty Thousand Leagues Under the Sea*, the mysterious gondola floating deep in the vast ocean. Like a theater stage, it faces the salon, "which has remained the pinnacle of luxury, calm and beauty," muted by heavy wall hangings, draperies and door curtains, upholstered in damask and velvet, filled with a jungle of potted plants and bathed in an intoxicating humidity. Dior later would insist on having flowers delivered twice a week to the apartment on Boulevard Jules-Sandeau, carried by slipper-clad emissaries from the florist Paule Dedeband. He regularly filled his interiors with a "profusion of reassuring kentia palms," which were in fashion at the turn of the century, before being replaced by the prosaic and meandering philodendron in the 1950s.

We could perhaps link the ideal of a well-upholstered, warm and protective cell to a fondness for dark velvet-lined alcoves, where Dior liked to place his sofas (as in his "favorite room" on the Boulevard Jules-Sandeau) as well as, more surprisingly, his beds and even his bathtubs. (Was it coincidence or inspiration that the same style also appears in the apartment in Marnes-la-Coquette that Jean Marais decorated and had photographed at the same time?)

The other childhood world, more real than many aspects of everyday life, was that of Charles Perrault's *Fairy Tales*, illustrated by Gustave Doré and bound in gold and red leather. Dior didn't know it yet, but he shared a fascination for these stories with his future friends Jean Cocteau and Christian Bérard; in 1946 they would inspire the voluptuous, misty atmosphere of Cocteau's *Beauty and the Beast* (the forest came from *Puss in Boots*, the staircase from *Donkeyskin* and the "lunar light" from *Tom Thumb*). This is more than a mere coincidence or a generational effect, because Doré's imagery—a world that is both pleasant and threatening, familiar and unexpected, dark and baroque—is one of the most successful examples ever created of a transcendent world. This suspension of the laws of reality played a key role in Dior's life, reappearing often and in multiple forms.

He tried to give substance to this constellation of signs and omens using all possible means, up to and including consulting clairvoyants (including one "very secret fortune-teller, called the Grandmother") and backing up the predictions of one with a second opinion: "the mere fact that her verdict agreed with that of my own fortune-teller gave me the necessary impetus to act," he noted seriously when he was creating his couture house.

BÉRARD

Dior rediscovered a sense of wonder, a "magic world of passion and nostalgia," in the work of a painter who focused on the ephemeral trappings of the theater world: Christian Bérard. ("His drawings taught one to transform daily life into a magic world of passion and nostalgia. I bought as many of his sketches as I could, and covered the walls of my room with his inspired paintings.") They are both now linked in history via Bérard's many drawings of Dior models, by his sketch of the façade for Avenue Montaigne and his recommendations concerning the boutique's design—for which the painter created just the right tone of disarray, suggesting the use of toile de Jouy, inspired by Watteau's *L'Enseigne de Gersaint*, and the shops of the eighteenth-century *marchand-merciers*. In hindsight, Bérard, who illustrated an era, is often viewed within the narrow scope of this legacy. A calligrapher capturing a snapshot, a virtuoso, a master of the *alla prima* technique, he was ultimately an early victim of his own extraordinary expertise. The second Bérard, the man of the theater and of fashion who flourished in the 1940s, ended up eliminating any trace of those "youthful years," this utopian period for Dior. It was a time when the young artist, a recent graduate of the Académie Ranson, became friends with the man who was not yet a couturier, but who was trying his hand at his "first profession: director of an art gallery."

PICASSO AND AFTER

While Dior was fascinated with architecture and houses before shifting to fashion, he was also drawn to painting, and very nearly made this his field. People often forget that once he had completed his military service, he joined forces with one of his friends, Jacques Bonjean, with the reluctant support of his parents, "to open a little gallery at the end of a rather squalid cul-de-sac off the Rue de la Boétie." This simple and relatively ephemeral gallery had a certain importance in the history of modern art; the discreet but significant role that Dior and Bonjean played—along with Pierre Colle, a former student of Max Jacob who would become an exceptional gallery owner—in the artistic economy of the period.

While the stated ambition of the undertaking was to exhibit "the masters we admired most: Picasso, Braque, Matisse, and Dufy"—in other words, the finest representatives of a modernity that had not totally taken hold—Dior and his friends were also aware of the dangers of blindly adhering to the diktats of a reified modernism, with the "simplified still lifes of the Cubists" or "abstract geometric figures." The ultimate goal of this adventure was to introduce, among the well-known artists, "the painters we knew personally and already held in high esteem: Christian Bérard, Salvador Dalí, Max Jacob, the Berman brothers."

A seminal exhibition held at the Galerie Druet, in 1926, and the participation of the critic Waldemar-George, among others, crystalized this new sensibility under the imperfect term "neo-romantic," best represented—through their diversity but also their contradictions—not only by Bérard, Eugène and Leonid Berman, but also by the somber Pavel Tchelitchew and the meticulous Kristians Tonny. Returning to figurative work, influenced by the hallucinatory visions of De Chirico's Italy, the poignant melancholy of Picasso's pink and blue periods, the memory of seventeenth-century French painting and certain echoes of Surrealism, the neo-romantics offered their own response to the question posed by the continuing radical experimentation that had been ongoing since the turn of the century. Their "anti-modernism"—which could also be termed neo-mannerism—was a step beyond, presented as the revival of a kind of painting that, in their eyes, had sunk into the repetition of a formula that had remained unchanged for a quarter of a century.

It is not hard to see how this aesthetic, which harked back to a certain tradition while incorporating the most current trends in art, could, in its sophistication and its approach, appeal to the refinement of the often limited palette and profoundly nostalgic sensibility of Dior. Yet it would be a mistake to reduce this movement to that of a return or a "reaction," because these young painters saw themselves as expressing their era, and initially enjoyed the support of the ultimate avant-garde icon, Gertrude Stein.

LOUIS XVI IN 1956

In Bérard, in his lyricism, restrained romanticism, sense of declining baroque and theatricality, Dior found a kindred spirit and one of the people who would help him formulate his idea of style. This community of mind—or of aesthetic sense—was also shared among more obscure people that Dior always included in his personal sphere. Victor Grandpierre, who first showed up during the Occupation in Cannes, at the charades played in the Mac-Avoy home, was the son of one of the major figures of eclecticism, an architect who designed hotels and the pseudo-Louis XVI follies that Dior loved so much. Less well known now than other figures from the era, he nonetheless played a significant role in setting the trends of the day, working, for example, on the design of Louise de Vilmorin's legendary "Salon Bleu" at Verrières, or creating the photographic prints—a composition of all types of objects—for the disturbing *Écho des fantaisies* that de Vilmorin paired with handwritten poems.

"But where," wondered Dior, as he was about to open his couture house, "was I to find the man capable of transforming my dreams into reality, within the limits of my modest budget?" A dream that he imagined as "a decorated, but non-decorative, atmosphere"—a blend, with no pretense of (historic) authenticity or (stylistic) purity, but entirely defined by a subjective coherence, which would, once again, be nothing other than "a 1910 version of Louis Seize." This was a decorative approach deeply connected to his generation, but also rooted in a certain past, formed of strata and sediments.

"Victor Grandpierre," wrote Dior, "had been brought up in the right traditions: and he did in fact prove to be the very man I was looking for. I sent such a pressing letter to him at Cannes, where he was on holiday, that he instantly left for Paris, and set to work trying to put into practice the very confused ideas which I sketched out to him. […] He created the 'Helleu' salon of my dreams: all in white and pearl grey, looking very Parisian with its crystal chandeliers."

And because "our tastes coincided wonderfully, and we were both equally happy recapturing the magic years of our childhood," Grandpierre was commissioned not only to create the iconic décor on Avenue Montaigne, but also that of the "tiny boutique which I intended to be a copy of the eighteenth-century shops which sold luxurious trifles," and went on to work on most of the interiors that Dior would later occupy.

VOGUE REGENCY

Grandpierre's approach to decorating, his sense of history and his knowledge of styles that inspired so many harmonic connections for Dior made him an exemplary figure in the cultural world and high society already discussed; the exact configuration of all this deserves to be fully explored one day. Art patrons (the Noailles, the de Beaumonts), authors

Christian Dior and Victor Grandpierre during the work done prior to opening the Dior salon, 1946.

Walter Carone, redesign of the
Colifichets boutique, decorated
by Christian Bérard with toile
de Jouy, 1950. Shop manager
Carmen Colle, in the foreground, fits
a dress onto a wicker mannequin.

(Cocteau, Louise de Vilmorin), artists (Bérard, Jean and Valentine Hugo), wealthy aesthetes (Charles de Beistegui, Arturo López-Willshaw, Tony Gandarillas), architects and decorators (Emilio Terry, Jean-Michel Frank), to mention but a few, all had something in common: they had assimilated—and sometimes even initiated—the lessons of modernism, practicing a sort of easy-going syncretism, while refusing to adhere to a single doctrine. A taste for allusion, the use of classical forms, a touch of whimsy and a fondness for a kind of baroque tempered any inclination to adopt the narrow criteria of a functionalist orthodoxy.

It is probably impossible to separate these individual examples from the tensions that started rippling through the artistic culture in Europe in 1925. The "neo-romanticism" displayed by Dior was only one of many visible reactions to the tired ideas of formal abstraction and increasingly geometric forms. An echo of this also appears in the antagonism that lasted through the 1950s between the Union des Artistes Modernes, advocates of new forms, and the Société des Artistes Décorateurs, which included such remarkable designers as Ruhlmann, André Arbus and Jean-Charles Moreux, who emphasized sophisticated, often precious materials, the highest quality craftsmanship, and a reinvention of the classical and baroque legacy. While Dior does not seem to have ever worked directly with these designers (with the exception of Lina Zervudachi, whose wicker mannequins he would use in his shop windows), he clearly approved of their approach. Another proof of the affinity can be found in his work with the Jansen company (more on this later), repository of a new "French style," for which several of these designers worked.

A CERTAIN SENSE OF STYLE

This playful, historicist and highbrow style had a caustic counterpart in England. Dior certainly appreciated the decorative irony, the blend of styles and the ornamental excesses adopted by Cecil Beaton and his friends (Oliver Messel, Rex Whistler, Stephen Tennant), although without daring to take on some of its more erratic manifestations, reserved for the British style. In its freedom, curiosity and fundamental irregularity, this sense of style had very little in common with the "English taste"—tartan-lined walls, mahogany furniture, whatnots and petit-point tapestries—which represented "good" or perhaps mediocre taste in mid-twentieth-century France. Static, highly coded and blandly bourgeois, it was the ultimate example of the "decorated" interiors that Dior firmly opposed with his own style.

A second dissuasive element was the culture of the ersatz, of the fake or counterfeit material that appeared with the restrictions imposed by mass production, the immediate corollary of modern economies based on an absence of authenticity.

Given all this, all that mattered to the creator of the New Look, "even in the greatest of luxury," was one cardinal value: "simplicity, the simplicity that was the widespread good taste in the France of the past." It is a quality that is not defined as the opposite of complexity, but instead maintains the multiple traces of a singular path, the mark left by a person in and through his interior, reflecting his own biography in spaces and in objects. So when he was faced with a job as intimidating and as exciting as furnishing and defining the interior that best reflected his own personality—"with the money

I received from my first collection"—that of the Coudret mill in Milly-la-Forêt, he only transformed and consolidated what was necessary, and took enormous pleasure in removing the elements—large modern windows and brand new roughcasting—added by the previous occupants. In the end, he achieved a "livable in" and "lived-in" interior, at the expense of some trompe-l'œil and rapidly executed re-creations dictated by his urgent needs, through the use of salvaged materials and tiles, as well as "that which I desired more than anything: the impression of simplicity and of a place inhabited for a long time."

The interior as a refuge, a "shelter and protection," was also a self-portrait, and as such, was dual in tone: "1956 Louis Seize," retrospective and current, old and modern, a contradiction in terms that the couturier viewed as "a contemporary and therefore sincere version."

TWO INTERIORS

In Dior's biography, the apartment on Boulevard Jules-Sandeau occupied a middle ground between two interiors, each of which met the specific needs and different purposes of the moment, and which were interdependent. The first, the Coudret mill in Milly, created a natural link with his provincial childhood and the memory of trips to the countryside. It featured a group of buildings, stables and barns around a horseshoe-shaped farmyard; it fulfilled his dream of "a house something like those houses in the provinces, those whitewashed convents with their well-polished parlours, where children are brought to talk politely to their relations, of which I preserve tender memories." Tiles and original beams contrasted with the plush Louis XVI and Louis-Philippe furniture, the whitewashed walls of the sitting rooms and the guest rooms lined with printed fabrics and decorated with petit-point carpets. Directoire fireplaces and screens, mahogany beds protected by a canopy of muslin and a few rustic eighteenth-century pieces heightened the sense of cozy intimacy of what started out as a "ruin in a marsh." The symbolic center of this refuge, in the mill's former machinery room, transformed into a sitting room, was the tapestry next to the piano and the couturier's drawing table: every guest had to add a few stitches to the design.

The garden also added considerably to Milly's charm ("I wanted it to look like the peasants' gardens which decorate the sides of the roads in my native Normandy"). It was painstakingly expanded by transforming the marshes and the forest.

The second place, in contrast to this enclosed garden of flowers and medicinal herbs, both in terms of time and space, was the forty-eight-square-meter ornamental pool and fifty-hectare field of the Château de La Colle Noire, which Dior purchased in 1950 near the village of Callian in the Var *département*, not far from where his father had lived. Once again, he felt it was essential to recreate an interior that felt as if it were lived in, that reflected transformations that had occurred over time, with furniture and objects added by successive generations—an impression the owner constantly sought to create.

A paved entry of gray, pink and green pebbles; gray and white woodwork leading to an entrance with large midnight blue curtains; and a large crystal chandelier hanging over a Regency desk all added a certain sense of majesty that was missing from the more rustic décor of Coudret. Upstairs, between the bathrooms fitted with mirror-lined alcoves painted with fake gray and white marble and furnished with Empire and Directoire elements, was a series of "Louis-Philippe," "neo-Egyptian," "Louis XVI" and "ceramic" rooms (named for the faience decorating the fireplace).

Blue and white cretonne, black and white toile de Jouy, red floral-patterned fabric, light-colored furniture, opaline glass, Empire-style mahogany and painted eighteenth-century furniture, plush upholstery and beveled mirrors created a different cachet in each room—with niches and alcoves, a recurrent element with Dior, forming a common theme linking the disparate sophisticated aspects.

Dior by Dior ends with a description of this interior, then in the midst of renovation, where the couturier wrote his book, by candlelight, "which cast amusing shadows on the ceiling." The images we have of this décor, taken several months after the death of the man who wanted to "bring things full circle"—although fate decided otherwise—radiate the same sense of comfort and *gemütlichkeit* that was so important to him. Paradoxically, the master of the graphic, structured silhouette and of the constrained, gently corseted body sought only ease and relaxation in his interiors, or rather the "overall softness that suits my roundish self," as he wrote.

A HOME OF HIS OWN

As opposed to these two country homes, concurrent in time, and his professional locations—the salons on Avenue Montaigne—the apartment on Boulevard Jules-Sandeau was where Dior really lived, "a townhouse for me, as urban and cozy as Milly has been rural and simple." A lair with an elaborate blend of styles, with disparate elements that mutually enhanced one another: "a Matisse drawing was to hang side by side with a Gothic tapestry, a Renaissance bronze, a Jacob ornament." It was a statement by example that once again illustrated a recurring creed: "Good taste was much less important than my own taste, for after all, living in a house that does not suit you is like wearing someone else's clothes." It's clear that the "clothing" of Passy closely fit the body and spirit of the couturier. Yet the very eclecticism and enthusiasm of Dior's choices reveal a particular quality, a preference for a specific style

Willy Maywald. Moulin du Coudret.
Christian Dior's house in Milly-la-Forêt.

Aerial view of La Colle Noire.
Christian Dior's house in Montauroux.

that was very much to the forefront here: that of the 1750s through the 1850s, a crucial, hybrid period marked by transitional styles, where the elegant curves of one declining culture were replaced by the forms of a revived antiquity, and the painted wood of the Directoire gave way to the light wood inlays of the Charles X style, then varnished papier-mâché cutouts. These styles, which "good taste" in France and in England had considered to be minor or negligible up to then, were revived in various circles, including those of Dior, and of Beaton and Sitwell across the English Channel.

Victor Grandpierre played his usual role, designing the private rooms in the house, a protected and secret refuge. His work overlapped with that of another long-time friend, Georges Geffroy, an unintentional agent of Dior's good fortune. A major figure in the French decorating world at the time, he contributed to the sitting rooms and the reception areas, in collaboration with Pierre Delbée from the Maison Jansen.

From the start, Jansen stood out for its excellent interpretations of eighteenth-century French styles. It played a major role in early twentieth-century decoration, particularly because a return to the expertise and high quality of classical cabinet-makers immediately attracted the attention of British and American clients, including Ogden Codman and Edith Wharton, who wrote a seminal manual of proper interior design, *The Decoration of Houses*, for American readers. (Jansen was also commissioned for work at this time by another eminence of transatlantic decoration, the fanciful society figure Elsie de Wolfe.) After the death of Jean Henry Jansen in 1928, Delbée (who would decorate Jackie Kennedy's White House in the 1960s) became director of the company that he had joined in the late 1920s, and went on to become its president, starting in 1961.

THE ENCLOSED GARDEN

It is hardly surprising that a staunch defender of French style like Dior would identify with this respect for tradition and the clear lacquered and inlaid furniture produced by Jansen. But his sense of whimsy, his fondness for combining elements and his taste for nostalgic daydreaming transcended the unequivocal aspect of this style, the characteristic that Americans pegged as "classical chic." His specific passion for variety (which, people say, inspired him to use unmatched teacups and saucers, to play with new combinations) and his fondness for shimmer and softness and patterned fabrics played a crucial role in the design of his interiors, particularly those in the Boulevard Jules-Sandeau apartment: cotton prints, floral patterns and velvet covered the furniture and walls, filtered the lights, covered the beds and hid or revealed rooms and alcoves. From the entry, beige door curtains edged with a Greek motif led to emerald-green shantung curtains inside; in the sitting room, decorated by Geffroy, was an imposing crystal chandelier, the inescapable kentia palm, a Sèvres porcelain athenienne against the wall hangings in a shade that Dior dubbed "willow shoot." Deep green ribbed fabric curtains concealed a silver bathtub in the bathroom; a nineteenth-century floral fabric lined a corridor; garnet-colored silk covered the canopy of a bed; the chairs were upholstered in cherry-red velvet; and an embroidered Chinese silk wall hanging in the smoking room was half hidden by a pair of straw-colored door curtains. In the couturier's favorite room, where he had himself photographed, two alcoves lined with ruby-red velvet, each with curved sofas set on either side of a fireplace, framed a portrait of the couturier by Bernard Buffet, a painting by Bérard, and a collection of fifteenth-century sculptures, Persian bronzes, faience and antique coins.

A small bouquet, two silver chandeliers, a magnifying glass, a few small *objets de vertu*; sitting on the edge of a banquette with a teacup in hand, Dior is immersed in reading a newspaper, enjoying the harmony of this décor that reflects his own image, forgetting Christian Dior to become simply Christian once again, and recreating, in this place as in all the others he created, an "enclosed garden," the peaceful haven of his childhood.

Christian Dior in his apartment at 7 Boulevard Jules-Sandeau in Paris, ca. 1950.

Left: Eugene Kammerman, model Renée Breton at the fashion show in the haute couture salon at 30 Avenue Montaigne, 1953.

1. All quotations come from *Dior by Dior: The Autobiography of Christian Dior*. London. V&A Publishing. 2nd ed., 2007.

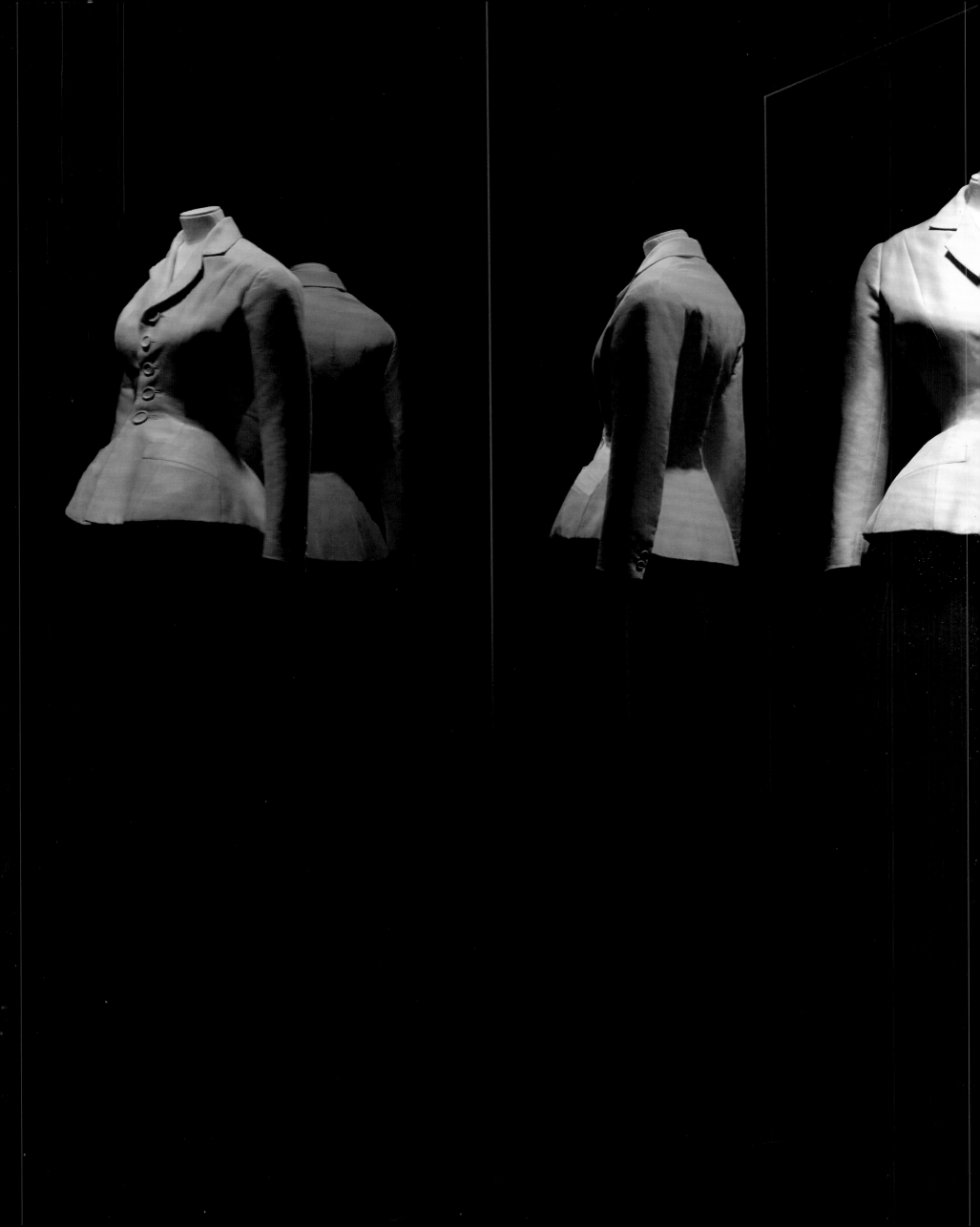

Christian Dior. *Bar* suit. Haute Couture, Spring-Summer 1947,
Corolle line. Afternoon suit. Shantung jacket.
Pleated corolla skirt in wool crêpe by Gérondeau et Cie.
Paris, Musée des Arts Décoratifs, UFAC collection,
gift of Christian Dior, 1958. Inv. UF 58-29-1

The *Bar* suit is the most iconic model in Christian Dior's New Look collection. The name is an allusion to the bar of the Hôtel Plaza Athénée, a favorite with café society ladies sporting elegant afternoon suits. The *Bar*, worn by the model Tania, was not the best selling of the ninety-six New Look designs, with just twenty-one sales (seven to private customers and fourteen to stores for the right to reproduce the design). Top sellers included *New York* (sixty sales), *Maxim's* (fifty-five sales), *1947* (forty-five sales) and *Amour* (thirty-four sales). But the *Bar* got the most press coverage and was hailed as the quintessence of the famous *Corolle* line. Dior had attempted a similar silhouette with the *Welcome* suit in 1946 when he was assistant to Lucien Lelong, but he took stylization to extremes with the *Bar*, exaggerating the curved lines of the "flower-woman." According to designer Christian Bérard, the original idea was inspired by "huge pleated skirts like those the Marseilles fishwives wear, long, and with tiny bodices and tiny hats."[1]

Another radical decision was for the wasp-waisted jacket to be worn next to the skin, without a blouse. The skirt was lengthened to cover the legs, the peplums of the jacket ultra-flared to make the waist look smaller. Dior compensated for the lack of rich materials in the postwar period with the luxury of extravagant lengths of fabric: the *Bar* suit skirt required 5.5 meters of 1.4 meter-wide wool fabric. And Pierre Cardin bought cotton wool from his local pharmacy to pad the jacket peplums. This ideal of femininity heralded the styles of the 1950s. The rectangular forms of the 1920s and the square shapes of the 1940s were succeeded by curves, with the slender silhouette of the Belle Époque reincarnated as a gliding figure in swirling skirts. The *Bar* suit introduced a posture reminiscent of the Romantic period with cinched waist, rounded back, slightly sloping shoulders and forward-jutting hips. The model had a dancer's grace, her skirt sweeping the spectators' legs as she passed, overturning ashtrays and catching men's eyes. As France emerged from the ruins of war, a reawakened sensuality was accompanied by a form of femininity given shape by the "architect" Dior.

From 1947 on, the major French, British and American couture houses drew inspiration from this singular silhouette. Over the decades, every creative director at Dior has paid homage to the *Bar* suit, the fashion house's archetypal signature design. Creators from the 1980s to the present day have used it as a reference that expresses the essence of Haute Couture.

FLORENCE MÜLLER

---

1. *Town & Country*, February 1957, p. 51.

Christian Dior

COLLECTION PRINTEMPS 1947

———

Les lignes de cette Première Collection de Printemps sont typiquement féminines et faites pour mettre en valeur celles qui les portent.

2 Silhouettes principales :

La silhouette " COROLLE " et la silhouette en " 8 "

" COROLLE " : dansante. très juponnante, buste moulé et taille fine.

" 8 "   : nette et galbée, gorge soulignée, taille creusée, hanches accentuées.

Les jupes allongées nettement, les tailles marquées, les basques de jaquettes souvent écourtées, tout contribue à élancer la silhouette.

Seules les robes de fin de journée ou de grand soir sont largement et doucement décolletées.

L'asymétrie, le trop grand emploi du drapé et l'entrave ont été volontairement évités.

Coloris dominants :   Marine - Gris - Grège et Noir.

Quelques teintes discrètes :   Royal kaki.
Bleu de Paris.
Terre de Paris.

Quelques tons éclatants :   Rouge Scream.
Vert Longchamp.
Rose Porcelaine.

Imprimés exclusifs :   Pois et carrés sur twills de teintes discrètes.
Imprimé " Jungle " sur crêpe et mousseline.

Les chapeaux volontairement simples, précisent la silhouette voulue.

Pat English, the model Tania wearing
the *Bar* suit at the presentation of Christian
Dior's first collection, Spring-Summer 1947.

Left: Program of the Spring-Summer
1947 collection (*Corolle* and *En 8* lines).

Following double page, left: Txema Yeste,
ensemble from the Spring-Summer 2016 Haute
Couture collection, model Maartje Verhoef.
The sprigs of lily-of-the-valley add a reference
to the *Bar* suit, in celebration of Christian Dior.

Right: Patrick Demarchelier, *Diosera* ensemble,
Spring-Summer 1997 Haute Couture collection,
model Sui He. This was the first design that
John Galliano created as a tribute
to the *Bar* suit of 1947; he modernized it with
a miniskirt and offbeat accessories.

Christian Dior. *Pompon* suit. Haute Couture,
Spring-Summer 1947, *En 8* line. Wool afternoon
suit, embroidered fringes. Paris, Dior Héritage,
gift of Mme Nolasco. Inv. 1987.9

"The lines that make up this first spring collection are typically feminine
and designed to make the women who wear them look their very
best," says the catalog of the New Look collection for Spring-Summer
1947. The two "main shapes" were *Corolle*, "swirling lines with very full
skirts, close-fitting bodices and nipped-in waists,"[1] and *En 8*, "clean-
cut rounded lines, prominent bust, tiny waist, accentuated hips."[2]

Pompon, a plain black afternoon suit, illustrates the graphic effect of
the *En 8* line. Darts between the breasts emphasize and define the bust.
The waist is belted, and diagonal pocket flaps draw attention to the hips.

"The art of couture [...] can only survive in perpetual evolution,
in a movement that displaces and replaces lines according to a designer's
taste and the intangible trends in the air," claimed the fashion magazine
L'Officiel, pointing out that "Christian Dior sketches and creates his own
designs."[3] In his autobiography, Dior underscored the fact that his work
as a designer consisted of using his own research sketches to define his lines.

Christian Dior added to the *Corolle* line for his next collection in
Fall-Winter 1947 and, the following spring, combined the *Zig-Zag* and
Envol lines. Thereafter, he presented one new line with each collection:
*Ailée, Trompe-l'œil, Milieu du siècle, Verticale, Oblique, Naturelle, Longue, Sinueuse,
Profilée, Tulipe, Vivante, Muguet, H, A, Y, Flèche, Aimant* and *Libre. Fuseau*,
his last line, was introduced with the Fall-Winter collection of 1957.

The importance of drawing was unusual, as not all couturiers could
draw. By copying illustrations from magazines, Dior taught himself
to produce quick, descriptive sketches of figures in movement, with
an expressive élan that then had to be rendered in fabric. The ensuing
construction of a garment in the couture atelier was a complex
process. Constricted or augmented stylized curves were broken
down into polygons of fabric, often stitched onto structures such as
bustiers or whalebone under-bodices; loose volumes, on the other
hand, were composed of folds, pleats or layers like those of a tutu.

Dior's inspiration often came from ballet costumes. Although the *Corolle*
silhouette is often taken as the synthesis of his style, the *En 8* silhouette—
represented by *Pompon*—was also essential, as the flower-woman emerged
from both these lines. With a design based on the basque corset introduced
by Marcel Rochas in 1946, Christian Dior's *En 8* line was an allusion
to the silhouette of the 1900s, when his mother was young; but it also evoked
the exaggerated pin-up silhouette of American cartoons and films noirs.

The New Look had a great impact in the United States.
Rita Hayworth, star of Charles Vidor's *Gilda* (1946), was in Paris
to promote the movie in May 1947; she "enthusiastically adopted the
two Dior silhouettes: one straight and figure-hugging; the other very
flared and floaty."[4] She ordered twelve designs, including *Pompon*.

ÉRIC PUJALET-PLAÀ

1. Catalog of the Spring-Summer collection, 1947.
2. Ibid.
3. *L'Officiel de la couture et de la mode*, no. 301–302, 1947, p. 73.
4. *Elle*, June 24, 1947, p. 4.

Christian Dior, sketches for the Haute Couture collections for
Fall-Winter 1948 (*Ailée* line), Spring-Summer 1949 (*Trompe-l'œil* line),
Fall-Winter 1951 (*Longue* line) and Spring-Summer 1955 (*A* line).
These sketches reflect the Dior style through the predominance
of the line, which strongly expresses the shape and movement.

Right: Horst P. Horst, portrait of Rita Hayworth, 1947. She is wearing the
Maxim's dress, Spring-Summer 1947 Haute Couture collection (*En 8* line).
Lila de Nobili illustrated this dress for *Vogue Paris* (see page 33).

Christian Dior. *Diablesse* dress. Haute
Couture, Fall-Winter 1947. *Corolle* line.
Pleated wool afternoon dress. Granville,
Musée Christian Dior. Inv. 1999.5.1

For his second collection, in Fall-Winter 1947, Christian Dior developed the designs in
the *Femme Fleur* and *Femme Tige* lines, taking up the key themes that had made the New
Look such a hit and adding the occasional touch of piquancy to the nature-inspired
theme. Diablesse expresses the darker side of feminine allure; the red chosen by
Christian Dior—called "Satan" in the collection catalog—is a deep, dark red like that
of molten lava, and a perfect match for the emphatic curves of this wool afternoon dress.

Diablesse is characteristic of the silhouette of the collection with its soft shoulders,
slender waist, full bust and new-length skirt that preserved the seductive mystery of the legs.
The close-fitting bodice, which clings to the bust, has buttons down the front like a shirt-
waist, then extends in pleats from hip to calf. A twirl of the skirt, with its deliberately
irregular hemline, brought the fabric to life. The swing of the pleats as the model
walked created a free and easy effect: Christian Dior wanted the dresses in this line to play
down the fuss factor (to "dress down dressiness"[1]).

Diablesse had a special significance among the 123 designs created for the collection, with
a particular role to play in the staging of the show. About halfway through a presentation,
Dior liked to introduce spectacular effects that became known as his "coups de Trafalgar,"
moments that captured the attention of clients and journalists alike. The chosen designs,
which were often red, were especially striking and set the overall tone for the collection.

Dior was quick to realize that red was his lucky color—it was, after all, the color of
the kisses planted on his cheeks at the end of each show! What sweeter reward for the
founder of the fashion house at 30 Avenue Montaigne? From 1949 on, one of these reds
would be forever associated with the name of Christian Dior: Rouge Dior, whose success
boosted the 1955 launch of a first lipstick line with eight colors ranging from bright red
to orange, enabling women to match their lipstick to their outfit and allowing Christian Dior
to assert his skill as a colorist and his passionate desire to make all women beautiful.

VINCENT LERET

1. Catalog of the Fall-Winter 1947 Haute Couture collection.

Left: Guy Bourdin, Dior lipstick, 1972.
Above: Tim Walker, Marion Cotillard
wearing a "Dior red" cashmere *Bar* coat,
Fall-Winter 2012 Haute Couture collection.

Christian Dior. *Fête* gown. Haute Couture.
Spring-Summer 1948. *Envol* line.
Silk faille evening gown. Granville,
Musée Christian Dior. Inv. 1996.1.3

The color of this silk faille ball gown from the *Envol* line is "boreal pink"—
a shade defined by the couturier as a painter might describe the tones of his
soft-color palette. Named *Fête*, it has a tight-fitting, short-sleeved bodice above
an ankle-length skirt with a burst of pleats at the back. Christian Dior
described the dynamic allure of the *Envol* line in the show's catalog:
"an unequal distribution of fullness creates the impression of flight with every
step and dips dramatically at the back." Inspired by the voluminous fashion
of the late Belle Époque, when he was a child, the highly inventive designer
used a geometric cut and tightly woven fabric of high quality to give the gown
a flowing but fitted look. In the black pencil sketch released to the press, the
profile view of the silhouette accentuates the sharp lines of the different
volumes at the back of the gown and the faux-casual arrangement of the folds
at the hips. According to the collection's dressmaking records, the rigorous
construction of the *Fête* skirt required over sixteen meters of fabric.

This gown, with its simple bodice and swirling skirt, designed as a piece
of "ephemeral architecture"—as Dior described his work in his memoirs[1]—
was intended to add a sway to a woman's step. It was an incentive to dance
at a ball, to express the "new joie de vivre." Suited to the flower-woman
silhouette with its rounded shoulders, bare neck and high, shapely bust, the
tight-waisted gown flares over the curve of the hips with a bustle effect;
the legs remain mysteriously hidden under the long skirt, which ends in a train.
Although Dior did not use the term "tournure" (bustle) in his writing,
preferring the word "pouf" to describe the bunched fabric at the back of his
retro-style gowns, he had not forgotten the designs of historical inspiration
that he drew in the prewar period. The ideal beauty imagined by Dior to banish
the mood of the war years was embodied in the revolutionary New Look,
successfully launched at the opening of his couture house in 1947. In its issue
dedicated to the spring collections of 1948, *L'Officiel de la Couture et de la Mode*
enthusiastically described it as "Paris rediscovered."[2] And the *Fête* gown,
sketched by fashion illustrator Pierre Grisot, had pride of place in this celebration.

MARIE-SOPHIE CARRON DE LA CARRIÈRE

1. Christian Dior, *Dior by Dior: The Autobiography of
   Christian Dior*, London, V&A Publishing, 2nd ed., p. 189.
2. *L'Officiel de la couture et de la mode*, 1948, no. 313–314, p. 74.

Following double page, right:
actress Odette Joyeux in a
Christian Dior costume for the
film *The Four-Poster*, by Roland
Tual, 1942. Christian Dior was
clearly inspired by Auguste
Renoir's painting *La Loge*, 1874,
London, The Courtauld Gallery.

Christian Dior. *Petit Dîner* dress.
Haute Couture, Fall-Winter 1948,
Ailée line. Faille late afternoon dress.
Paris, Dior Héritage. Inv. 1989.14

Petit Dîner looks like an ideal outfit for an elegant, not-too-formal supper party—but the large scallops of gathered silk faille on either side of the straight skirt would make it difficult to remain comfortably seated for the duration of a meal! The dress's name was perhaps ironic; although the collection catalog described it as a "late afternoon dress," it was probably intended for cocktail parties.

These social gatherings, at which guests remained standing with their drinks and nibbles, became popular after World War II. Leading afternoon into evening, a cocktail party required a dress that was short but "dressy"—and paradoxically, it is the touch of *déshabillé* in an outfit that gives it a dressy look. A cocktail dress also had to suit the season and reflect the tone of the collection. *Petit Dîner* has a deep V neckline and short sleeves, showing just the right amount of bare skin for a Fall-Winter outfit intended to be worn in a cool drawing room. The simply constructed bodice with seamless armholes, the tight folded belt and the scallops of the skirt accentuate the gently sloping shoulders, slender waist and curved hips. As a result, the body is stylized to suit the New Look, and the different reliefs—smooth taffeta, tight drapes and flounces—give the required dressiness to the strict, black silhouette.

"This season, the focus has shifted away from skirt lengths to their cut and the distribution of fullness, with lines now vigorous rather than undulating and soft. This fullness, more or less moderate, allows the wearer total freedom of movement, never hindering her steps."[1] The skirt is characteristic of the *Ailée* line from the 1948 Fall-Winter collection. It is composed of two overlapping, symmetrical panels joined on the bias, with one end of each rolled over at the hips to fall in a scallop shape at the front or back. The draped belt accentuates the corkscrew effect of the cut. The *Ailée* line was designed to make the silhouette "as youthful and casual as possible."[2]

Petit Dîner was a modern cocktail dress for an ideal wardrobe—a wardrobe put together according to the different sequences in a fashion show. The cocktail dress appeared on the catwalk after suits and day or afternoon dresses and before dinner dresses, short then long evening gowns, ball gowns and, finally, gala gowns—an order of presentation reflecting Dior's nostalgia for customs that were somewhat outdated by 1948. Social occasions therefore determined forms, according to a hierarchy of specific materials, volumes and production methods: simple, slender designs and those of sometimes masculine inspiration, such as suits, were for daytime wear and were often made of wool or matt cotton; floaty, luxurious, low-cut designs for evening wear were made of silk with shining embroidery and sometimes required vast amounts of fabric. The former were mostly produced by the tailoring atelier, the latter by the "flou" dressmaking atelier which created *Petit Dîner*—Dior dressmaking incarnate.

ÉRIC PUJALET-PLAÀ

1. Catalog of the Fall-Winter collection, 1948.
2. Ibid.

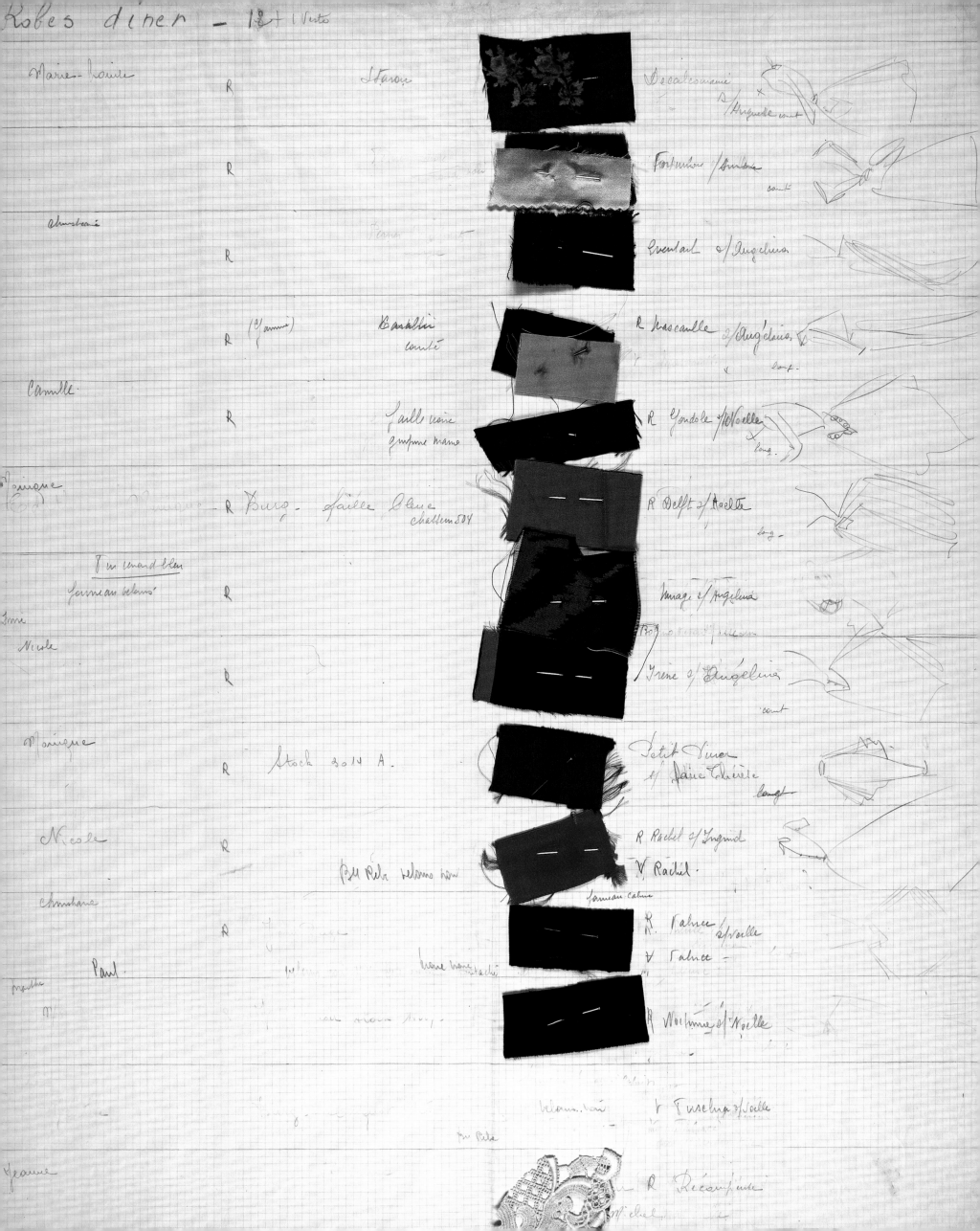

Above: Henry Clarke, *Raout* dress, Spring-
Summer 1956 Haute Couture collection
(*Flèche* line), model Dovima.

Left: Page for the "dinner dresses" created
from the chart for the Fall-Winter 1948
Haute Couture collection (*Ailée* line). A chart
provides a wealth of information: atelier name,
fabric manufacturer, sample, sketch, and so on.

Christian Dior. *Arizona* coat. Haute Couture.
Fall-Winter 1948. *Ailée* line. Rodier wool
coat. Paris. Dior Héritage. Inv. 1997.1

This coat caused a sensation when it was presented in 1948. It featured in a drawing by Pierre Louchel for the magazine *La Femme Chic*,[1] was photographed by Richard Avedon for *Harper's Bazaar*, and appeared in many magazines as an emblem of the fashion season. In *Harper's Bazaar* it was described as "Dior's big bright red coat, one of the best big coats in the collections. A loose bolero worked into the tailoring gives an altogether new line around the shoulders."[2] *L'Officiel de la Mode* stressed its "winged movement," quoting from the description of the season's flagship line in the press release issued by the House of Dior.[3] According to the couturier, "The dropped line of the shoulders is emphasized by a new sleeve cut, which often creates a wing-like and lifting effect that puts more emphasis on the bust than in previous seasons. Our aim was to make the silhouette as youthful and casual as possible, which is why we named it: 'the Winged Line.'"[4]

The garment's name and "travel coat" style evoked the distant plains of Arizona and its loose fit was a promise of comfort for women on the go—but its cut and its ember-red color proved that Dior did not reserve his spectacular effects just for evening gowns. *Arizona* was produced in the "Paul" atelier and presented by the model Gabrielle; it has no buttons and closes with a large scarf collar which is knotted around the neck, focusing attention on the wearer's face. The high, double-pointed collar and downward flare of the coat suggest movement; when in motion, it has a beautifully billowing silhouette. Movement was one of Christian Dior's favorite themes; he explored how the inherently changing nature of a fabric could create different effects depending on the wearer's movements and the displacement of air. Dior's ability to capture live movement and transcribe it in the form of an ideal silhouette was perfectly in phase with the spirit of an age that had adopted fast travel, outdoor sports and a dynamic view of femininity.

The beauty of this design still fascinates today. John Galliano opened his Summer 2011 show, dedicated to the artist René Gruau, with a stunning new version of *Arizona* in which the scarf collar was replaced by a pearl gray bow that brought the artist's ink drawings to life with "ostrich feather brush strokes." Galliano partly covered the coat with dégradé tulle in shades "from light to dark like a painting technique."[5]

In 2012, Jean-Baptiste Mondino chose *Arizona* for a series of portraits of the actress Marion Cotillard, showcasing the elegance of the 1950s in a contemporary mise-en-scène. The French actress, awarded an Oscar for her portrayal of Édith Piaf in Olivier Dahan's film *La Vie en Rose* (*La Môme*), was happy to oblige, stressing the extent to which "Monsieur Dior was an imaginative designer who invented, reinvented, was always in phase with his time."[6] The following year, Raf Simons borrowed the lines of the *Arizona* coat for the "memory dresses"[7] in his Winter 2013 ready-to-wear collection.

FLORENCE MÜLLER

1. *La Femme chic*, October 1948, p. 41.
2. "Topcoats—Full skirts or full backs," *Harper's Bazaar*, October 1948, p. 180.
3. "Naissance d'une mode," *L'Officiel de la mode*, no. 319–320, 1948, p. 71.
4. Press release for the Winter 1948 Haute Couture collection. Dior Héritage.
5. Press release for the Spring-Summer 2011 Haute Couture collection. Dior Héritage.
6. Jean-Pierre Lavoignat, *Dior* magazine, no. 1, 2012, p. 38.
7. Press release for the Winter 2013 Ready-to-Wear collection. Dior Héritage.

Following double page, left: Arik Nepo.
dress from the Fall-Winter 1948
Haute Couture collection (*Ailée* line).

Christian Dior. *Miss Dior* dress. Haute Couture,
Spring-Summer 1949, *Trompe-l'œil* line.
Short evening dress embroidered with flowers by Barbier.
Paris, Dior Héritage. Inv. 2003.85

"A short evening dress embroidered with a thousand flowers." This was the catalog description of the *Miss Dior* design from Dior's *Trompe-l'œil* line—one that showed the couturier to be a master of illusion, a magician of the new springtime of French fashion.

It is hard to see any fabric under the mass of blossoms on this dress, designed to enhance the form of a "flower-woman," its thousand flowers reminiscent of the "mille e tre" conquests of Mozart's *Don Giovanni*. It was an impossible quest, a folly dreamt up by Dior, for whom there could never be enough perfume and flowers to welcome clients to his showrooms. This evening dress is an impressionist composition, a distant echo of Monet's garden. Above all, it is a dream— the dream of an alchemist for whom perfumes were dresses, and dresses emerged like genies from a bottle.[1] *Miss Dior* is a flowered design in three dimensions, with a corolla silhouette. The couturier's fifth collection was sublimated by the "blossoming," "fullness," "natural curves" and "movement" of his designs, echoed by the sinuous lines of the bottle containing the *Miss Dior* perfume, launched in 1947. In the grandiose, poetic language of his exquisite couture, he speaks to us of the primroses of spring, of the constant renewal of the earth, conjuring images of the garden that first inspired him—that of his Granville childhood, where he discovered the beauty of nature under the fond gaze of his mother Madeleine. With this dress, Dior seems to have scattered a rainbow of flowers onto an empty field, transforming it into a luxuriant garden. Are the flowers attached to the dress? Embroidered? Were they randomly scattered like seeds on the ground? Was Dior's intention to plunge us into a tangled garden or a carefully constructed composition? We can almost hear the humming of bees, dizzy with pollen. And flowers, after all, are expert in the arts of trompe-l'œil and attraction. "Make me a perfume that smells of love," said Christian Dior to his perfumer.[2] What joy to embrace a woman wearing the *Miss Dior* dress and the perfume of the same name!

The couturier-perfumer took his obsession with flowers to extremes with *Miss Dior*. The hazy blooms on the dress—in pastel pink, white, a little mauve and violet and a touch of lilac—merge together to make the garment a pure abstraction. Like a bouquet of wild flowers, the *Miss Dior* perfume was a tribute dedicated in 1947 to Christian's sister Catherine, a former member of the Resistance who devoted her postwar life in Grasse and Paris to flowers. The *Miss Dior* dress recalls the early morning atmosphere at the flower stalls in the Halles Baltard in central Paris, where Catherine worked as a producer of blooms for the cut-flower industry.

The graceful, fragile silk flowers on the *Miss Dior* dress also evoke the wear and tear of time—the enemy of every creator. The designer tells us that, though bouquets soon fade, memories associated with love and perfume live forever. *Miss Dior* is a touching work of art, and a masterpiece of floral perfection.

FRÉDÉRIC BOURDELIER

1. Christian Dior, interviewed by the
   Fashion Group, ca. 1950. Dior Héritage.
2. Extract from the personal notes of Dior's friend,
   the journalist Alice Chavannes de Dalmassy.

Claude Monet, *Le Jardin de l'artiste à Giverny*,
1900, oil on canvas. Paris, Musée d'Orsay.

Left: Jean Chevalier, Christian Dior poses with the
model Simone (wearing the *Miss Dior* dress), 1949.

Christian Dior. *Gruau* gown. Haute Couture,
Fall-Winter 1949, *Milieu du siècle* line.
Satin ball gown. Paris, Dior Héritage. Inv. 2013.3

With this gown, Christian Dior kept his promise to his friend
and collaborator René Gruau, but reserved a surprise for him too.
The two men knew each other well; they first met in the offices
of *Le Figaro* in the mid-1930s, and saw eye to eye on the subject
of elegance. René Gruau's skill as an illustrator for French and
Italian fashion magazines had brought him work in advertising and
he already had a successful career behind him; newcomer Christian
Dior was rapidly earning his stripes as a designer by selling his
sketches of hats to fashion houses. In 1935, some of his illustrations
were published in the women's section of *Le Figaro*. Dior and Gruau
met, became friends and envisaged working together in the future.

Christian Dior designed the *Gruau* gown in 1949, during the
summer—a season when "it is delightful to imagine the freshness
of a winter morning."[1] Made in white satin for the show, this ball
gown is a pinnacle of elegance, reflecting all the sophistication
of Dior's designs. A suit would not be good enough for Gruau.
He deserved a gown that could embody the charisma of his
drawings and the impact of his style.

Readers of fashion magazines could always recognize a René
Gruau illustration by its originality. In March 1949, they were
the first to see the drawings Christian Dior had commissioned
from his friend for the *Miss Dior* perfume. Gruau's illustration
showed an elegant swan wearing a huge black bow and a string
of pearls—no perfume bottles or dresses in this first drawing.
The aristocratic grace of a creature that symbolized eternal
youth in the eighteenth century met with instant approval
from Christian Dior, who immediately sent Gruau a telegram
saying, "I'm absolutely thrilled, your drawings are marvellous."[2]

Dior's 167 designs for the Fall-Winter collection of 1949 included
the *Gruau* and the *Cygne Noir*, a satin and velvet evening gown
that also perfectly reflected the identity of *Miss Dior*. Like Gruau's
Miss Dior swan, Dior wanted the dresses in his new collection to be
worn with plenty of gemstones and pearls to add a touch of sparkle.

The style of both the *Gruau* and the *Cygne Noir* gowns stemmed
from a desire for novelty and nonchalance. Accessories were
all-important to achieve a range of stylish and subtle effects: hats
shaded the eyes; skirts could spin like windmills; evening gloves
were unbuttoned at the shoulder. Christian Dior revived a repertoire
of feminine gestures that particularly appealed to René Gruau,
who captured them brilliantly in his illustrations.

VINCENT LERET

1. Christian Dior, *Je suis couturier*, Paris,
   Éditions du Conquistador, 1951, p. 52.
2. Congratulatory telegram from Christian Dior
   to René Gruau, March 11, 1949. Dior Héritage.

René Gruau, drawing for the perfume
Miss Dior, 1949.

Right: First *Miss Dior* amphora, 1947.

Left: René Gruau, drawing for the
Gruau dress, Fall-Winter 1949 Haute
Couture collection (*Milieu du siècle* line).

Christian Dior. *Junon* gown. Haute Couture.
Fall-Winter 1949. *Milieu du siècle* line.
Long crinoline evening dress embroidered
with sequins by Rébé. Paris, Dior Héritage.
Inv. 1989.21

Claire Poe Newman was an American blonde beauty whose pinup proportions were perfectly suited to Dior's *Junon* ball gown. "I have to have it," she told Christian Dior when catching sight of the fairy-tale tulle dress. And since Claire Poe Newman had an nineteen-inch waist, she managed to fit into the Haute Couture sample size, originally worn by Alla, one of Dior's star models.

A former model, Newman had been one of *Life* magazine's more memorable cover girls in 1944, as well as doing advertisements for Camel cigarettes and Hanes stockings. Her husband, Robert Newman, was a well-traveled charmer and Southern gentleman whose New Orleans-based family owned countless plantations in Louisiana. After viewing his first ever Dior collection in 1948, Newman ordered thirteen Dior suits, ball gowns, cocktail dresses, and casual outfits. "Each Dior model my wife tried on enthralled us," Robert Newman later wrote. "They were everything I had hoped for, plus a touch, to me at least, of the erotic."[1]

During the next ten years, the Newmans returned to Paris and ordered outfits. They amassed a collection that was exhibited in the Louisiana State Museum show *Dior, Merchant of Happiness: the private collection of Mrs. Robert J. Newman*, in New Orleans 1988. Describing Christian Dior as "a quiet, unobtrusive man," Claire Poe Newman wrote that the designer "never pressured" them but "did suggest" and "was happy when I chose the ones he thought were good for me."[2] The *Junon* ball gown became a favorite that Claire Poe Newman donned at special occasions such as Grace of Monaco's engagement party, held at the Waldorf Astoria in New York 1956. A photograph taken in Saint Moritz shows her wearing the dress simply with natural hair and no jewelry. No doubt because the petals of the dress's crinoline skirt were more than enough, having been superbly embroidered by Rébé with an otherworldly mix of dark blue and green sequins.

Right from the start, Dior adopted the crinoline style. It was a daring and some felt foolhardy decision, considering that it was just after World War II, when fabric was still being rationed. Indeed, the British press annihilated him for his extravagant disregard. Nevertheless, the stubborn-minded Dior soldiered on and proved to be quite the expert, having designed all the nineteenth-century costumes for Claude Autant-Lara's film *Lettres d'Amour* in 1942. Not only did the voluminous crinoline flatter, making the waist look tiny, but its immediate allure defined ethereal femininity and achieved Dior's romantic aim of making his clients "flower-like."[3] A swiftly embraced signature style, it inspired other designers of the House of Dior, such as Gianfranco Ferré and John Galliano, to create dresses with the crinoline.

NATASHA FRASER-CAVASSONI

1. Natasha Fraser-Cavassoni. *Monsieur Dior: Once Upon a Time*, New York, Pointed Leaf Press, 2014, p. 124.
2. Ibid., p. 129.
3. Christian Dior. *Dior by Dior: The Autobiography of Christian Dior*, London, V&A Publishing, 2nd ed., p. 22.

Franz Xaver Winterhalter, *Madame Rimsky Korsakov*,
oil on canvas, 1864. Paris, Musée d'Orsay.

Richard Avedon, *Theo Graham, Le Pré Catelan*,
August 1949. *Vénus* and *Junon* dresses, Fall-Winter
1949 Haute Couture collection (*Milieu du siècle* line).
The *Vénus* and *Junon* dresses, with their petal
covered crinoline skirts, are the perfect
expression of the flower-woman created by Dior.

Christian Dior. *Auteuil* suit. Christian Dior-New York,
Fall-Winter 1949. Flecked wool suit, mother-of-pearl
buttons. Palais Galliera, Musée de la Mode de la Ville
de Paris, gift of Fougea, 1973. Inv. GAL1973.27.7

The *Auteuil* suit, in fine, steel-gray wool, resembles a pencil sketch with its
half-belted jacket and pencil skirt. Its structured cut sprang from the fluid
silhouette of Christian Dior's second collection for the American market.
The double row of buttons follows the diagonal line of the darts that flatter
the bust and slim the waist; the pockets accentuate the natural swell of the hips.
The half-belt at the back is the perfect finishing touch to the vigorous design
of the jacket; the pencil skirt follows the dead-straight line of the ensemble.

The "Christian Dior-New York" brand was launched in the United States
a year after the couture house opened in Paris. Targeting an American
clientele, it presented a twice-yearly collection of over 130 original designs,
different from those that were shown on Avenue Montaigne. In a period
dominated by the artistry and excellence of Haute Couture, Christian Dior-
New York was an attempt to prevent the manufacture of copies, an area in
which Monsieur Dior would brook no compromise. This new line, made in
French or American fabrics in the United States, adopted the ready-to-wear
principle that was soon to transform the fashion industry—a revolution that
the inventor of the New Look was one of the first to perceive and predict.
His commitment to the battle against copiers of what he called "auteur
fashion" inspired him to imagine new strategies, such as the creation of a
New York brand. With this American yet eminently Parisian vision, a Dior
boutique was opened on the corner of Fifth Avenue and Fifty-seventh Street.
Over twenty collections were successfully presented there, disseminating
but never exactly copying the style of the couturier, who drew inspiration
from urban architecture for the plumb lines of his future designs.

OLIVIER SAILLARD

TWENTY CENTS

MARCH 4, 1957

TIME

HIGH FASHION
The Paris Designers

THE WEEKLY NEWSMAGAZINE

CHRISTIAN
DIOR

$6.00 A YEAR

[REG. U.S. PAT. OFF.]

VOL. LXIX NO. 9

Cover of *Time*, March 4, 1957. Dior is the first
couturier to appear on the magazine's cover.

Left: Norman Parkinson, *Vendôme* dress,
Christian Dior New York Fall-Winter 1949 collection,
model Wenda Parkinson (born Rogerson).

Christian Dior. Special creation, c. 1950.
Cotton piqué ball gown adorned
with ivy, burgundy velvet belt.
Paris, Dior Héritage. Inv. 1987.92

"After women, flowers are the most divine creations," said Christian Dior.[1]
Gardens held a particular fascination for the designer, beginning with that
of his childhood home, the Villa Les Rhumbs in Granville. No other
couturier used flowers with the force and expressiveness of Dior, who had
his dresses printed or delicately embroidered with bouquets, sprays, branches,
garlands or plant motifs. In the case of this design, the simple, light fabric
of a summer ball gown was embellished with ivy. Dior transformed the
delicacy of these floral details into the expression of rediscovered femininity.

Flowered décolletages and rounded corollas paid tribute to the couturier's
memories of three special places: Granville, Milly-la-Forêt and Montauroux.
Perched on a Normandy clifftop overlooking the sea, the Villa Les Rhumbs
where Christian Dior grew up remained his unparalleled Garden of Eden.
Its grounds, landscaped in the English style by his mother Madeleine, are one
of the few early twentieth-century "artist's gardens" to have survived.
In 1948, he created a wonderful garden at the house in Milly-la-Forêt where
he liked to spend his weekends, but it was in La Colle Noire, near Grasse, that
Dior found his ultimate earthly paradise. In the different climate of the south,
he recreated the "enclosed garden" that was the peaceful haven of his
childhood, "bringing things full circle" in the hope that there he might
"one day forget Christian Dior, *Couturier*, and become the neglected private
individual again."[2]

LAURENCE BENAÏM

1. Christian Dior, *Christian Dior's Little Dictionary of
   Fashion*, London, Cassell and Company Ltd., 1954, p. 31.
2. Christian Dior, *Dior by Dior: The Autobiography of
   Christian Dior*, London, V&A Publishing, 2nd ed., p. 192.

Louise Dahl-Wolfe, Christian Bérard and Christian
Dior in Fleury-en-Bière, 1946. Dior loved to play
cards, especially solitaire. Artist Christian Bérard
was one of his closest friends and advisors.

Romaine Brooks, *Spring*, oil on canvas,
ca. 1912. Paris, Lucile Audouy private collection.

Christian Dior. *Coup de Théâtre* gown. Haute
Couture, Spring-Summer 1951, *Naturelle* line.
Taffeta gala gown covered with tulle by
Hurel, gold lamé lace ribbon, taffeta belt. Paris,
Musée des Arts Décoratifs, UFAC collection,
gift of Mme Raoul Meyer, 1956. Inv. UF 56-43-1

"Unless there is something outstanding to be seen, I take little pleasure in entertainments,"[1] confided Christian Dior. *Coup de Théâtre* came on stage as part of a collection dedicated to drama and theater, as reflected by the names of other designs: *Côté Cour, Côté Jardin, Entracte, Fauteuil d'Orchestre, Intrigue, Marivaux* and *Pantomime*. The catalog announced the oval as its "underlying theme," on which *Coup de Théâtre* is a variation, with rings of glittering gold encircling the gown to "follow the natural curves of the female body." The gradually widening rings suggest a view of the gown from above, accentuating its monumental quality and recalling the decorative style of "Infanta" gowns.

This creation would fit perfectly with the tiered and gilded balconies of an Italian-style theater. And Christian Dior adopted a method used by costume designers: enlarging details to make them visible from a distance. The bow at the waist is huge. The ivory taffeta gown is covered with black tulle—a layering that creates shimmers and shadows, heightening the brilliance of reliefs and the depth of folds and amplifying the slightest movement. "There are salon optics, just as there are theatre optics,"[2] said Dior. His design is a gown that plays with the shift from stage to ballroom. *Coup de Théâtre* might be worn by Molière's Donna Elvira: "Do not be surprised, Don Juan, to see me at this hour, and in this dress."[3]

Theatrical references were inherent to Christian Dior. It was in the field of costume that he first gained recognition as a designer, as he reported in his autobiography: "When Marcel Herrand asked me to design the costumes for Sheridan's *School for Scandal* in 1939, I was working anonymously at Piguet. These were the first costumes to which I put my name."[4] The historical nature of the costumes in question, inspired by eighteenth-century England, gave Dior an opportunity to experiment with the effects of billowing skirts. The enjoyment of dressing up he had demonstrated since childhood must also have fired his imagination, and his friendship with the painter, fashion illustrator and set designer Christian Bérard was another incentive to associate costume design with the history of theater and drama: Bérard often worked for the renowned French actor-director Louis Jouvet, and his partner was Boris Kochno, former assistant of Sergei Diaghilev. Many of Dior's contributions to stage and drama were connected to his circle of friends. In 1947, Louis Jouvet presented an original two-part program at the Théâtre de l'Athénée in Paris, beginning with the world premiere of Jean Genet's *The Maids*—with stage sets by Bérard and costumes by Lanvin—followed by Jean Giraudoux's last play *The Apollo of Bellac*, whose young heroine Dominique Blanchar wore the *Chérie* dress from the New Look collection.

ÉRIC PUJALET-PLAÀ

1. Christian Dior, *Dior by Dior: The Autobiography of Christian Dior*, London, V&A Publishing, 2nd ed., p. 189.
2. Ibid., p. 80.
3. Molière, *Dom Juan*, IV, 6, monologue by Donna Elvira.
4. Christian Dior, op. cit., p. 189.

Roger Berson, Christian Dior and Nathalie Philippart during
rehearsals for Roland Petit's ballet *Les Treize Danses*
at the Théâtre des Champs-Élysées, November 12, 1947.

Roger Berson, Leslie Caron, Nelly Guillerm and Christian Dior
during rehearsals for the ballet *Les Treize Danses*, November 12, 1947.

Right: Boris Lipnitzki, Dominique Blanchar and Louis Jouvet
in Jean Giraudoux's play *L'Apollon de Bellac*, April 1947.
Dominique Blanchar is wearing an adaptation of the *Chérie* dress,
Fall-Winter 1947 Haute Couture collection (*Corolle* line).

Christian Dior. *Mexique* gown.
Haute Couture, Fall-Winter 1951,
Longue line. Tulle evening dress with
embroidered gold, fish-scale motif.
Paris, Dior Héritage. Inv. 2009.1

Mexico has been interwoven throughout Dior's seventy-year history. Romantic and imaginative, the country implies exuberance, as demonstrated by this 1951 evening gown, as well as fashion shows presented in the Mexican capital. It also calls to mind the Spanish-speaking John Galliano, who created a Mexican-inspired collection in 2002 and referred to the traditional Mexican saddle when designing his decade at Dior celebratory handbag.

Christian Dior's passion for the country began in his first collection when he introduced *Mexico*, a printed day dress. Surrounded by stylish Mexicans, one of his best friends was Carmen Corcuera, who hailed from one of Mexico's grandest families and who in 1938 married Pierre Colle, Christian Dior's partner in his second gallery.[1] A friend of Balthus, Carmen Colle was well connected in Parisian art circles. When hiring her to manage his Colifichets boutique, Dior said, "Give me a grand dose of the Popocatépetl."[2] María Félix, Mexico's most famous movie star, also became a keen Dior client. Renowned for her enviably teeny waist and superb figure, Félix remained Dior's best poster girl, particularly in 1950 when he signed a contract with Palacio de Hierro, Mexico City's key department store, authorizing them to choose and reproduce his Haute Couture outfits twice a year.

During the 1950s, the South American market became supremely important to Christian Dior, boosted by major international clients like Eva Perón, the wife of Argentina's president. Not only was there serious wealth, but his thoroughly feminine designs suited his South American clientele, who were prepared to spend hours squeezed into his corsets. Their infectious enthusiasm was reflected in the names of his dresses, which included *Havana*, *Acapulco*, *Brazil*, *Argentina*, *Columbia*, *Uruguay* and *Venezuela*. Certain clients traveled to Paris; otherwise South Americans sought out Dior's agents, whose salons had the right French ambiance, with appropriate armchairs and lighting, evoking features of the Paris boutique. For instance, Dr. Humberto Solis sold Dior's Haute Couture gowns and products at El Encanto, his exclusive salon in Havana, Cuba, as did a certain Severiano Garcia in Los Gobelinos, a major department store in Santiago, Chile.[3]

Nevertheless, Christian Dior's ultimate boutique was in Caracas, Venezuela, then viewed as one of the most sophisticated capitals in the world. Situated on Avenida Francisco de Miranda (the city's equivalent to Paris's Avenue Montaigne), it occupied the same space as Cartier and boasted highly specialized personnel trained in France. Dior attended its opening in 1953—underlining the boutique's significance—and the following year a Red Cross charity fashion show took place that highlighted his fashion house's three-month South American tour. The glamorous event was held in the garden of La Vega, the magnificent home of one of his top clients, María Teresa Herrera-Uslar, the Dowager Marquesa de Torre Casa, often referred to as Mimi de Herrera.[4]

NATASHA FRASER-CAVASSONI

1. Natasha Fraser-Cavassoni, *Monsieur Dior: Once upon a Time*, New York, Pointed Leaf Press, 2014, p. 49.
2. Ibid., pp. 152, 49.
3. Ibid., p. 160.
4. Ibid., p. 133.

Willy Rizzo, Mimi de Herrera with the Dior models at the La Vega
hacienda in Caracas, before the presentation of the new Christian Dior collection, 1953.

Right: Eva Perón during ceremonies for the Argentinian
national holiday, in 1950. She is wearing the *Bach* dress,
Spring-Summer 1950 Haute Couture collection (*Verticale* line).

Christian Dior. Evening gown. Haute Couture. 1951.
Bodice and belt of silk organza over silk satin,
skirt of seven layers of silk, net and silk organza;
embroidered with raffia, sequins of pressed pulp laminated with straw,
metal sequins, diamanté beads and mother-of-pearl shells.
Museum of London, gift HRH Princess Margaret,
Countess of Snowdon, 1968. Inv. 62.6/2a,b,c

On November 22, 1951 the journalist Pierre Macaigne told readers of *Le Figaro* that his childhood dreams of princesses in white ball gowns, smiling graciously while dancing in illuminated salons, had finally come true the previous night.[1] That evening Republican Guards stood to attention while Princess Margaret, younger sister of Queen Elizabeth of Britain, ascended the staircase of the Cercle de l'Union Interalliée on Rue du Faubourg Saint-Honoré to attend a charity ball. The "petite princesse," as the French press dubbed her, wore a beautiful white gown ordered from Dior for her twenty-first birthday in August that year.

The dress, from the *Oblique* line, was not the first the Princess had commissioned from Dior. During a visit to 30 Avenue Montaigne in 1949, the nineteen-year-old Margaret had thanked the couturier "for creating the New Look" and had ordered a gown of "white strapless tulle" with "a vast satin bow at the back" which she later recalled as her "favourite dress of all."[2] For her official birthday photographs in 1949 and 1950 the Princess observed the unwritten rule that royal women should patronize British fashion and wore Norman Hartnell. For Cecil Beaton's photographs for the princess's coming-of-age, however, Margaret could not resist wearing her latest Dior gown, its seven-layered skirt spread out on the royal settee.

Dior is said to have asked his royal client whether she felt more like a gold or a silver person.[3] The princess seems to have felt golden but surprisingly Dior did not employ precious metal thread for the gown's embroidery but raffia, pressed pulp laminated with straw, as well as metal sequins, diamanté beads and mother-of-pearl shells. Wearing her Cinderella dress, the Princess opened the ball to Cole Porter's "Night and Day" and continued to dance until the early hours of the morning, asking the trumpeter Aimé Barelli to play "La Vie en Rose" for her.[4]

The following day Margaret paid another visit to Dior. She also attended the designer's charity fashion show at Blenheim Palace in England in November 1952, probably the last time the couturier and his royal client had a chance to talk. The Princess remained a Dior client almost to the end of her life. While Margaret's visit to Paris in 1959 might have been the last time she ordered couture, she also put together a wardrobe of ready-to-wear garments bearing the Dior label.[5] The close association between Princess and couturier was relatively short-lived but mutually beneficial. The New Look silhouette perfectly suited the Princess's figure, and her connection with the French fashion house helped to establish her as a fashion icon. The anglophile Christian Dior must have relished dressing Margaret, whom he called "a real fairy princess, delicate, graceful, exquisite."[6]

BEATRICE BEHLEN

1. Pierre Macaigne, "Soirée de Paris. Au bal du Cercle interallié *avec une princesse de rêve....*" *Le Figaro*, No. 2, 240, 22 November 1951, title page.
2. Theo Aronson, *Princess Margaret: A Biography*, London: Michael O'Mara Books, 2001, p. 115 (based on a conversation with Princess Margaret); Angela Huth, *The Englishwoman's Wardrobe*, London: Ebury Press, 1986, p. 14.
3. Marie-France Pochna, *Christian Dior: The Man Who Made the World Look New*, New York: Arcade Publishing, 1996, p. 162 (source not provided).
4. Marion Crawford, *Princess Margaret*, London: George Newnes, 1953, p. 64; André Lacaze, "Le Bal de Margaret," *Paris Match*, 1 December 1951, p. 20.
5. Lent to the Royal Ceremonial Dress Collection, Historic Royal Palaces, by Lord Linley and Lady Sarah Chatto: 3400416, green velvet coat by Christian Dior, London, worn 1975; 3400413 black silk dress by Christian Dior, London, worn 1979; 3400451 cream wool knee-length cape, Christian Dior Boutique, 1997; 3400446, fur coat, Christian Dior-New York, worn 1982–1993.
6. Christian Dior, *Dior by Dior: The Autobiography of Christian Dior*, London, V&A Publishing, 2nd ed., p. 161.

Princess Margaret accompanied by Sir Oliver Harvey as she arrives at the Bal du Cercle de l'Union Interalliée, a benefit for the Hertford British Hospital in Paris, November 21, 1951.

Princess Margaret at the presentation of the Fall-Winter 1954 Haute Couture collection at Blenheim Palace, November 3, 1954.

Opposite: Cecil Beaton, official portrait of Princess Margaret for her twenty-first birthday. She is wearing the dress that Christian Dior designed exclusively for her.

Christian Dior. *Trianon* gown. Haute Couture,
Spring-Summer 1952, *Sinueuse* line. Evening gown
in organdy by Jean Page, embroidered with lamé,
metallic sequins and silver beads. Palais Galliera,
Musée de la Mode de la Ville de Paris, gift of Francine
Halphen-Clore, 1984. Inv. GAL1986.69.8

Christian Dior's collections included five different versions of the *Trianon* gown, the first of which was part of the Spring-Summer collection of 1949. These long, voluminous and richly embroidered evening gowns reflect the couturier's fascination for the Enlightenment. *Fête à Trianon* and *Bal à Trianon* are examples of the corseted gowns that Christian Dior brought back into fashion; the evening dresses, formal gowns and cocktail dresses of the 1950s recall the pannier dresses of the eighteenth century. From the late 1940s on, both Christian Dior and Pierre Balmain—who had met while working as assistant designers for Lucien Lelong—contributed to the return of opulence to evening wear, using heavy taffeta, sumptuous satin, imperial velvet and magnificent silk faille to create bodices with nipped-in waists and billowing skirts like those worn at Versailles. Girdles helped create the new silhouette, with constraining corsets replaced by cleverly concealed whalebone. Horsehair padding at the hips and many-layered underskirts rivaled historical sack-back gowns and court dresses.

In addition to these exuberant forms, the colors were also inspired by the palette of the eighteenth century: "Marie Antoinette blue," "Bertin pink" (from the name of the famous fashion merchant), "Versailles" gold and white, "Trianon gray," "Dauphin green," "cheveux de la reine ('queen's hair') blond" and "royal red." The use of lace, guipure and embroidery of all kinds also reflected a return to ornamentation.

In his *bureau de reveries* ("office of daydreams")—an eighteenth-century expression adopted by the couturier—Dior the demiurge recreated the atmosphere of a bygone age, a period that the first half of the twentieth century, with its Scheherazade cushions, had dispelled from his imagination. With its preciously ornamented, light-colored fabric, *Trianon* illustrates Dior's intentions as a couturier, decorator and painter. For the salons of his couture house, the alcove of his bedroom and the pages of his sketchbooks, Christian Dior desired the return of splendor. His sinuous designs, in fabrics that were dry and stone-colored by day, acquired nobility in the evening with their opulence of form and color. Dior was truly the king of 1950s fashion.

OLIVIER SAILLARD

Clifford Coffin, *Coquette* dress photographed at the
Grand Trianon, Fall-Winter 1948 Haute Couture collection
(*Ailée* line), model Wenda Parkinson (born Rogerson).

Christian Dior. *Vilmorin* dress.
Haute Couture, Spring-Summer 1952, *Sinueuse* line.
Afternoon dress in silk muslin, embroidered
by Rébé with flowers in canvas and cotton. Paris,
Musée des Arts Décoratifs, UFAC collection,
gift of Patricia López-Willshaw, 1966. Inv. UF 66-38-26

This dress appeared on the cover of the special Easter 1952 issue of *Elle* magazine, alongside another similarly embroidered dress worn by aspiring young model Brigitte Bardot. The youthfulness and freshness of the design stem from its delicacy, its light colors and the lovely embroidery of daisies on a soft and natural-looking ground. The Musée des Arts Décoratifs holds the many embroidery samples produced by René Bégué (known as "Rébé") to show how this effect could be attained. The dress still has the pencil marks that outlined the irregular embroidery pattern on the organza to ensure that it created the trompe-l'œil effect of a daisy-sprinkled lawn.

The embroidery also flatters the curves of the body: the highest reliefs and most intense colors, on either side of the belt, fade imperceptibly toward the neckline and hemline. The resulting silhouette resembles a spray of flowers tied in the middle, spreading up toward the décolletage and down to reveal the line of the legs. The neckline of the low-cut, tight-waisted bodice features a collar of ethereal organza reminiscent of the eighteenth-century *fichu menteur*—a historical reference which, together with the simple, beautiful illusion of the embroidered daisies, evokes the Queen's Hamlet at Versailles. The humble daisy, heralding the arrival of summer, expresses the bucolic aspect of Dior's floral inspiration. The *Vilmorin* afternoon dress may have been the designer's interpretation of the springtime view of the garden at his "Rousseauesque" cottage[1]—the Coudret mill at Milly-la-Forêt—and was probably also inspired by the walled garden of his childhood home in Granville. The name of the dress is also associated with Dior's childhood: the Vilmorin seed company, founded near Paris in the eighteenth century, must have been known to the Diors who ran a prosperous fertilizer business in Granville. The Vilmorin catalogs were Dior's favorite reading material when he was a boy.[2]

Besides expressing the designer's love of flowers, the *Vilmorin* dress could be a tribute to Parisian socialite, fashion columnist and writer Louise de Vilmorin (1902–1969), who was also the companion of André Malraux. The intelligentsia liked to gather in her "salon bleu" at Verrières-le-Buisson; this Louis XVI drawing room with blue upholstery, adorned with charming, antiquated family ornaments, was a reference in terms of interior decoration. It evidently inspired the floral print wallpaper that Christian Dior used for the drawing room of his last retreat, the Château de La Colle Noire in Montauroux. The springtime theme of the *Vilmorin* dress, inspired by several real or imaginary gardens, designates youth as an aesthetic ideal. Its "budding" beauty heralds the growing influence of the baby-boom generation that would revolutionize taste in the decades to come.

ÉRIC PUJALET-PLAÀ

1. Christian Dior, *Dior by Dior: The Autobiography of Christian Dior*, London, V&A Publishing, 2nd ed., p. 190.
2. Ibid., p. 168.

Cover of a catalog by Vilmorin-Andrieux & Cie, Spring 1905. In his memoirs, Christian
Dior describes how these seed catalogs were his favorite bedtime reading material.

Right: Cover of *Elle*, March 24, 1952. *Vilmorin* and *Andrieux* dresses, Spring-
Summer 1952 Haute Couture collection (*Sinueuse* line). The *Vilmorin*
dress is worn by Sylvie Hirsch, the *Andrieux* dress by a young Brigitte Bardot.

ELLE

Joyeuses Pâques

NUMÉRO SPÉCIAL DE PAQUES

LES CONFIDENCES DE 6 FEMMES QUI SE CONNAISSENT BIEN,

le MAQUILLAGE DE PRINTEMPS et

VOUS AVEZ RENDEZ-VOUS AVEC L'AMOUR, par Françoise Giroud

N° 330 - 24 MARS 1952

60 Pages - 50 Frs

Christian Dior. *Palmyre* gown. Haute Couture. Fall-Winter 1952, *Profilée* line. Evening gown in satin by Robert Perrier, embroidered with Swarovski crystals, metallic thread, gemstones, pearls and sequins by Ginesty. Paris, Dior Héritage. Inv. 1996.2

Palmyre, a long princess gown with a bustier bodice, illustrates "the dynamic precision of planes and automobiles"[1] characteristic of the *Profilée* line. The hang of the shiny acetate satin highlights the contrast between the unadorned and embroidered areas, accentuating the radiating pleats that frame the hips like a fuselage but open out into "panniers" like those of eighteenth-century court gowns.

The embroidered decoration of pearls, rhinestones and gold thread by Ginesty creates the impression of a busk point below the waist; despite the contemporary inspiration for the *Palmyre* design, this splendor firmly places it in the category of sumptuous historical gowns used to bring a show to its climax. "Short evening dresses, long sheath dresses, full-skirted dresses, finally the grand ball dresses encrusted with embroidery—I myself decide the order in which they are to be shown, rather as a fireworks artist launches the various pieces in his repertoire."[2] The skillfully embroidered cobalt blue and turquoise floral scrolls on the light-colored fabric are an evocation of the decoration on Ottoman Iznik pottery. The embroidery spreads across the gown symmetrically on either side of a central panel with arabesques, like the painted decoration on a large earthenware vase whose handles would be the wearer's bare arms and shoulders. This comparison merits a brief digression. Iznik pottery appeared in sixteenth-century Turkey in an attempt to imitate the Chinese porcelain pieces that arrived via the Silk Road. The style of these ceramic wares was popularized in Europe in the nineteenth century through the works of Eugène-Victor Collinot and Adalbert de Beaumont, who also spread knowledge of them with their encyclopedia of oriental decorative arts (*Encyclopédie des arts décoratifs de l'Orient*), published in 1881. Dior must have been familiar with the distinctive style of Iznik decoration and its compositions of tulips, hyacinths, carnations and roses through Étienne de Beaumont, the grandson of a famous ornamentalist inspired by the Orient. Dior had been friends since the 1920s with de Beaumont, who held a "Kings and Queens Ball" in 1949 that Dior attended dressed as a lion. The *Palmyre* gown may have been partly inspired by de Beaumont's family background and personality—especially his love of dressing up.

The Oriental luxury of this ball gown is a blend of authentic exactitude and creative fancy. It appeared in a photograph in American *Vogue* in September 1952, against the backdrop of the Pavillon Colombe in Saint-Brice, property of the Duchesse de Talleyrand—a rococo setting, somewhere between the Bosporus and the China Sea, in which it evoked all the exoticism of the *Amorous Indies* or the *Persian Letters*.

ÉRIC PUJALET-PLAÀ

1. Fall-Winter 1952 collection catalog.
2. Christian Dior, *Dior by Dior: The Autobiography of Christian Dior*, London, V&A Publishing, 2nd ed., p. 125.

Peter Lindbergh, ornament created with
Swarovski crystals, *Princesse Lucknow* dress, Fall-Winter 1997
Haute Couture collection, model Charlotte Connoley.

Christian Dior. *Sonnet* gown.
Haute Couture, Fall-Winter 1952.
Profilée line. Ottoman ball gown.
Paris, Dior Héritage. Inv. 2012.9

The *Sonnet* ball gown, with its surprisingly contemporary look, has a purity of line that evokes the minimalism of today. The structured cut and sturdy ottoman fabric accentuate both the outline and the key features of the silhouette. The design is characteristic of the *Profilée* line, intended by Dior to create a "clean-cut and defined silhouette that reflects contemporary life, as expressed by a resolutely modern technique. […] For the woman of today has her own tastes and proportions, very different from the tomboy of yesteryear. […] Today's women are as curvy as modern cars."[1] This gown is a perfect expression of the relationship between sketch and cut, such an important part of the couturier's creative process; after all, Christian Dior had gained entrance to the world of Haute Couture through his talent as a designer-illustrator.

In 1935, his drawing skills saved him from the downward spiral occasioned by the economic crisis and his father's bankruptcy. After living in a wretched attic room above the Bœuf sur le Toit bar, Dior was invited to share the apartment of his friend Jean Ozenne on Quai Malaquais. With the encouragement of Ozenne—a future stage actor who was earning a living as a fashion designer at the time—and of his American friend Max Kenna, Dior learnt to do fashion sketches and managed to sell his first designs to the milliners Esther Meyer, Agnès, Rose Valois and Claude Saint-Cyr. Sales to fashion houses followed—Patou, Schiaparelli, Rochas, Nina Ricci, Maggy Rouff, Balenciaga, Molyneux, Worth and Paquin—and, finally, *Le Figaro* newspaper and *Le Jardin des Modes* and *Vogue* magazines published his sketches of the season's fashions. Some of these—such as the page in the *Figaro* of May 4, 1939 showing the new summer blouses—were signed with his name.

Dior's love of drawing persisted when he was a couturier: "I scribble everywhere, in bed, in my bath, at meals, in my car, on foot, in the sun, in electric light, by day and night. […] My dresses take shape all around me. […] Suddenly, one such flash of inspiration gives me an electric shock. I am possessed, and embroider endless variations on one theme. The next morning, it is the turn of another line—which has perhaps come to me during the night—to give me the signal."[2]

In the preliminary sketches he called his *petites gravures*, Dior indicated the key elements of the cut, hang and direction of the fabric to help the *premières d'atelier* (head seamstresses) create the muslin models. What mattered most in his view was that "they [the drawings] should be expressive. The great mistake of the fashion schools is teaching their pupils simply to turn out finished drawings or abstract patterns. In order to excite the enthusiasm of a *première*—or mine, for that matter—a sketch must suggest both attack and allure; it must already suggest a living line; it must be redolent with movement."[3] In a series of photographs taken at the Roubaix-Tourcoing woolen mills, *Elle* magazine presented the *Sonnet* gown in the middle of the loom room.[4] And for *L'Officiel de la Mode*, the *Sonnet* gown with its full skirt and low neckline held a promise of nights spent dancing "in dark, billowing silk."[5]

FLORENCE MÜLLER

1. Press release for the 1952 Fall-Winter collection.
2. Christian Dior, *Dior by Dior: The Autobiography of Christian Dior*, London, V&A Publishing, 2nd ed., 2007, p. 62.
3. Ibid., p. 63.
4. *Elle*, November 24, 1952, p. 27.
5. *L'Officiel de la mode*, December 1952, no. 369–370, p. 74.

Willy Maywald, Christian Dior drawing, ca. 1950.

Right: Frances McLaughlin, dress from the Fall-Winter
1952 Haute Couture collection (*Profilée* line), model Gigi.

Insert: Christian Dior, drawing made for Claude Saint Cyr,
belonging to a collection of 100, 1937–1938. Collection
Christine Labrune, daughter of milliner Claude Saint Cyr.

Christian Dior. *May* gown. Haute Couture, Spring-Summer 1953, *Tulipe* line. Ball gown in organza, embroidered with leaves and flowers by Rébé. Paris, Musée des Arts Décoratifs, UFAC collection, gift of Mme de Bord in memory of her mother Mme Lazard, 1978. Inv. UF 78-33-1

With the *Tulipe* line—the emblematic silhouette of the 1953 Spring-Summer collection—Dior's work probably reached its apotheosis in terms of suppleness and fluidity. And the ball gown called *May*, number 115 in that collection, is surely one of the most vibrant expressions of the couturier's passion for flowers—a passion dating from his childhood.[1] Dior was well aware of the pitfalls of an ill-considered approach to floral motifs, no matter how attractive. His dictionary entry for "Flowers" is as follows: "They [flowers] are so delicate and charming, but they must be used carefully."[2] Moreover, the cultural history of textiles embroidered, woven, painted or printed with "natural" or "fantasy" plant motifs is so rich that the imagination of any artist working with them is inevitably inspired, not only by the materials themselves, but by depictions of them in other media such as painting.

The program for the show featured a description of the characteristics of the *Tulipe* line: "blossoming of the bust," "impression of breathable comfort," "contraction of the hips," "natural shoulders" and an "unfettered look." The ivory organza was an ideal choice for the purpose of the gown and the glorification of the *Tulipe* silhouette.

The name of the gown, *May*, refers to its embroidery. The "pretty month of May" (*le joli mois de mai*) of traditional French songs is evoked by the embroidered clover—a humble, common plant whose spreading stems and trifoliate leaves wind their way among flowering grasses. Even non-specialists can easily distinguish the two different species on this sunny, soft green ground: red clover and strawberry clover, expressed in colors ranging from pale pink to crimson and purple, with flower heads of different shapes, globular or slightly elongated. This vegetation is skillfully scattered over the organza: sparsely toward the hem of the gown; more thickly from knee-level upward; blossoming in a cluster on the bodice.

Although the bucolic inspiration of this elegant embroidery recalls the eighteenth century, the arrangement of the motifs, which appear to have been freely and spontaneously scattered over the organza, is more reminiscent of "modern" artistic trends exemplified by the beautiful silk scarves designed in 1907 by René Lalique—especially *Champ de Blé* and *Champ de Marguerites*, manufactured by the Bianchini-Férier company in Lyon.[3] Above all, the *May* gown evokes the elegant ladies whose gestures and movements, captured by the Impressionists, enhanced the floral fabrics of their gowns through the effects of light. The model Alla, who presented *May*, must have resembled a living allegory of Spring—like Jeanne Demarsy, the lithe-figured young actress chosen in 1881 by Édouard Manet as the embodiment of Spring[4] in a light-colored dress sprinkled with delicate bouquets of blue and yellow wildflowers.

PHILIPPE THIÉBAUT

1. Christian Dior, *Dior by Dior: The Autobiography of Christian Dior*, London, V&A Publishing, 2nd ed., p. 168.
2. Christian Dior, *The Little Dictionary of Fashion: A Guide to Dress Sense for Every Woman*, London, Cassell and Company Ltd., 1954, p. 31.
3. These four scarves were exhibited at the salon of the Société des Artistes Français in 1907, and purchased the same year by the Union Centrale des Arts Décoratifs.
4. Édouard Manet, *Jeanne (Spring)*, 1881, Los Angeles, J. Paul Getty Museum.

Below: Henri Cartier-Bresson, model Alla having the *May* dress fitted before the fashion show, 1953.
Following double page: Tierney Gearon, *New Junon*, *Brise de mémoires*, *Essence d'herbier* and *Souvenir d'automne* dresses, Spring-Summer 2017 Haute Couture collection, models Laura Toth, Blanca Padilla, Julie Hoomans and Romy Schönberger.

Christian Dior. *Mazette* dress. Haute
Couture, Fall-Winter 1954, *H* line.
Wool dress with a mink collar.
Paris, Dior Héritage. Inv. 2003.83

The name of this dress, *Mazette*, is a French exclamation denoting surprise and just a hint of fear. Christian Dior's 1954 Fall-Winter collection was a volte-face in relation to the New Look: "The *H* line introduces a radically different silhouette based on the lengthening and reduction of the bust. The parallel lines that form the elongated letter H provide the structure for dresses, suits and coats."[1] The *H* line, dubbed the "String Bean" line or the "flat look" by the press, gave the impression of flattening the bosom.

Mazette reflects this stylization. It has an under-bodice of whaleboned net, on the front of which is a wool panel that fills the dress's open neckline, rather like a square modesty piece. The plunging, rollover, mink stole collar covers the bosom where it creates a contrastingly smooth, flat effect. The dress is cut like a frock coat, with a crossover fastening and no drapery. It is composed of a number of organza-lined wool panels placed on either side of the waist seam. The buttons down the left side form the legs of the letter "H" that gave the line its name.

The *Mazette* dress garnered particular attention because of its defining *H* line characteristics: verticality and an undefined bust line. In response to advocates of the high-busted look who criticized the *H* line, at a press conference in September 1954, during the shooting of *Gentlemen Marry Brunettes*, Christian Dior invited the voluptuous actress Jane Russell to wear the dress—which she did, demonstrating that "if a woman's got it you can't do anything to suppress it."[2]

Mazette looks to us today like a hybrid garment, rooted in the 1950s but foreshadowing the decade to come. According to the collection program, this black dress was to be worn under a coat that also had a mink collar, creating a highly sophisticated and sensual daywear outfit. Without the coat, the *Mazette* afternoon dress looked rather like a fur-collared coat worn with nothing but lingerie underneath (the under-bodice features a garter belt). The short, set-in sleeves add a dressy touch to what would otherwise be a coat dress, and prefigure the mini dresses of the following decade, often embellished with buttons.

ÉRIC PUJALET-PLAÀ

1. 1954 Fall-Winter collection catalog.
2. *New York World-Telegram and Sun*, September 17, 1954.

Christian Dior

AUTOMNE-HIVER 1954

LIGNE H

SILHOUETTE HANCHÉE

L'heure **H** a sonné d'une ligne entièrement différente basée sur la **longueur** et l'**amenuisement** du buste, c'est sur les parallèles qui forment la lettre **H,** toute en hauteur, que se construisent robes, tailleurs et manteaux.

Si la taille reste toujours à sa place, c'est par les emmanchures **verticales,** par la poitrine **peu marquée** et **haut placée,** par de nombreux effets de drapés ou d'empiècements placés sous la taille, au départ de la **hanche,** que nous avons obtenu cet effet de buste long s'appuyant sur les hanches, qui est la marque de la saison.

Nous avons étudié un gainage nouveau du corps, en souplesse, parfois indépendant de la robe, qui contribue pour une large part à cette silhouette.

Toute la Collection, que les jupes soient larges ou étroites, s'inspire de la même construction.

Les cols sont fréquemment remplacés par des drapés et ne sont jamais importants.

La poitrine **haut placée** entraîne nécessairement des décolletés beaucoup plus **réservés.**

Si les robes ne sont pas tout d'une pièce, elles sont souvent formées d'une jupe et d'un haut, non pas chemisier, mais en forme de vestes-chemises souplement ajustées et descendant jusqu'aux **hanches.**

Les blouses se sont, elles aussi, allongées au lieu de s'arrêter dans la jupe.

Les basques des tailleurs sont plus longues et ont tendance à s'évaser sous une taille que rien n'entrave.

Jane Russell wearing the *Mazette* dress during
a photo shoot organized by the House of Dior
and United Artists for the promotion of the film
Gentlemen Marry Brunettes. This press presentation
was aimed at convincing journalists that the
H line was not eliminating feminine curves.

Left: Press release of the Fall-Winter
1954 Haute Couture collection.

In 1955, Christian Dior designed the Chinese-inspired *Surprise* for the Duchess of Windsor. An intriguing choice considering all the racy rumors about her youth spent in Shanghai in the 1920s. Nevertheless, the Duchess wore it incessantly.

She was so enamored by Christian Dior's designs that her royal husband declared, "the Duchess loves Paris because it is not too far from Dior."[1] Famous for saying "you can never be too rich or too thin," the American-born style icon lacked the curves that inspired the couturier but he recognized that she had innate elegance and was prepared to spend afternoons ensuring a seamless fit.

Yet in many ways, Marc Bohan's pared-down style was better suited to the Duchess's purist needs. On one occasion, she suggested that they do away with the outfit's pockets. Bohan quickly did so. In general, the Duchess liked blue and beige tones "but neither apricot nor grey," he said. During the day, she preferred outfits brought together by a jacket and avoided wool because "it made her feel hot." At night she chose "evening dresses that were short" and "made of light fabrics" like pleated chiffon, faille and taffeta.[2]

Nowadays, Dior is worn by a host of stylish Chinese actresses such as Gong Li, Zhang Ziyi, Maggie Cheung, Shu Qi, Angelababy, Sun Li and Ni Ni. But the house's history with China began with Christian Dior. During his childhood, his vivid imagination was stirred by the magic and mystery of the Far East. Although he never went to China, he demonstrated his fascination when choosing names for outfits such as *Pékin*, *Shanghai*, *Chinoiseries*, *Nuit de Chine*, *Hong Kong* and *Bleu de Chine*.

In Beijing in 1986, at the Great Wall Sheraton hotel, Frédéric Castet, Dior's fabled fur designer, presented the Winter collection to an audience of 800 people. Eight years later, Dior opened its first boutique in China in Shanghai. In his 1997 Spring-Summer Haute Couture collection John Galliano evoked Shanghai's 1930s glamour, and in 2003 he created an entire Chinese collection that included acrobats. A decade later, the designer Raf Simons unveiled his second Dior Haute Couture collection on the Bund.

Meanwhile, a series of elaborate artistic encounters with China have included exhibitions like *Christian Dior and the Chinese Artists* in 2008, *Lady Dior As Seen By* in 2011, *Esprit Dior* in 2013, and *Le Théâtre Dior* and *Miss Dior* in 2014.

NATASHA FRASER-CAVASSONI

1. Suzy Menkes, *The Windsor Style*, London, Grafton, 1987, p. 95.
2. Laurence Catinot-Crost, *Wallis la magnifique! L'extraordinaire destin de la duchesse de Windsor*, Paris, Atlantica, 2005, p. 301.

Christian Dior. *Bal de Printemps* ensemble.
Haute Couture, Spring-Summer 1956, *Flèche* line.
Coat embroidered with floral motifs in floss silk
by Rébé, embellished with gold sequins. Shantung
cocktail dress. Paris, Dior Héritage. Inv. 1987.7

For the 1954 premiere of the Hitchcock film *Rear Window*, Grace Kelly wore a gown by Dior. At the party to celebrate her engagement to Prince Rainier III of Monaco, held at the Waldorf Astoria hotel in New York, the star wore a Dior gown in white satin fit for a true fairy-tale princess, a dazzling vision to all who saw her. From then on, Grace of Monaco stayed true to the House of Dior. To seal the bond between Marc Bohan and the princess, at the Monaco Red Cross Ball in 1961 the Dior perfume company presented her with a magnificent eighteenth-century Chinese lacquer casket containing a luxury edition of the perfume *Diorissimo*, a set of bath oils and a selection of fourteen lipsticks.

Grace of Monaco wore the *Bal de Printemps* ensemble to conceal her figure when she was pregnant with her daughter Caroline. This design from the *Flèche* line, with its loose-fitting back and high waistline, perfectly illustrates the "child's coat style."[1] The motif of bouquets by the embroiderer Rébé recalls Dior's predilection for rustic floral decoration.

Marc Bohan asked Princess Grace to be the honorary patron of the first Baby Dior store, inaugurated on November 7, 1967 at 28 Avenue Montaigne. Wearing the *San Francisco* suit, she was greeted by two little cherubs: Delphine de Rohan-Chabot and Hubert Chalmeton de Croÿ, dressed in black velvet with white ruffs, who presented her with flowers and sugared almonds. Accompanied by Marc Bohan, she cut the inaugural ribbon of this tiny four-by-five-meter boutique, decorated with wicker and white cotton piqué by Victor Grandpierre. The window display by Jean-François Daigre featured a huge knitted stork with outspread wings. Bohan's five-year-old daughter Marie-Anne was his inspiration for the collections for babies and toddlers aged from birth to four years old.

Caroline and her sister Stephanie are also regular, high-profile clients of the House of Dior, and Princess Charlene of Monaco has continued the tradition since her wedding to Prince Albert II of Monaco in 2011. The many Dior designs she has worn include a clover-embroidered, long white gown designed by Maria Grazia Chiuri for Dior, which highlighted the princess's diaphanous beauty at the Princess Grace Awards in October 2016. To celebrate its close links with the Principality, under the high patronage of HSH the Princess of Monaco, the House of Dior organized a spectacular *Croisière* show in Monte Carlo in May 2013, with the sea as its backdrop.

FLORENCE MÜLLER

1. Collection catalog, Spring-Summer 1956.

Elliott Erwitt, Grace Kelly wearing a white satin
Dior dress at a ball celebrating her engagement
with Prince Rainier of Monaco, at the Waldorf
Astoria Hotel in New York, January 6, 1956.

Right: Yousuf Karsh, portrait of Grace Kelly,
1956. She wears the *Colinette* dress, Fall-Winter
1956 Haute Couture collection (*Aimant* line).

Christian Dior. *Opéra Bouffe* gown.
Haute Couture, Fall-Winter 1956.
Aimant line. Short evening gown
in silk faille by Abraham.
Paris, Dior Héritage. Inv. 2009.6

When he founded his couture house at 30 Avenue Montaigne in Paris, Christian Dior introduced a look, a style, a form of optimism. Together with the lily-of-the-valley that instantly became the emblematic flower of the House of Dior, the rose evoked the ideal of the Dior spirit. With the *Opéra Bouffe* design, it appears in the form of a gown with rosebud-shaped drapery. The rose symbolizes the designer's nostalgia for his mother Madeleine's rose garden at his childhood home in Granville. It also signified a love of the earth incarnated by his sister Catherine, who, active in the Resistance, was deported to Ravensbrück on August 15, 1944, returning in May 1945 to rebuild her life in Callian, in the south of France, where she cultivated the roses from which she made a living.

The rose also evokes the first Dior perfume, *Miss Dior* (1947), a fragrance with which the rooms of the couture house were sprayed for the inaugural show on February 12, 1947. *Miss Dior* was an ode to the elegance of the *Parisienne*, celebrated in the Spring-Summer collection of 1947: "I designed clothes for flower-like women, with rounded shoulders, full feminine busts, and hand-span waists above enormous spreading skirts."[1] By redesigning the female body, Christian Dior wanted Paris to recover the sparkle of which it had been deprived by the Occupation. And so Paris once more became the center of attention, the epicenter of style. Together with the New Look, the couturier launched a sensual and olfactory manifesto with the rose as its symbol: the art of seduction, a new guide to the language of love, incarnated by the *Roseraie* gown and many others, from *Rose Pompon* (Spring-Summer 1953) to *Roses de Brabant* (Spring-Summer 1957). Dior himself designed half of the sixty or so rose-inspired Haute Couture creations produced between 1947 and 1996, not forgetting designs such as *Schumann* (Spring-Summer 1950) with its spray of white muslin roses on the back from bodice to hip.

In the work of Christian Dior, roses have many facets, creating a garden of promises reflected in the sky. They appear in a whole palette of colors—*Boréal, Ibis, Nuage Pâle, Flamant, Rose Bonheur*—with reddish shades too, such as the deep pink that was renamed *Rose de Noël* for the *Vivante* line of Fall-Winter 1953. The rose theme is an endless source of inspiration, recurring in all the creations of the House of Dior from jewelry to cosmetics. Like an elixir, the Dior rose is a lesson in happiness, a fantasy woven from memory and desire.

LAURENCE BENAÏM

---

1. Christian Dior, *Dior by Dior: The Autobiography of Christian Dior*, London, V&A Publishing, 2nd ed., pp. 22–23.

Pat English. *Amour* dress. Spring-Summer
1947 Haute Couture collection (*En 8* line).

Christian Dior. *Salzbourg* gown.
Haute Couture, Fall-Winter 1956,
Aimant line. Evening gown
in silk faille by Coudurier.
Paris, Dior Héritage. Inv. 1987.71

Salzbourg is a typical Christian Dior gown in that its apparent form, artfully draped and knotted at the front, is actually structured on a hidden whalebone bodice held up from the waist. The hang of the silk faille accentuates the cut, with a waist "set in the Dutch fashion"[1] (i.e. in its natural position, but expanded). The silhouette forms an isosceles triangle, with the warp thread of the fabric in the front center of the skirt. The lack of a waist seam creates an austere line like that of the "princess gowns" worn in official processions and at the royal courts of Europe in the 1900s.

Despite its voluminous horsehair and tulle skirt, the gown reflects an inspiration quite different from that of the "flower-woman" of a decade earlier. The femininity of the imposing monochrome pink is probably related to the arrival of young designer Yves Mathieu-Saint Laurent at the Dior studio in 1955. Hired to work with the designer Paul Mathieu, the future great couturier soon made his mark on the collections, and this gown may have been due to his talent; the stylized silhouette prefigures the Empire-waisted "Goya" gowns he designed a few seasons later. The detail of the knot with its fringed ends recalls a communicant's armband, giving the design a ceremonial— or ritualistic—dimension. Like the fringed scarf that accompanied the gown, the knot also creates an illusion of structure, emphasizing the nap of the fabric to detract attention from the artful cut required by the shape of the décolletage. The goal was to create the illusion that the gown was simply draped and knotted, like a negligee tied with a bow around a slim and curvy waist, or like the wrapping paper around a bunch of flowers.

The *Salzbourg* gown is in keeping with the overall theme of the 1956 Fall-Winter collection which, with *Adagio*, *Bayreuth*, *Bel Canto*, *Covent Garden*, *Opéra*, *Rhapsodie* and *Scala*, evokes Dior's love of assonance, music and musical environments. Dior was a classical music lover who played the piano; he was also a close friend of Henri Sauguet, who frequented the group of composers called "Les Six." In 1948, Sauguet composed an impromptu waltz in honor of *Miss Dior*; he also composed the *Pie Jesu* for Dior's funeral in 1957. And Christian Dior gave the name *Sauguette* to an afternoon dress in his 1952 Fall-Winter collection. The Cardinal de Richelieu outfit worn by Sauguet the same year, and probably made in the Dior ateliers, is held by the Musée des Arts Décoratifs. Dior's personal record collection also reflects his love of Bach, Brahms and Mozart. *The Magic Flute*, *Don Giovanni* and *The Abduction from the Seraglio* are evidence of Dior's love of opera, casting a lyrical light on his work. Bianca Castafiore, the opera singer in Hergé's *Adventures of Tintin*, hints at this with her reference to a certain "Tristan Bior."[2]

ÉRIC PUJALET-PLAÀ

1. Program of the Fall-Winter collection, 1956.
2. Hergé, *The Castafiore Emerald*, 1963.

Henry Clarke, *Jazz* dress, Spring-Summer 1948 Haute Couture collection
(*Trapèze* line). The name of the dress and the style of the photograph reflect
the importance of jazz among young people at the time; Yves Saint Laurent
drew on this to revive the spirit of Haute Couture.

Right: Norman Parkinson, *Mozart* dress, Spring-Summer 1950 Haute Couture
collection (*Verticale* line), model Maxime de La Falaise (born Maxine Birley).

Christian Dior. *Salle Pleyel* gown. Haute Couture,
Fall-Winter 1956, *Aimant* line. Silk velvet
evening gown, fringed silk satin belt, *obi* style bow.
Paris, Dior Héritage. Inv. 1989.5

The program for the Spring-Summer collection of 1956 notes the
presence of numerous draped scarves—the principal accessory
of the *Salle Pleyel* evening gown. The waist is encircled by a wide,
corset-like belt, tied at the back with a large, flat bow resembling
an *obi* kimono sash. In Christian Dior's childhood memories,
Japan was associated with the hall at the family house in Granville,
which was "decorated in imitation pitchpine picked out with
bamboo borders. In the same way over the doors there was a kind
of pagoda roof of bamboo and straw. Large panels painted in
imitation of Japanese prints adorned the whole staircase. These
versions of Utamaro and Hokusai made up my Sistine chapel."[1]

Although few French fashion houses ventured into the Japanese
market, Christian Dior signed a contract with the Daimaru
company in 1953, according to which Japanese buyers and
designers would come to the Paris shows to choose the Dior
designs that would then be made in the Japanese ateliers. A series
of shows were presented in October 1953 in Osaka, Kyoto,
Kobe and Tokyo to launch the operation, and a growing number
of Dior designs were given Japanese-inspired names: *Jardin
Japonais* in the Summer 1953 collection and, for Winter 1954,
the *Outamaro* ensemble, the *Rashomon* frock coat (a reference
to the filmmaker Akira Kurosawa) and the *Tokyo* dress, made
in Nishijin fabric by the Tatsumura textile company in Kyoto.

The partnership between Japan and the House of Dior
culminated with an order for three bridal outfits for the
wedding of Michiko Shoda and Crown Prince Akihito.
On April 10, 1959, after the traditional Shinto ceremony at which
she wore a kimono, the princess wore the Dior gowns produced
by the Daimaru ateliers using exclusive Tatsumura fabrics.
Christian Dior designed them, but it was Yves Saint Laurent who
supervised their production. Dior's designs were intended as a
form of stylistic interaction between East and West. The ensemble
that Michiko wore for the carriage ride was composed of a very
Parisienne tight-waisted gown and a coat with kimono sleeves.
Two other gowns were designed for the congratulatory
ceremonies: one with a four-layered collar recalling the multi-
layered ceremonial kimono, and another, European-style dress
decorated with traditional *shibori* designs.

The creative directors who succeeded Christian Dior continued
to draw from the traditional stylistic vocabulary of Japan. John
Galliano paid a vibrant tribute to Hokusai and *Madame Butterfly*
with his Spring-Summer collection of 2007. Loyal to the founder
of the House of Dior, he created a mix and match effect by
combining elements of the New Look with kimonos, origami,
geishas and Hokusai's famous wave. In Winter 2013, Raf Simons
reinterpreted the architectural lines of the kimono and *obi*,
using the *shibori* technique and a decoration of Japanese seals.

FLORENCE MÜLLER

1. Christian Dior, *Dior by Dior: The Autobiography of
Christian Dior*, London, V&A Publishing, 2nd ed., p. 169.

Willy Maywald, the model Renée Breton presents
the *Voyageur* ensemble to a Japanese delegation,
Fall-Winter 1955 Haute Couture collection (*Y* line).

Right: Patrick Demarchelier, *Konnichi-Kate*
ensemble, Spring-Summer 2007 Haute
Couture collection, model Catherine McNeil.

Christian Dior. *Muguet* dress. Haute Couture, Spring-Summer 1957, *Libre* line. Organdy dress embroidered with lily-of-the-valley by Barbier. Paris. Dior Héritage. Inv. 1993.3

Christian Dior and lily-of-the-valley—or the story of a man and a flower, an intimate exchange between a designer and a good luck symbol, a humble flower that never left the creator's side. Every May, Christian Dior's favorite plant had pride of place in the plush interior of the couture house on Avenue Montaigne. Dior's seamstresses (*les petites mains*) pinned sprigs of lily-of-the-valley to their outfits—as did "Monsieur," who wore one on the lapel of his gray suit. Like a trusted companion, the lily-of-the-valley also found its way into the finely crafted reliquary that Christian Dior kept hidden in his jacket pocket.

Lily-of-the-valley was a recurrent theme in the couturier's work; despite its apparent simplicity, Dior dedicated a whole collection to this charming flower for his Spring-Summer show in 1954, and when it also became a perfume with *Diorissimo* two years later, Christian Dior designed the white organdy *Muguet* gown embroidered with the flower's beautiful little bells made by Maison Barbier.

From 1956 on, Christian Dior divided his time between Paris and the Château de La Colle Noire in Montauroux in the south of France, near the Sainte-Blanche property in Cabris of perfumer Edmond Roudnitska, who had planted a special bed of lily-of-the-valley for research on the *Diorissimo* perfume. While Christian Dior was designing the *Muguet* gown, his perfumer was endeavoring to create a fresh, green perfume suggesting youth and springtime. The couturier and perfumer may have been working with different materials, but their quest was the same: a couture perfume for a fashion style as vibrant as its emblematic flower.

This turned out to be a surprisingly complex task. Lily-of-the-valley is a "mute" flower whose fragrance cannot be extracted; more amenable flowers had to be found to recreate its scent. Like Dior's "ephemeral architecture," Edmond Roudnitska developed a perfect harmony between the floral notes of lily-of-the-valley, jasmine and ylang-ylang to create a young, fresh lily-of-the-valley fragrance. The perfumer's olfactory design mirrored the couturier's work with fabrics.

Dior dresses and perfumes were in unison. Both couture and fragrance left the New Look behind them, aiming for a different kind of elegance: one that no longer spread like a corolla but remained slightly closed, like the little pearly bells of spring. The *Diorissimo* perfume and *Muguet* gown represent a tribute to the spirit of Dior, to the charming and sensitive bond between the nature of a man and the essence of a flower, coming together to create the luxury of the fresh and joyful scent of spring, all year round.

VINCENT LERET

Top: Gérard Uféras, Roger Vivier bronze-green satin
mule for Christian Dior, decorated with lily-of-the-valley
and rose leaves on the upper part, Spring-Summer 1955.

Bottom: Laziz Hamani, *Diorissimo* perfume
in its Baccarat crystal bottle designed in 1956.

André Ostier, Patricia López-Willshaw (in the *Festival* dress, Fall-Winter 1956 Haute Couture collection, *Aimant* line), Arturo López-Willshaw, Francine Weisweiller (in the *Muguet* dress), Édouard Dermit and Jean Cocteau during a ball at the home of Charles de Beistegui, Château de Groussay, March 18, 1957.

Christian Dior. *Plaza* dress. Haute
Couture, Fall-Winter 1957. *Fuseau*
line. Bouclé wool dress. Granville,
Musée Christian Dior. Inv. 2009.5.2

The cut of the *Plaza* day dress, in black bouclé wool, is like that of a suit. The waistline is accentuated by a double bow at the front and by the loose fit of the bodice. Two rows of buttons structure the bodice and continue down the skirt, creating the effect of a double-breasted jacket and wrap-around skirt. The year was 1957, ten years after the New Look with its *Bar* suit, designed by Christian Dior for late afternoon wear in the bars of grand hotels. The name of this suit-style dress is *Plaza*, like the hotel and bar that inspired the original suit—so things had come full circle, like the belt around this dress! But silhouettes had changed in the space of ten years. The name of this line is *Fuseau*, the French word for "spindle," which indicates how different it was from the curvaceous *Corolle* and *En 8* lines of 1947.

Christian Dior's collections featured fourteen designs called *Plaza*—which shows how fond he was of the eponymous hotel. He is said to have deliberately chosen to set up his couture house a short distance away on the same avenue. The townhouse at 30 Avenue Montaigne held obvious appeal for the couturier with its ironwork balconies, scrolls and mascarons, and Christian Dior had fallen in love with it long before imagining he would open a fashion house there one day. But his love of the architecture was not the only reason for his choice: the House of Dior also needed to be located in a neighborhood frequented by ladies "from the most elegant ranks of society."[1] The two establishments on either side of Avenue Montaigne shared the same view of French-style luxury and the same international clientele—a wealthy clientele that came to spend a few months a year in a luxury hotel in Paris, the undisputed capital of Haute Couture, where they had only to cross the street to be outfitted in the latest fashions. Marlene Dietrich was a regular guest at the Plaza when she wasn't spending weekends at Christian Dior's country home in Milly-la-Forêt—after being introduced by Jean Cocteau, the couturier and the star had become close friends. Dior dressed her both on and off screen; she even threatened Alfred Hitchcock with "No Dior, no Dietrich!" to obtain a Dior screen wardrobe for the shooting of *Stage Fright*. They remained close until Dior's death. Marlene Dietrich spent the last years of her life in her apartment at 12 Avenue Montaigne—between the House of Dior and the Plaza—where she is said to have left over three thousand outfits, 400 hats, 430 pairs of shoes, pajamas, nightgowns, and even a Christian Dior cap.

JÉRÔME HANOVER

1. Christian Dior, *Dior by Dior: The Autobiography of Christian Dior*, London, V&A Publishing, 2nd ed., 2007, p. 139.

Marlene Dietrich congratulating Christian Dior after his fashion show, 1955.
Willy Maywald, Marlene Dietrich in the front row of a Christian Dior show, 1955.
Left: Jack Garofalo, Christian Dior on the balcony of 30 Avenue Montaigne, 1957.

Yves Saint Laurent for Christian Dior. *Bonne Conduite*
dress. Haute Couture, Spring-Summer 1958, *Trapèze* line.
Smock dress in speckled wool by Rodier. Paris, Fondation
Pierre Bergé–Yves Saint Laurent. Inv. HC1958E032R

"Trapeze-shaped smock dress in gray speckled wool by Rodier with a Claudine collar, embellished with a bow at the front"[1]: the *Bonne Conduite* dress is clearly the most emblematic of the *Trapèze* collection presented by Yves Saint Laurent for Dior on January 30, 1958. This was the first collection designed by Dior's former assistant after the couturier's death on October 24, 1957 in Montecatini. An austere but ingenuous spring collection, represented by dresses whose names evoke childhood (*Jeudi*, *Refrain*, *Dame Tartine*) and by the disillusioned youth of Françoise Sagan's *Bonjour Tristesse*. A spring collection in the form of a manifesto, for a line "whose elegance derives primarily from its austerity and purity of construction."[2] The Parisian press gave a triumphant welcome to the twenty-one-year-old couturier, the youngest in the world: "Triumph for the House of Dior, Long Live *La Femme Trapèze*," declared the newspaper *L'Aurore*.[3] Edmonde Charles-Roux, editor of *Vogue Paris*, chose the *Bonne Conduite* dress for the cover of the March 1958 issue. According to *L'Officiel de la Mode*,[4] "the success, or should we say the triumph, of a very young man who was a teenager only yesterday has confirmed the worldwide prestige of French haute couture with brio. Parisian chic, hard hit last October by the tragic death of Christian Dior, had lost its magician and was undergoing a tough ordeal. The miracle has occurred." Yves Saint Laurent hit the cover of *Paris Match* on March 1, 1958: "Dior without Dior." The break with the past was complete: in 1947, Christian Dior had designed ball gowns for flower-women, a postwar new beginning; in 1958, Yves Saint Laurent celebrated the arrival of the Swinging Sixties, with their promise of progress and emancipation.

Like a mobile in space, the *Bonne Conduite* dress was to the twentieth century what the loose *robe battante* (invented by Madame de Montespan to conceal her pregnancies) was to the seventeenth: the waist is hidden, as it is with the *Innocente* dress, designed to give the wearer a more ingenuous look… Then there were the *Sainte Nitouche* dresses that preceded Yves Saint Laurent's *Belle de Jour* style. *Bonne Conduite* is a gateway, an invitation to join the movement of change. January 1958 saw the birth of the electric car and the launch of the Explorer 1 satellite; everything was shifting and changing. Asserting himself as Dior's heir, Saint Laurent drew inspiration from the flappers of the 1920s with their unfettered forms. In the winter of 1957 there were already signs that *Bonne Conduite* was on its way, with a sack dress heralding the "Now Look," a style reasserted by Saint Laurent in 1966, with the creation of Saint Laurent Rive Gauche.

LAURENCE BENAÏM

1. Program of the Spring-Summer Haute Couture collection, 1958.
2. Ibid.
3. *L'Aurore*, January 1988.
4. "Permanence de la Haute Couture Française,"
   L'Officiel de la mode, no. 431–432, March 1958, p. 191.

Following double page, left: Willy Rizzo, cover of *Paris Match*, March 1, 1958. Yves Saint Laurent presenting two characteristic dresses from his collection, recognizable by their trapeze shape, worn by models Victoire and Christine.
Right: William Klein, cover of *Vogue Paris*, March 1958, model Gunila.

PARIS MATCH

N° 464 SAMEDI 1ᵉʳ MARS 1958 **50** Fr.

Afrique du Nord **60** fr. — Maroc **65** fr. — G. B. **1** 6 — Belg. **10** fr.
Suisse **0.90** — Canada **25** cents. — Esp. **12** peset. — Turquie **85** piast.

DIOR SANS DIOR
Pour sa première collection
Yves Saint-Laurent, 22 ans,
lance la ligne « trapèze ».
Victoire et Christine pré-
sentent ici deux modèles
inédits de printemps.
Photo Rizzo

VOGUE

PARIS
dicte
une
mode
jeune

les
collections
de
printemps
1958

F **600**

NUMÉRO SPÉCIAL · MARS 1958

What happened to the well-behaved young man behind the *Trapèze* line? Only one year later, Yves Saint Laurent had already made his intentions clear as creative director of Christian Dior. With the color black, first of all: a deep, kohl black, the mysterious black of the heroines of Manet and Goya. And with silhouettes all a-flutter, like the *Marilyn* dress in black taffeta by Buche, draped in ruffles at the hips.

Marilyn, the name of a shining star: *Some Like It Hot* premiered in New York on March 28, 1959, at Loew's Capitol Theater on Broadway. Marilyn Monroe arrived with her husband, Arthur Miller, in a dazzling iridescent white gown. She both shocked and fascinated puritanical America, appearing in the film almost topless, with just a sprinkling of rhinestones to keep the censors at bay…

Yves Saint Laurent excited, provoked and galvanized in his own way. By the time of his fourth show on Avenue Montaigne in July 1959, he was clearly more of a night bird than a humble disciple of Dior. In Marcel Carné's 1958 movie *Les Tricheurs* (*The Cheaters*)—an evocation of Parisian Left Bank bohemia, to the jazzy strains of Fats Domino, Stan Getz, Oscar Peterson and Chet Baker—Pascale Petit is "Mic," a liberated young woman… who wears Dior. Dior cocktail dresses were given names such as *Tricheuse*, *Lolita*, *Zazie* and *Motard*—an "absolute bombshell," according to *Elle* magazine,[1] which referred to the "suspense of the hemline," nurturing the fascination for the young couturier with his slightly decadent form of classicism. At a time when he was launching his first Haute Couture biker jackets, Yves Saint Laurent added to the bemusement with his reference to the scandalous star that Hollywood loved to hate because she ruffled puritanical feathers.

Yves Saint Laurent would present another *Marilyn* dress in the 2000s—a flowing white silk number worn by a model who smoked her way along the catwalk in the Salon Impérial at the InterContinental Hotel. But for the time being, his diva was none other than the petite and insolently feminine Victoire, with her black chignon and slender waist, grieving after the death of Christian Dior—"the father of my dresses." She played an increasingly important role for Yves Saint Laurent. According to the program of the *1960* line (Fall-Winter 1959), "The whirlwind of modern life has created a new woman":

"The need for a **new** fashion
The need for a **new** woman
A **new** attitude
New bases."

This short evening dress, which demonstrates "the return of lace flounces and shirring in the *Chouterie* style,"[2] resonated with the "fierce make-up" and draped, "candy bag" capes. Yves Saint Laurent was having fun, provoking and seducing with the only weapon at his disposal: his creative hypersensitivity.

LAURENCE BENAÏM

1. *Elle*, September 7, 1959, p. 39.
2. Program of the Fall-Winter 1959 Haute Couture collection.

Mannequin
d/ Nicole
269.

Taffetas
canard
annulé

Irving Penn, *Marilyn* dress, Fall-
Winter 1959 Haute Couture collection
(*1960* line), model Isabella Albonico.
Insert: Yves Saint Laurent, sketch of the
Zénaïde dress from the Fall-Winter 1959
Haute Couture collection (*1960* line).

Yves Saint Laurent for Christian Dior. *Labia* gown.
Haute Couture. Fall-Winter 1959. *1960* line.
Silk taffeta evening gown. Chantilly lace ruffles. Paris.
Fondation Pierre Bergé–Yves Saint Laurent.
Inv. HC1959H100R

Created by Yves Saint Laurent for the House of Dior, the *Labia* dress suggests the mystery of Venice and the Bal de Beistegui held at the Palazzo Labia on September 3, 1951. European society's most memorable ball, it was given by Charles de Beistegui, a host of astounding wealth and taste. Preparing for the occasion, he spent 150 million old French francs on the seventeenth-century baroque palazzo that he had acquired in 1948. His chief aim was restoring the frescos in the palazzo's ballroom. They recorded Cleopatra's life and were created by Tiepolo, the renowned Venetian painter.

The Bal de Beistegui's guest list included Hollywood film stars Gene Tierney and Orson Welles, the heiress Barbara Hutton and Winston Churchill. The dress code was eighteenth century and masks were encouraged. Arriving by gondola on the Grand Canal, notable entrances included Lady Diana Cooper posing as Cleopatra, Patricia López-Willshaw appearing as an Empress of China with masked footmen in her wake and Christian Dior with Salvador Dalí creating an eerie Phantoms of Venice parade. Daisy Fellowes created a sensation with a Christian Dior dress made of champagne-colored chiffon with a subtle leopard-skin print.[1] Wearing pheasant feathers in her hair, she presented herself as the Queen of the Red Indians in eighteenth-century America. Her group, consisting of her two daughters, Emmeline and Rosamund, David Herbert, Alec de Casteja and Princess Stanislas Radziwill, was entirely dressed by Dior. "The color scheme was yellow, beige and different shades of brown," said David Herbert, the English aristocrat."[2] Radziwill, who played the role of the first white settler, wore a billowing ball gown. "It was made of white tulle, and looked as if it was a striped dress, due to its gold ribbons," she said.[3] Another Dior-clad beauty was Mary, la Baronne Alain de Rothschild.[4]

Operette, *Danse* and *Monaco* were just a few of the many ball dresses that Christian Dior dreamt up for his clients. Meanwhile, being a recognized member of the *mondain*, Dior was noted for his personal costumes. At the Bal des Rois et des Reines hosted by Étienne de Beaumont in March 1949, the designer appeared as the King of the Jungle. And when the celebrated art patron Marie-Laure de Noailles—a client and close friend from Dior's art gallery period—gave her Bal de la Lune sur la Mer in January 1951, the couturier created her barmaid outfit and joined her by going as a waiter. Five years later, at Noailles's next event—the Bal des Artistes—the couturier came dressed as Jules Amédée Barbey d'Aurevilly, the Norman novelist.

In homage to Christian Dior's taste for dressing up, and considering his profound respect for artists, John Galliano organized the ultimate Bal des Artistes in Versailles to celebrate Dior's sixtieth anniversary in July 2007. In January 2017, to celebrate seventy years of the New Look and to mark Maria Grazia Chiuri's first Haute Couture collection, a masked ball was held in the enchanting setting of the Musée Rodin.

NATASHA FRASER-CAVASSONI

1. Nicholas Foulkes, *Bals: Legendary Costume Balls of the Twentieth Century*, Paris, Assouline, 2011, p. 162.
2. Ibid.
3. Natasha Fraser-Cavassoni, *Monsieur Dior: Once upon a Time*, New York, Pointed Leaf Press, 2014, p. 139.
4. Ibid.

Christian Dior dressed as a lion at the Bal
des Rois et Reines hosted by Comte
Étienne de Beaumont in Paris, March 1949.

Left: Cecil Beaton, Daisy Fellowes wearing a Dior
dress at a ball hosted by Charles de Beistegui
at the Palais Labia in Venice, September 3, 1951.

Yves Saint Laurent for Christian Dior. *Chicago* ensemble.
Haute Couture. Fall-Winter 1960, *Souplesse, Légèreté, Vie*
collection. Jacket in imitation crocodile skin trimmed with
mink. Bouclé wool skirt. Paris, Dior Héritage. Inv. 2013.22

The *Chicago* ensemble—a bouclé wool skirt and a black crocodile
skin jacket jacket trimmed with mink—is emblematic of Yves Saint
Laurent's Fall-Winter 1960 Haute Couture collection for Dior.

Commenting on the collection, the press praised its pioneering
look but gave voice to a certain unease. *Elle* magazine associated
these "unconventional, rash, excessive, young"[1] designs with the
"beatnik" look—a name by which the collection is still known today.

The names of the designs—*À Bout de Souffle, Aimez-Vous Brahms,
Cinecitta* and *Dolce Vita*—referred to contemporary films and novels,
and above all to the youth culture of the day. At the age of twenty-
four, Yves Saint Laurent was inspired by the popular culture of his
own generation, and this collection represented a new direction.

American *Vogue* editor Jessica Daves evoked the "surprises" and
"controversies" of the latest Paris collections, commenting on the
perception of women reflected in designs by the great French
couturiers.[2] Cardin's woman was "mondaine, contemporary," while
Dior's was "avant-garde." The lines, the toque hats and especially
the black leather jacket of the *Chicago* ensemble were particularly
innovative aspects of a collection that was mocked by some fashion
journalists. Though she stressed the audacity of the designs,
Jessica Daves was openly critical; in her view, the human body
was "ingenuously disregarded" by a line composed of a "long torso
with no hint of waistline, ending at various points below the
hips in little balloon skirts […] startlingly short." The toque hats
also came in for some harsh criticism; in the American article,
they were compared to "a little Vermont boy's winter headgear."

The controversy focused on the *Chicago* jacket, because it
recalled the kind of black leather jacket worn by "bad boys" and
rebels—and especially by Marlon Brando in *The Wild One*. It was
described as "the farthest-out garment in the world," and as a
"challenge." French *Vogue* printed an image of the imitation
crocodile skin jacket to illustrate the question "yes or no to the
black jacket?", suggesting that the leather jacket, a symbol of
masculinity and non-conformism, was bound to be controversial.[3]

This Yves Saint Laurent collection, characterized by its tubular
line and short skirts and clearly inspired by street clothes and
youth culture, heralded the fashions of the 1960s. But it was too
much for couture clients, and the young couturier's boldness
met with a disapproval that hastened his departure from Dior.

DENIS BRUNA

1. *Elle*, September 2, 1960, pp. 40–41.
2. Jessica Daves, "Paris. Surprises, controversies, allure in the new
   collections," American *Vogue*, September 15, 1960, pp. 221–239.
3. 1960–1961. "Une mode controversée," *Vogue Paris*,
   September 1960, pp. 168–169.

Above: Irving Penn, *Chicago* dress,
Fall-Winter 1960 Haute Couture
collection (*Souplesse, légèreté, vie*),
model Dorothy McGowan.

Following double page: William Connors,
Elle, September 2, 1960.

Anticonventionnels, téméraires, excessifs, jeunes, voilà comment sont les beatniks des Etats-Unis, voilà comment sont les tenues de cette page. (Pour ceux qui veulent en savoir plus, les plus illustres des beatniks, cousins de nos existentialistes et de nos surréalistes, sont auteurs, poètes, cinéastes, et fanatiques de jazz. "Beat" veut dire mesure de jazz, ou, "battue", (the beat generation), et le suffixe "nik" est né avec Spoutnik, Lunik et autres niques).

Les beatniks :
un
air "chic-nik"

Un blouson de vison (excessif !) noir et blanc. A retenir : les larges rayures horizontales, l'absence de col, le fourreau de crêpe de laine, noir comme l'humeur des beatniks. Dior.

Chevreau noir et renard argenté (téméraire). V ceinturée, portée sur une robe en même chevr comme du satin, ajustée et sans manches. Ja

40

Chevreau noir et tricot blanc (un poème !), le cardigan est dou-
blé de tricot blanc à grosses mailles. Jupe droite. Pull-over
sans manches, décolleté en V, en même tricot. de Rauch.
Crocodile noir et vison noir (un défi), ce blouson de super
luxe qui imite le ciré, est porté sur une robe très sobre
en crêpe noir. Chapka de fourrure noire. Christian Dior.
Agneau noir et tweed (une bonne idée) une blouse à enco-
lure crantée et poches gilet, portée avec un tailleur de tweed
à jupe droite. Toque en cuir, ourlée de vison noir. Estérel.

41

From 1947 on, filmmakers and actresses often commissioned
their movie wardrobes from Christian Dior. The couture house's
filmography comprises over a hundred films by famous directors
including Luis Buñuel, Stanley Donen, Terence Young, Jean-Luc
Godard, Charlie Chaplin, François Truffaut, Costa-Gavras,
Claude Lelouch and Woody Allen. Before he created his fashion
house, Christian Dior had designed costumes for a number
of films, such as Roland Tual's *Le Lit à Colonnes* (*The Four-
Poster*, 1942), Claude Autant-Lara's *Lettres d'Amour* (*Love Letters*,
1943) and René Clair's *Le Silence est d'Or* (*Silence is Golden*, 1946).
Once he was caught up in the whirlwind expansion of his couture
business, he often refused to create special designs, preferring to
dress actresses in outfits from his current collections. His actress
clients included the divine Marlene Dietrich for Hitchcock's *Stage
Fright* (1950), the unforgettable Nicole Stéphane for Jean Cocteau's
Les Enfants terribles (*The Holy Terrors*, 1950) and the stunning Ava
Gardner for Mark Robson's *The Little Hut* (1957). Later examples
of screen elegance signed Dior include Brigitte Bardot in
Michel Deville's *L'Ours et la Poupée* (*The Bear and the Doll*, 1970),
Isabelle Adjani in Jean-Jacques Beineix's *La Lune dans le Caniveau*
(*The Moon in the Gutter*, 1983) and Sophia Loren in *Arabesque*
(Stanley Donen, 1966) and Robert Altman's *Ready to Wear* (1994).

In 1969, Marc Bohan designed an exceptionally elegant
wardrobe to be worn by Elizabeth Taylor in Joseph Losey's
Secret Ceremony. The star was playing the role of Leonora, a
London prostitute involved in a strange relationship with the
rich heiress Cenci (Mia Farrow). The fifteen or so outfits
designed by Dior for the film included a white jersey tunic, a
white rabbit fur cape, a beige twill raincoat, a jersey sweater
and miniskirt, a black poplin raincoat, a white satin negligee,
an embroidered orange organza evening gown, a purple velvet
tunic dress, a yellow crêpe dress, a long beige lace dress, a long
white damask dress, a beige poplin 7/8 coat, a beige poplin shorts-
and-sweater ensemble, a white organdy coat and pajamas, a
fuchsia and green printed georgette dress—and all the
accessories that went with them!

Elizabeth Taylor responded enthusiastically to Marc Bohan's
arrival at Dior; she ordered twelve dresses from his first collection, drawings of which were printed in the press. The same year,
the star wore the *Soirée à Rio* gown to receive her Oscar for Best
Actress for her performance in Daniel Mann's film *Butterfield 8*.
In this gown, characteristic of the season's "romantic globe dresses
with billowing skirts," Liz Taylor hit the cover of *Life* magazine
on April 28, 1961.[1] And Olivia de Havilland, another Dior
regular, wore the same gown at the party held to celebrate
the twenty-first anniversary screening of *Gone with the Wind*.

FLORENCE MÜLLER

1. Program of the *Slim Look* collection, Spring-Summer 1961.

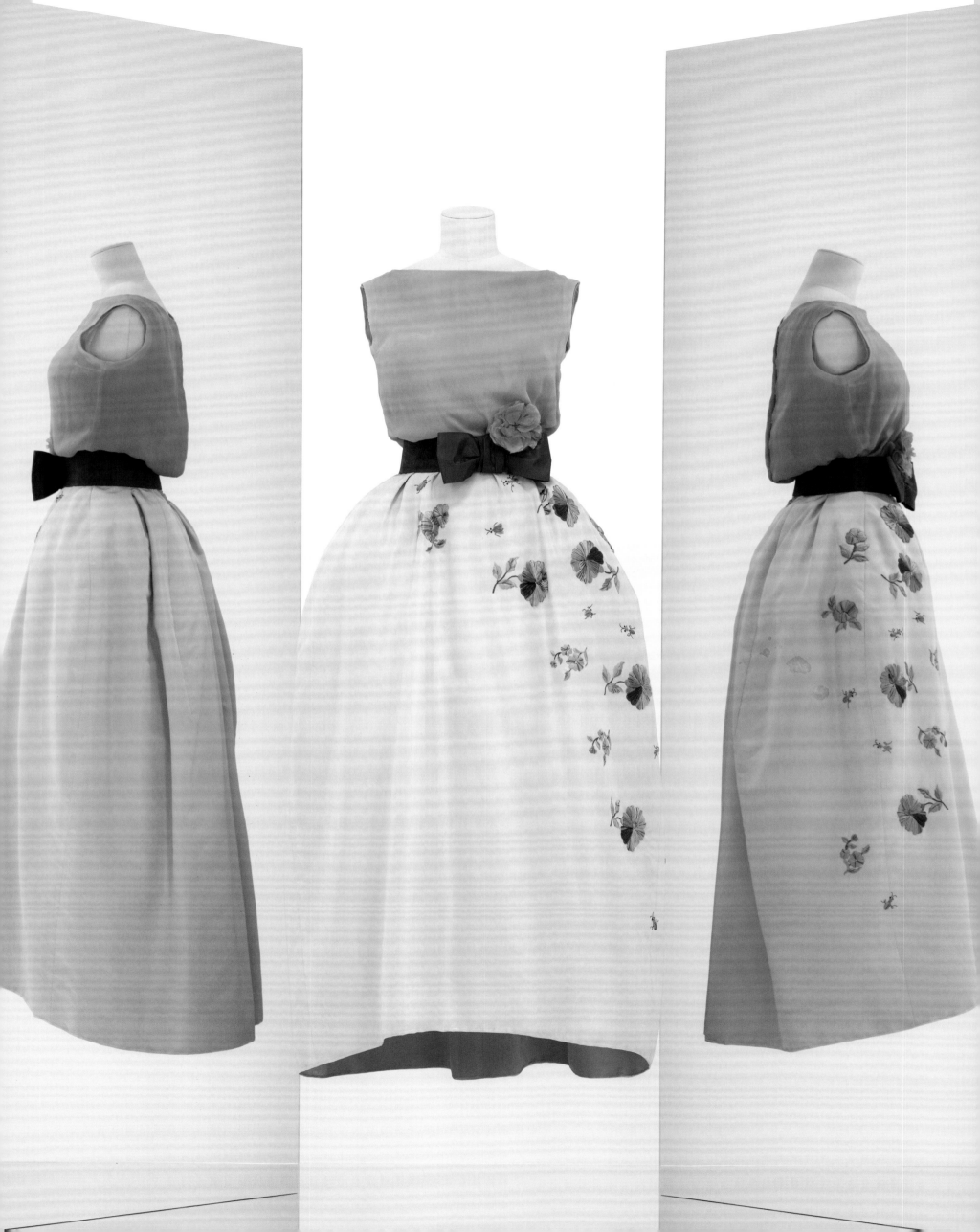

Brigitte Bardot in a Dior dress, in Michel
Deville's film *The Bear and the Doll*, 1970.

Sophia Loren in a Dior dress in
Stanley Donen's film *Arabesque*, 1966.

Mark Shaw, Elizabeth Taylor in the *Soirée à Rio*
dress, Spring-Summer 1961 Haute Couture
collection (*Slim Look*). She wore this dress when
she received the Oscar for Best Actress, 1961.

Marc Bohan for Christian Dior. *Miss Dior* dress.
Haute Couture, Spring-Summer 1961,
Slim Look collection. Short evening dress
in organdy embroidered with lily-of-the-valley,
moiré ribbon belt decorated with flowers.
Paris, Dior Héritage. Inv. 2012.96

Christian Dior was very close to his younger sister Catherine, with whom he shared a love of gardening. His collections sometimes included a dress that was called *Miss Dior* in her honor. His admiration for Catherine—a former member of the French Resistance, who was awarded the Croix de Guerre—inspired the *Miss Dior* perfume, created in 1947. For his first *Slim Look* collection in Spring 1961, Marc Bohan established a youthful new silhouette that was slender, supple and slim-waisted. His *Floralies* dresses were printed with hundreds of flowers, and two dresses in embroidered fine white linen were dedicated to innocent girlhood: one bearing the name of his daughter *Marie-Anne*, the other, *Miss Dior*, named in tribute to Catherine Dior. This charming "little girl" dress is an example of the bell-shaped "globe dresses" that were one of the novelties of the season's collection.[1]

The first women's ready-to-wear line launched by Dior in 1967 was also called *Miss Dior*. The collection was entrusted to Philippe Guibourgé, assisted by the young designer Adeline André (who would gain recognition in the 1980s). In 1968, the brand was sold at 143 outlets in France, Switzerland, Italy, Germany, Belgium, Sweden, Norway...[2] It was made at the Dior factory in Orléans and comprised some sixty designs. Prices ranged from 300 to 800 French francs (compared to 3,500 to 6,000 French francs for an Haute Couture dress). It was presented to buyers nine months before the Haute Couture collection, and was therefore a means of testing the trends of the moment. The Miss Dior brand was a hit with young women who could treat themselves to something of the magic of Dior at more affordable prices.

The French actress Frédérique Cerbonnet-Véran, who appeared in films by Éric Rohmer and Maurice Pialat, and her mother Jacqueline Quéffelec-Cerbonnet, a former dancer at the Opéra-Comique and a friend of Zizi Jeanmaire, were both fans of the brand and owned a complete Miss Dior wardrobe: clothes, bags, shoes, belts, scarves, jewelry... Mother and daughter swapped outfits, playing with the many "mix and match" possibilities. Their addiction to the brand shows the extent to which it captured the spirit of the times for young women.

FLORENCE MÜLLER

1. Program of the Spring-Summer collection, 1961.
2. Interview with Marc Bohan and Philippe Guibourgé for *L'Express*,
    "Chez Dior," February 1, 1968, typewritten. Dior Héritage.

Miss Dior : une collection de prêt à porter toute nouvelle, lancée le 11 septembre à Paris, vingt ans après la création de la maison Christian Dior. Des modèles entièrement dessinés et fabriqués par Dior, dans leur atelier et leur usine : donc un prêt à porter qui bénéficie d'une coupe haute couture. Des prix abordables, un style élégant, facile à porter, raffiné dans les détails, conçu pour un maximum de femmes, de tous les âges. En vente à Paris, mais aussi en province et à l'étranger.

**CHRISTIAN DIOR
LANCE
MISS DIOR**

Robin Butler, ravissante Américaine blonde, chargée des Relations plus courte. 180 F. Blouse à la raie en jersey angora rayé, 150 F. Co

ROBIN BUTLER

Fabriqué de Christian Dior à New York, à posé pour nous. A gauche, manteau en poil de chameau à mi-mollet et boutons de cuir, 680 F. Jupe assortie bons : une longue en jersey pure laine orange et boa de plumes de même couleur, 300 F. Coiffures Laurent. Où trouver ces modèles ? Voir page 9.

ROBIN BUTLER

**CHRISTIAN DIOR
LANCE
MISS DIOR**

Ci-dessus : un chemisier, classique de forme, en lamé jaune à boutons-pression dorés, gravés du mot "Miss Dior", 100 F. Jupe en jersey noir à g Bas fantaisie Christian Dior. Chaussures de satin noir, Dior. A droite : redingote croisée en flanelle grise, à col et poignets en agneau d

vous devant et poches verticales sur le côté, 400 F. Tibiet, 750 F. Entre Dior. Les adresses? Page 9.

Henry Clarke, the first *Miss Dior*
designs. *Vogue Paris*, October 1967.
Left: Gina Lollobrigida and Elizabeth Taylor
both wearing the *Miss Dior* dress at the
Moscow International Film Festival, 1961.

Marc Bohan for Christian Dior. *Gamin*
suit. Haute Couture, Fall-Winter 1961,
Charme 62 collection. Tweed suit.
Short double-breasted jacket.
Trapeze skirt and matching scarf.
Paris, Dior Héritage. Inv. 1997.35

The *Gamin* dress-and-jacket suit was part of Marc Bohan's second collection
for Christian Dior. After supervising the setting up of the London store, he was
called back to Paris in October 1960. This Parisian creation may have been an
interpretation of his impressions of "Swinging London": the black and white
mohair tweed, the cap and the wool scarf reflect a certain Anglophilia, accentuated
by the name "slim look": "The silhouette is supple, slim, with natural shoulders,
curvy waist, flat hips. The skirts gently flare [...] and end just above the knee."[1]

This suit was probably inspired by Bohan's observations of the school uniforms
and out-of-school clothes worn by London's youngsters. The short jacket, with its wide
collar and large gap between the two rows of buttons, has a slimming effect on the
bust. The look is young, even childish, and has a retro touch as it was also inspired
by the popular suits of the 1930s. The cut is symmetrical, without a waistline; the
neck is uncovered and the fabric sits on the shoulders and hips, creating a trapeze
silhouette. This geometrical effect is softened by slightly curved seams at the waist
and by the recurring circles: the visor; the large buttons; the circle of the skirt with
its underskirt of horsehair and organza.

The proportions of this day ensemble and the choice of color-block tweed (a sports
fabric) heralded the "Courrèges bombshell" of 1965 and made Bohan's style and view
of Haute Couture consistent with an era that saw the emergence of youth culture.
This outfit seems to focus on pattern and texture rather than silhouette. It recalls
the contemporary interest in black and white optical effects in fashion and the
arts, a theme Bohan would return to during his long career. His great successes
included his 1968 dresses and accessories printed all over with the Dior logo.

ÉRIC PUJALET-PLAÀ

1. Program of the Spring-Summer collection, 1961.

Willy Maywald, *Bistrot* dress, Spring-Summer 1961
Haute Couture collection (*Slim Look*).

Mark Shaw, *Vert Gazon*, *Gavroche* and *Flirt* dresses,
Spring-Summer 1961 Haute Couture collection (*Slim Look*).

Following double page: Richard Avedon,
*Roger Vivier, Raymonde Zehnacker, Marguerite Carré,
Mickey, Philippe Guibourgé, Marc Bohan, Mitzah Bricard,
Jacques Rouët, Kouka, Suzanne Luling and Yvonne
Minassian*, 1961. Mickey and Kouka are wearing the
Belle d'hiver and *Nuit blanche* ensembles, Fall-Winter
1961 Haute Couture collection (*Charme 62*).

Marc Bohan for Christian Dior. Haute Couture,
Fall-Winter 1967. Black wool crêpe evening dress
embroidered by Mesrine with wool, sequins and
rhodoid petals. Paris, Musée des Arts Décoratifs,
fashion and textile collection, gift of Hélène
David-Weill, 1998. Inv. 997.47.20.1

This design by Marc Bohan reflects a number of decorative influences: the wool embroidery illustrates the season's "naive peasant styles in brilliant colors,"[1] while the use of iridescent rhodoid discs adds a sparkle "in kaleidoscope tints."[2] This mini trapeze dress with its folksy, psychedelic decoration is a perfect example of its era. Since André Courrèges had endorsed the new skirt length with his revolutionary collection of Spring 1965, the mini had permeated the world of Haute Couture. Short dresses were now acceptable for both daytime and evening wear. Despite its ultra-modern features, this "little black dress" complies with the traditional conventions of evening wear and is classical in construction. The supple wool crêpe is fully lined and the circular form of the dress is supported by an underskirt with horsehair trim—rather like a mini version of the structure of 1950s petticoats—though such a shape usually required double-sided gabardine, used by Emanuel Ungaro for example.

This collection, the forty-second from the House of Dior, still conveys a sense of the technical expertise of Marguerite Carré, who used the tried and tested resources of Haute Couture to turn a fashion sketch into a dress. Marguerite Carré was one of Dior's closest collaborators from the New Look onwards; her mastery— of Patou's famous box pleats, in particular—was undisputed. For Bohan, she had to lighten her lining technique; the designer did not want the dresses to "stand up on their own": "I wanted things to be impeccable, to hang beautifully, but with a minimum of lining and organza."[3]

This dress by Bohan symbolized both the tradition and the modernity of Christian Dior. The sexual and geometric forms and abstract corollas embroidered on the black wool crêpe gave a clever new twist to the legend of the flower-woman. The daisies with their checkered centers may also have been a discreet tribute to the skill of the seamstress: the French word for "daisy" is *marguerite*. "Marc Bohan has taken charge of the enchanted world of Dior,"[4] asserted *Marie-Claire* magazine in September 1967; "Dior is still the world's fashion guru. The little townhouse on Avenue Montaigne has taken over five adjacent buildings. Turnover has increased one hundredfold in nineteen years."[5]

ÉRIC PUJALET-PLAÄ

1. Catalog of the Fall-Winter collection, 1967.
2. Ibid.
3. Marc Bohan, in the film *Dior, les années Bohan: Trois décennies de styles et de stars*, by Philippe Lanfranchi, 2009.
4. *Marie-Claire*, September 1967, no. 181 p. 67.
5. Ibid., p. 58.

Following double page, left: Arnaud de Rosnay, mini evening dress from the Christian Dior New York Fall-Winter 1968 collection, model Marisa Berenson. Right: Jeanloup Sieff, Anna Karina wearing a white organza mini-dress with culottes, edged with braids, Christian Dior Colifichets Spring-Summer 1968.

Insert: Marc Bohan, sketch of a dress from the Fall-Winter 1967 Haute Couture collection.

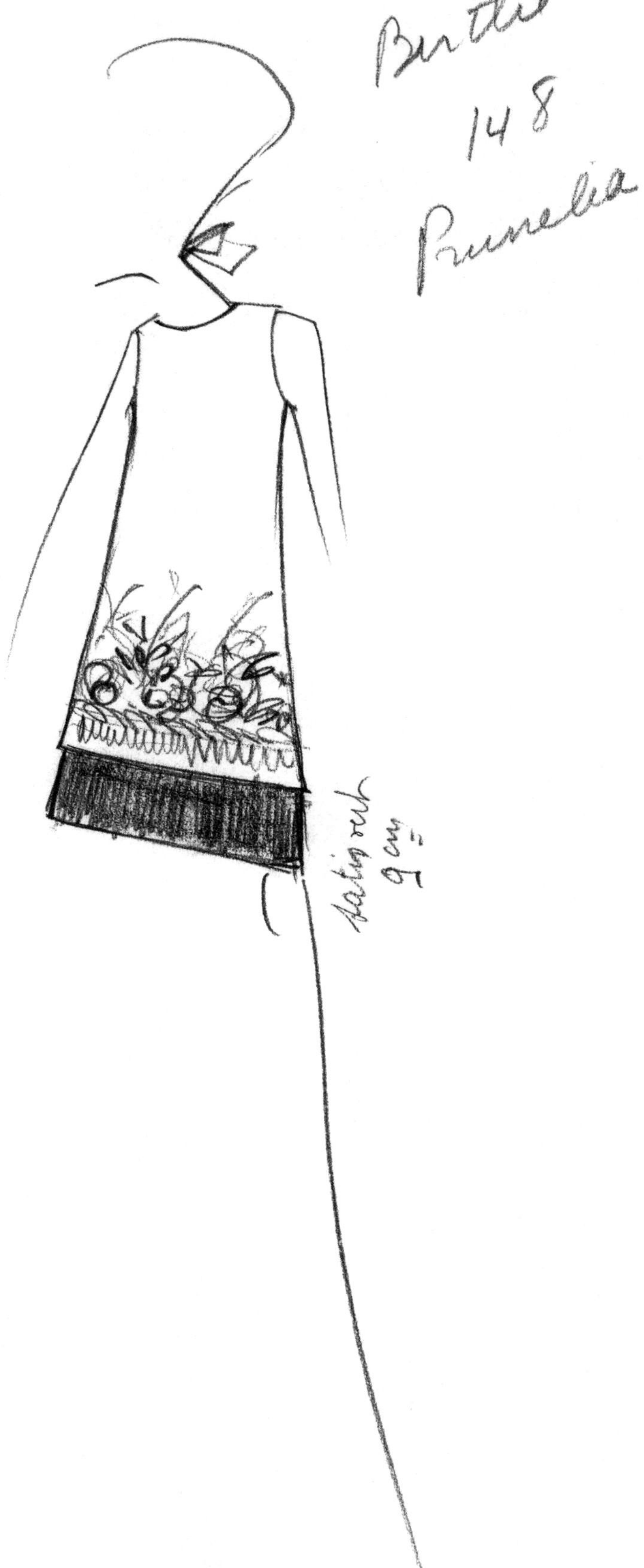

Berthe
148
Prunella

hauteur
9 cm

Marc Bohan for Christian Dior. 1981. Long taffeta bustier gown. Taffeta belt. Created for Isabelle Adjani, starring in the film *All Fired Up* by Jean-Paul Rappeneau. Inv. 1987.208

Jean-Paul Rappeneau's 1981 movie *All Fired Up* was one of the film projects on which the House of Dior worked. After the success of his first feature film, *The Savage*, the director asked Yves Montand to share top billing with Isabelle Adjani, who became famous after her role in *The Slap*, released in 1974.

All Fired Up was a dramatic comedy, the story of Victor (Montand), a self-serving, wily father who returns after an absence of several years to his family, where his eldest daughter, Pauline (Adjani) is watching over things. After pursuing several schemes, Victor manages to sell the family home despite Pauline's objections, to invest in a casino on the shores of Lake Geneva.

Catherine Leterrier was responsible for the costumes, with the exception of the dresses worn by Isabelle Ajani and Lauren Hutton in the film's final scene, during the opening of the casino. These two dresses by Marc Bohan for Christian Dior were made in the ateliers at 30 Avenue Montaigne. Their dramatic impact was considerable at this point in the film. Despite a number of difficulties, Victor has achieved his goal: the casino has finally become a reality, and Pauline walks through it in her long ivory satin evening gown, belted in the back. Wearing this light-toned dress, she appears as the triumphant victim of risky investments by a troublesome father who has nonetheless managed to regain his daughter's affection.

The extremely sexy look of the second Christian Dior dress, worn by Lauren Hutton, is the exact opposite of the one worn by Isabelle Adjani. Made of gold lamé, it features a very low-cut neckline. This dress alone, worn by Victor's new girlfriend, symbolizes the old demons of a frivolous but loving father who, suddenly forced to depart to take care of a shady deal, leaves his daughter Pauline alone to turn off the lights in the coveted casino.

After *All Fired Up*, Isabelle Adjani pursued a remarkable career of powerful roles that confirmed her personality as an uncompromising contemporary actress. In 1983, she joined forces with Alain Souchon, in Jean Becker's *One Deadly Summer*, in which she played an incandescent, vengeful seductress, receiving a César for best actress.

After conquering this fiery role, she became the mistress of ceremonies for the launch of two fragrances at the Château de Vaux-le-Vicomte, *Poison* in 1985 and *Dune* in 1991. *Poison* became an international success in the mid-1980s, enhanced in France by the aura of Isabelle Adjani.

VINCENT LERET

Yves Montand with Lauren Hutton and
Isabelle Adjani, both wearing dresses by Dior in
Jean-Paul Rappeneau's film *All Fired Up*, 1982.

Left: Dominique Issermann, Isabelle
Adjani wearing a design from the Spring-
Summer 1993 Haute Couture collection.

Black and white polka dots were a favorite motif in Christian Dior's ornamental vocabulary. The great couturier liked to incorporate them into his designs and wear them on his ties. His successors all returned to the graphic and rhythmic inspiration of these optical patterns. In the Fall-Winter 1986 collection, Marc Bohan reinterpreted the dots on a black faille with a galaxy of speckled white and black spots. A thick layer of pigment was printed on the fabric, using a pattern repeat of around twenty centimeters, most likely with a silk-screen process. This pattern reflects the spirit of the Fall-Winter 1984 collection, which was directly inspired by Jackson Pollock's drip paintings. The designer's approach was also similar to that of Popy Moreni and Tokio Kumagaï, who both made use of drip techniques in the early 1980s. At that time, fashion design was no longer reserved for Haute Couture, and ready-to-wear had become a major source for new ideas. Indeed, the line of this design by Marc Bohan resembles the mermaid dresses by such couturiers as Azzedine Alaïa, Thierry Mugler and Claude Montana. Finally, the use of the bow, resembling the obi of a kimono, reflects the Japanese influence.

With this dress, Bohan demonstrated a tremendous ability to encapsulate all these inspirations in a single well-balanced post-modern construction. The tight neckline counters the wide shoulders; cinched waist contrasts with the generous forms of the bow; the narrow skirt flares out at the bottom. The structure defines basic shapes (triangles, circles) along with more complex ones (loops, cones), creating full and empty spaces that cover and reveal the body (broad shoulders and large pockets with bare arms, a full bodice with a bare back). The interplay of oppositions creates a highly sculptural silhouette that sets off the pattern on the fabric. The black and white drip motif looks like a Pollock, but also resembles the speckled pattern that is characteristic of furniture designs by the Memphis Group. This dress seems to have been made by the tailoring atelier, and the cut repeats certain elements of the famous *Bar* jacket, like the vertical bust darts and large pockets. Bare skin appears in the center and all around this pointillist construction, which appears to be a dress, a sculpture and a painting.

In 1951, Cecil Beaton captured images of women wearing evening dresses in front of Jackson Pollock's large-format paintings. These famous photographs, published by *Vogue*,[1] probably gave Marc Bohan the inspiration for this hybrid gown that combines the vocabulary of a couturier, the vision of a photographer and the brushstrokes of a painter.

ÉRIC PUJALET-PLAÀ

1. *Vogue* (American edition), March 1951, pp. 158–159.

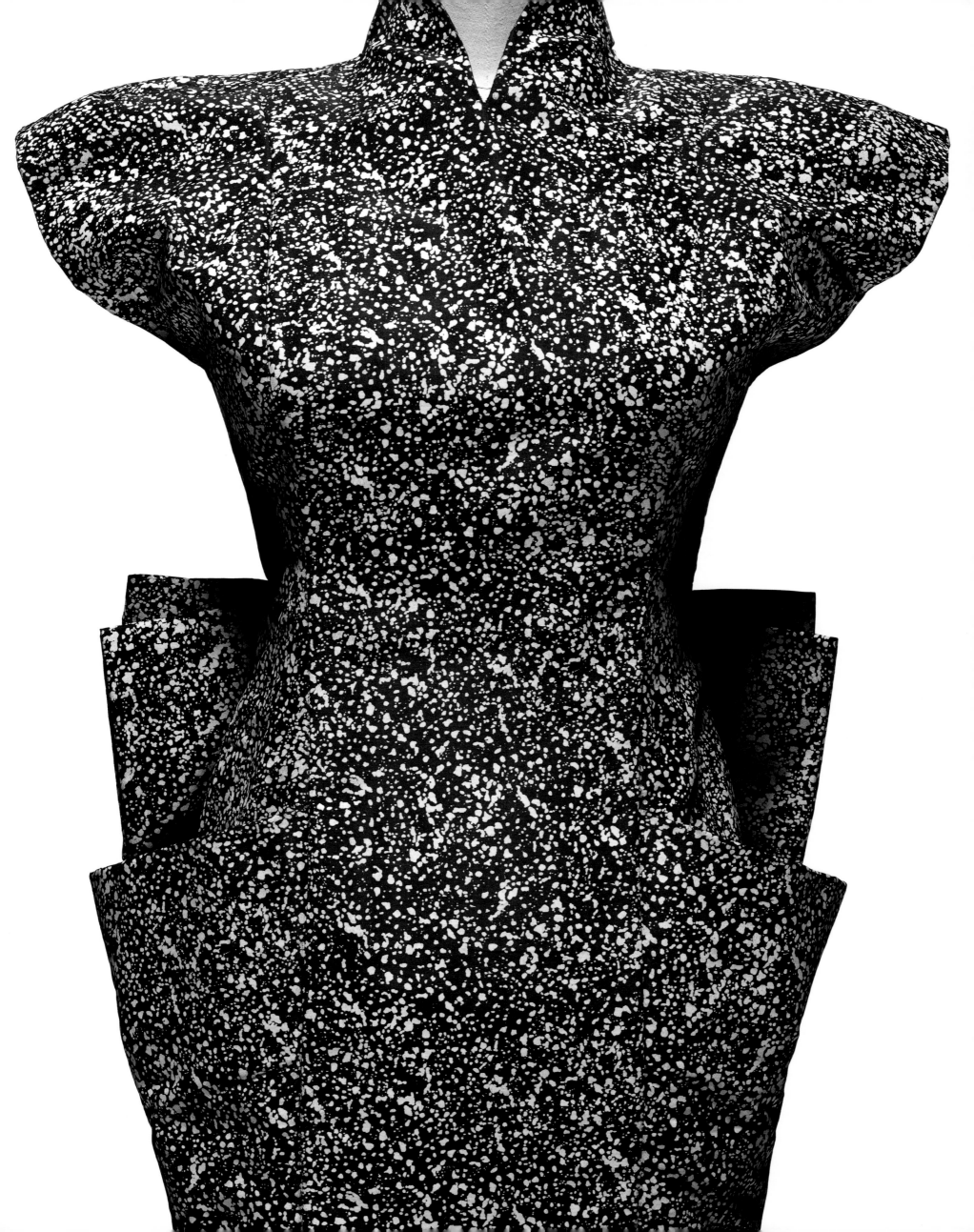

Marc Bohan for Christian Dior.
Haute Couture, Fall-Winter 1986.
Barathea suit, ornamental feathers.
Paris, Dior Héritage. Inv. 1987.186

Marc Bohan made garments meant to be worn in real life, not only for spectacular effect. The cut, balance and harmonious proportions mattered more to the couturier than being a part of the competition, chasing the trends that rattled the fashion world each season. But he still loved high style, as evidenced by this suit, with its superlative cut that emphasizes the waist and hips, in the tradition of the New Look. Black, gray and white formed Bohan's favorite palette. These unfailingly elegant colors followed the tradition of French-style "good taste." The ornamental feathers—a type of fragile adornment usually reserved for rarely worn evening dresses—reflect the luxurious spirit of Haute Couture; this decorative element adds an eye-catching touch of luxury.

This suit is part of a Marc Bohan collection that is particularly representative of the mid-1980s style: strong shoulders, highly defined belted waistline, jackets with short or long peplums. Day skirts are very short and the pockets stand out to accentuate the curve of the hips and narrow the waist. Cocktail dresses are draped on the sides. The masculine suits consist of loose-fitting double-breasted jackets, strict white shirts and tuxedo dresses and jackets with an interplay of black and white. Black barathea is a signature fabric in Haute Couture and tuxedo-style evening wear. One journalist quipped: "Marc Bohan has been captivated by feathers! I believe that there is a region somewhere on the planet where the roosters have lost their vigor, given the number of attributes they have lost!"[1]

The suit had nearly disappeared during the 1970s, amid the waves of popular protest. This garment, linked to a code of decorum, had been the uniform of the city girl since the early twentieth century. It returned in the early 1980s, alongside a retro trend inspired by the 1940s and 1950s. It helped to underscore the new status of women in society, women who fully embraced their independence, strong women who successfully juggled careers and family lives. By creating a more masculine silhouette, the 1940s-inspired padded shoulders symbolized the rise of the career woman.

FLORENCE MÜLLER

1. "La mode à Paris," *Le Soir*, July 30, 1986.

Horst P. Horst, suit from the Spring-Summer 1978
Haute Couture collection, model Mounia Orosemane.

Frank Horvat, Marc Bohan with five models
and Ellin Saltzman, editor of American
Glamour, wearing designs from the Spring-Summer
1964 Haute Couture collection, April 1964.

Right: Helmut Newton, suit from the Spring
Summer 1978 Haute Couture collection,
photographed on the Place du Palais-Bourbon,
in Paris, location of the *Vogue Paris* offices.

Marc Bohan for Christian Dior.
Haute Couture, Spring-Summer 1987.
Taffeta dress. Paris, Dior Héritage.
Inv. 1987.188

Paris. March 20, 1987. Her Royal Highness Princess Caroline of Monaco cut the ribbon for the inauguration of the renovated boutique at 30 Avenue Montaigne. She was wearing a fuchsia-pink silk taffeta evening dress that stopped above her knees. The draped bustier had a heart-shaped neckline; the skirt consisted of two overlapping pleated panels, like two rows of petals. That morning, the textile department of the Musée des Arts Décoratifs, then known as the Arts de la Mode, opened the exhibition *Hommage à Christian Dior, 1947–1957*—"the first ever retrospective devoted to the work of Christian Dior," touted the press release. One hundred fifty-four silhouettes and more than 300 documents (sketches, drawings, photographs, embroidery samples, swatch charts) provided an overview, thirty years later, of the ten years and twenty-two fashion shows by the founder of the Dior house.

Marc Bohan, who had been Dior's creative director for twenty-six years, also dreamed up an Haute Couture collection as a tribute to Christian Dior; it was called *Dior Toujours 1947–1987*, and gave pride of place to skirts with layered pleats, jackets with flared peplums, as well as shantung and every shade of pink. Hence the dress—very Dior in inspiration, and very Bohan in interpretation—that Princess Caroline wore that night. As a young woman of thirty, she jazzed it up with a long length of dotted Swiss silk, a metallic pouch and patterned black tights, a high-society Haute Couture punkette of the 1980s. "Caroline is fascinating because she dresses for herself. She is gorgeous, extremely charming, a divine silhouette. [...] She's a dream for a designer," Marc Bohan told Virginie Merlin in *Paris Match* the following week.[1] And he went on: "It's true that she's someone I adore designing for." The princess also participated as a friend in the commemorations celebrating the forty years of the house: the designer had known her since she was sixteen years old. They attended the Salzburg festival together, where Herbert von Karajan was conducting the orchestra, and were part of the same transgenerational group that loved to laugh, party and attend opera performances. He dressed her for every occasion, every season, as he had done for her mother, Princess Grace, and as Christian Dior had done before him—when she was still known as Grace Kelly.

JÉRÔME HANOVER

1. Virginie Merlin, *Paris Match*, March 1987.

 rely 28

Marc Bohan, sketch of the pink
taffeta dress, Spring-Summer
1987 Haute Couture collection.

Right: Stefano Casiraghi,
Princess Caroline of Monaco and
Marc Bohan at the inauguration
of the *Hommage à Christian Dior*
exhibition at the Musée des
Arts Décoratifs, March 20, 1987.

Andy Warhol, *Princess Caroline*, 1983,
mixed technique, synthetic polymer paint and
silkscreen ink on canvas. The Princess is
wearing a dress created by Marc Bohan for Dior.

Frédéric Castet for Christian Dior.
Tour Eiffel coat. Fashion furs, Fall-Winter 1988.
Mink coat. Paris, Dior Héritage.
Inv. 1987.411 and 2016.59, gift of Yvette Rossi

At the end of the rehearsal for the Fall-Winter 1988 fashion fur collection, Frédéric Castet announced that he was leaving Christian Dior. After joining the fur and tailoring atelier in 1953, replacing Pierre Cardin, and following a brief stint with Balenciaga, Castet returned to take charge of fashion furs in 1968. In 1973, he also launched Christian Dior Fourrure, a boutique presenting ready-to-wear clothes. His work elevated furs to a creative level never before achieved. The September 1988 show was his last in a long career and included "a tribute to the monuments of Paris,"[1] in the form of "four glossy, natural or transformed Saga mink coats,"[2] among them the *Tour Eiffel* coat, bearing the legend "Bonjour Paris." The other three coats represent the Sacré-Coeur, the Arc de Triomphe and the Opéra. All are created from a patchwork of colored fur, using great technical skill. But what stands out most in these designs is that the most expensive materials and master techniques were used for a kitsch interpretation of tourist clichés. This light-hearted, whimsical vision of fur was perfectly in sync with Frédéric Castet's goal: "I tried to revive the fashion for furs, which had been stagnating for years, to rejuvenate it and give it a touch of nonchalance. I freed it from its complexes. For me, fur should not represent an investment, but merely offer another option for changing an outfit."[3] This liberating manifesto certainly paved the way for other forms of stylistic freedom. Patrick Kelly's *Tour Eiffel* dresses the following winter, for example, appeared to echo these designs by Castet for Dior.

Castet invented a new approach to fur, making it lighter and treating it as a fabric like any other. Furrier techniques were adapted to produce all manner of variations, including fluid lettering (such as the extreme precision of the loop in the "r" of "Paris"). The colors used, five per coat, created landscapes, each with a different sense of light: *Arc de Triomphe*, for example, offered a night view down the Avenue des Champs-Élysées. It is an evening coat, while *Tour Eiffel* has a more casual cut and is a day coat on which the tower rises as a bright spot in a gray and white sky, dotted with pink snow.

Castet was very young when he first started working with Christian Dior, so his work was steeped in the very essence and styles of the house's inspiration. The unbridled luxury of his designs was perfectly in sync with the seasons and times of the day. The nonchalance with which he treated fur embodied the very heights of luxury.

ÉRIC PUJALET-PLAÀ

1. Program from the Fall-Winter 1988 fur collection.
2. Ibid.
3. From "Pour mieux connaître Frédéric Castet,"
   typewritten document, March 1974. Dior Héritage.

Horst P. Horst, Sophia Loren's lips are outlined in red mink on this coat from Christian Dior Fourrure, Fall-Winter 1980.
Right: *Tour Eiffel* coat, Fall-Winter 1988 fashion furs collection.

Boleslaw Edelhajt-Winczewski, Frédéric Castet
with his models wearing *Arc de Triomphe*,
Tour Eiffel, *Sacré Cœur* and *Opéra* coats from
the Fall-Winter 1988 fashion furs collection,
a tribute to the monuments of Paris.

Gianfranco Ferré, the robust Italian who became artistic director of Christian Dior in 1989, brought with him a love of opera and a distinct breed of exuberance. Baroque is the word. In art, the baroque shifted taste from the intellectual appeal of Mannerism to something more visceral, an appeal aimed plainly at the senses. Hence the term "baroque" can be applied to Ferré's work for Dior: opulent and sybaritic, lushly indulgent of the senses.

Dior himself adored grandeur, as the vast swathes of fabric that comprised a major part of his New Look amply attest. His own evening gowns were often outright operatic. Originally trained as an architect, Ferré shared Dior's love of those highly constructed silhouettes and of technically complex, elaborate clothing.

Only the third artistic director since Christian Dior's death, Ferré immersed himself in the house's archives prior to his debut. Ferré's resulting styles, while superficially similar to those of Dior—sketching the same silhouettes of broad skirt and minute waist—were, however, entirely different in attitude. Born from the indulgence of 1980s fashion with its overload of decoration and strong shapes, Ferré's baroque was an overload of the senses, incorporating passementerie, embroidery, printing and hand-painting, frequently in a single garment. While baroque can also be used to define Ferré's daytime clothing, it reached its ultimate expression in his evening ensembles, and the labour-intensive craftsmanship only feasible in Haute Couture.

Ferré's *Lady*, a gown from his debut Fall-Winter 1989 Haute Couture collection, epitomises this approach. He ended his debut Dior collection with a clutch of evening gowns in printed organzas and faille, girdled with embroidery, draped in chiffon, with silk flowers tucked into the back or waistline—here, a cascade of three-dimensional blooms tumble asymmetrically along a crinolined skirt of printed organza. Initially, the appearance is reverential of Dior's archive styles— but the audacity of the combinations of fabric, colors and decorations acutely reflect that particular moment in contemporary fashion.

Gianfranco Ferré's clothes spoke of abundance. He was a fan of the bold—the oversized bow, the expansive skirt, a gathered bustle. All had been used by Christian Dior, but were pushed to new extremes by Ferré, to register on the fashion stage of the late 1980s and early 1990s. His daywear occasionally surrendered decorative effect to practicality—for instance, the subjugation of the dramatic, illustrative line of a winged cuff to the requirement of a wrist to move readily within it. Yet in his evening wear, Ferré indulged pure fantasy—both his own, and those of his clients. Skirts were overblown to fantastical Scarlett O'Hara proportions below handspan waists, giving his women all the trappings of a fairy tale. It accurately reflected a conclusion drawn by Dior himself: "Deep in every heart slumbers a dream, and the couturier knows it: every woman is a princess."

ALEXANDER FURY

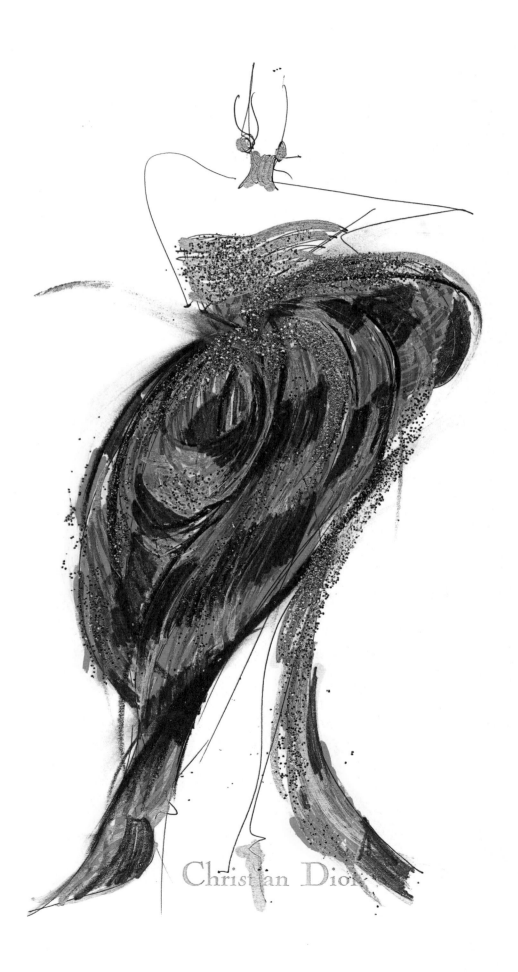

Christian Dior

Isabelle Adjani and Gianfranco Ferré during the
Spring-Summer 1993 Ready-to-Wear fashion show.

Left: David Seidner, dress from the Fall-Winter 1991 Haute
Couture collection (*Soleil d'Automne*), model Gisele Zelauy.

Insert: Gianfranco Ferré, sketch for the *Parade* dress, Fall-Winter
1992 Haute Couture collection (*Dans le secret d'un hiver vénitien*).

Gianfranco Ferré for Christian Dior. *Match* outfit.
Haute Couture, Fall-Winter 1989. *Ascot—Cecil Beaton*
collection. Three-quarter-length flared wool jacket
lined with printed organza. Piqué wool dress. Paris.
Dior Héritage. Inv. 1990.7

The notion of masculine combined with feminine seems very modern—and the
antithesis of Christian Dior's glorification of the divine female form, with its hourglass
waist and curved hips and bust. And yet the interplay of male and female was a constant
rapport within Dior's work. Like the tension between *tailleur* and *flou*, the two
opposing approaches to couture that round out a collection, Dior's work frequently
explored the notion of colliding the strict, rigorous and linear approach of the male
wardrobe with the sinuous and sensual feminine sphere.

That approach is most evident in his choice of fabrics, where Dior returned
again and again to textiles traditionally restricted to menswear tailoring—*fil-à-fil*,
Prince of Wales check, and most evidently the graphic houndstooth check, or
pied-de-poule. Practical but also decorative, evocative of British style and culture,
which Dior adored, the black-and-white houndstooth check in particular became
a Dior signature, one of the elements the couturier toyed with throughout his
career. Dior first achieved noted success in 1938, when he designed a full-skirted
dress of houndstooth check with a broderie anglaise petticoat edging for the
Robert Piguet couture house. It was inspired by *Les Petites Filles Modèles*, a French
children's book from the nineteenth century (the period echoed by its expansive
skirt, a precursor to the New Look of almost a decade later), and Dior dubbed
the dress *Café Anglais*. The dress caused a sensation—Christian Bérard, the artist
and friend of Dior, first introduced him to the journalist Marie-Louise Bousquet
as its creator. Bousquet may not have yet known Dior, but she knew his dress.

Ever superstitious, ten years after this *succès fou*, Dior employed houndstooth
check in his own-name debut, and in subsequent collections, like a talisman.
It rapidly became a key house motif, used by creative directors as diverse as
Gianfranco Ferré, John Galliano and Raf Simons, to underscore the identity of Dior.

Christian Dior, naturally, restricted the use of the fabric to daywear—suits, he felt,
were for morning to evening, but not for night. Nevertheless, he injected his tailoring
with as much glamour and invention as his grand evening gowns, manipulating flat,
spare, masculine fabrics into the highly constructed feminine shapes he adored.
His *Cocotte* suit of Spring-Summer 1948 is the most supreme example, a streamlined
houndstooth check coat-dress rising at the back into a structured, double-flounced
bustle. The masculine, used to create the sublimely feminine.

A similar taste for houndstooth check—as a contrast to, or even subversion of, the
overt femininity synonymous with Dior—was inherited by Christian Dior's
successors. They turn to houndstooth check specifically in their debut collections,
to emphasize a particular Dior code; or perhaps, like Monsieur Dior, as something
of a good-luck charm.

When the Italian Gianfranco Ferré created his first Dior Haute Couture collection
in 1989, he juxtaposed austere menswear fabrics—tweed, barathea, flannel, and
houndstooth check—with fragile lace, a subtle echo back to *Café Anglais*. His daywear
revolved around a palette of Dior grey, specifically in houndstooth, cut with a voluptuous
hand and a generosity that echoes Dior's own trademark exuberance. Contrasted with
bubbling blouses in voile, organza or silk, or tipped in embroidered lace, the combination
of male and female had lost none of its dynamite power in forty-two years.

ALEXANDER FURY

Clifford Coffin. *Cocotte* dress. Spring-Summer 1948
Haute Couture collection (*Zig-Zag* line). The name
and design of this dress recall the nineteenth-century
bustle dresses worn by demimondaines.

Left: Clifford Coffin, *Aventure* ensemble,
Spring-Summer 1948 Haute Couture collection (*Envol* line).

In 1989, Gianfranco Ferré joined the Parisian couture and ready-to-wear house, but continued to live in Milan. In 1974, this designer founded his own fashion label, which continued its activities throughout the years he worked at Dior. An outsider to the French spirit represented by Christian Dior's "flower woman," Ferré was deeply fascinated by the theatrically exaggerated and sumptuous style of the Parisian woman, as represented by Dior's collections. What Dior and Ferré shared was a love of architecture. The former had initially wanted to be an architect before becoming a couturier. As for the latter, he earned a degree in architecture in Milan. In 1955, during a conference at the Sorbonne, Christian Dior explained the importance of architecture in the construction of a dress: "As a couturier, I must follow the laws, the principles, of architecture."[1]

Shaped like a fluted ancient column, the long sheath dress in pleated white silk, named *Palladio* after the Venetian architect Andrea Palladio (1508–1580), was part of the *Au vent léger de l'été* collection for Spring-Summer 1992. Interviewed on Italian TV after the show, Ferré described his collection as being designed for a woman enjoying the air of Paris who likes to surround herself with colorful bouquets of flowers. He added that his own country was marvelous, even though it didn't have the same florists as in Paris. The reference to Palladio reflected the architect's influence on the neoclassical art of the second half of the eighteenth century. It owed a great deal to Palladio's architectural projects in sixteenth-century Veneto, imbued with a return to the ideals of ancient Greece and Rome and to the purity of classicism. According to the master of Vicenza, the classical order implied using columns as the basic component of any structure, but also the color white, symbolizing purity.

This return to antiquity was a source of inspiration for Ferré, who showcased Italy's past. This was embodied in the pared-down construction of the *Palladio* dress, which resembles the clean, straight lines of an Ionic column. In this case, the molded base, fluted column and capital with two volutes were transposed onto the elaborately worked fabric. The elegant embroidery by the Lesage house, applied around the base and neckline, structures the garment on either side of the soft flat pleats that create movement. In Greek architecture, a group of caryatids sometimes replaced the Ionic columns, as at Erechtheion, one of the Acropolis temples in Athens. A photograph from the archives of the couture house, dated December 1951, is a harmonious shot of eight models dressed in Christian Dior's "most beautiful dresses" posing in front of draped female statues which functioned as supporting columns in the Athenian temple.

MARIE-SOPHIE CARRON DE LA CARRIÈRE

1. *Conférences écrites par Christian Dior pour la Sorbonne,
1955–1957*, Paris, Éditions de l'Institut français de la mode /
Éditions du Regard, 2003, conference on August 3, 1955, p. 43.

John Galliano for Christian Dior. 1996. Satin and lace dress.
Special creation worn by Lady Diana at the Metropolitan Museum
of Art for the Costume Institute tribute celebrating Dior's fiftieth year,
in December 1996. Paris, Dior Héritage. Inv. 1996.59

This navy silk shift dress was John Galliano's first-ever design for the House of Dior. An auspicious start, it was a special order created for Diana, Princess of Wales, then one of the most famous women in the world, when she attended the Costume Institute's evening gala to celebrate Dior's fiftieth anniversary, held at the Metropolitan Museum of Art in New York in December 1996. Fitting in with her new "Sexy Di" image,[1] it inferred a negligee with its lace straps and drew attention to the princess's much-admired cleavage, toned silhouette and impressive height.

Galliano's meetings with the princess had been fun. "On a personal level, she had a gorgeous sense of irony, and was always one of the girls," he later recalled.[2] Meanwhile, it quickly became obvious that she needed simplicity and a lack of clutter, allowing her inner beauty and warmth to radiate. However, being a public figure who would be endlessly introduced to others, the princess required a dress that was feminine, non-constrictive and photogenic.

On the night, she teamed her dress with her ubiquitous pearl and sapphire choker and her irresistible pearly smile, and dazzled the attendees with her unforgettable charm. Often christened the People's Princess, Lady Diana was a winning mixture of grounded and accessible. As *Women's Wear Daily* later wrote on her sudden and shocking demise in 1997, "Diana had all the ingredients to become a fashion icon. But she had something else few others possess: the ability to walk into a room and instantly command the attention of every person in it."[3]

On the night of Dior's fiftieth anniversary, it was also noted that the Princess wore the *Lady Dior* bag, made in matching satin. Hanging on her wrist, it was aptly suited to her casual style. Indeed, Galliano's dress was a continuation of the princess's relationship with the fashion house that had initially begun with the *Lady Dior* bag. As often happens with an iconic accessory, there were various stages. In September 1995, when the Princess of Wales came on an official visit to Paris, Bernadette Chirac, the wife of the French president, gave her a quite new Dior bag. She became deeply attached to this accessory; she ordered several versions and wore it at various public appearances. In homage to the Princess, the bag was baptised *Lady Dior*.

NATASHA FRASER-CAVASSONI

1. *Women's Wear Daily*, Fairchild Publications, September 2, 1997, p. 4.
2. Ibid., p. 5.
3. Ibid., p. 1.

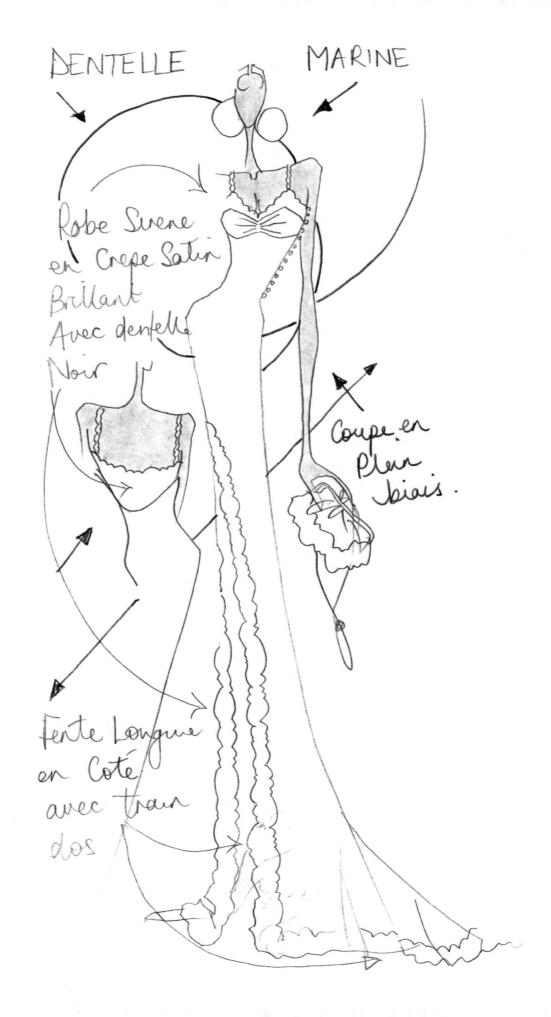

DENTELLE   MARINE

Robe Sirene
en Crepe Satin
Brillant
Avec dentelle
Noir

Coupe en
Plein
biais.

Fente Longue
en Coté
avec train
dos

Lady Diana at the Costume Institute gala celebrating the
fiftieth anniversary of the House of Dior, where she
inaugurated the *Christian Dior* exhibition at the
Metropolitan Museum of Art, New York, December 9, 1996.
Insert: Sketch of the design especially created for Lady Diana.

John Galliano for Christian Dior. *Kusudi* dress.
Haute Couture, Spring-Summer 1997. Long S-line mermaid
bustier dress in lace-veiled silk crêpe with corolla hemline.
Maasai beaded corset and high multicolor beaded choker.
Paris, Dior Héritage. Inv. 1997.27

Kusudi. Three syllables to embark on a journey to another world. In Swahili, this word means "intention." For John Galliano, the purpose of this dress was to showcase a full-blown, heightened femininity, but also one that was exotic and mysterious. This sheath dress in black silk crêpe, with black lace and a beaded corset, embodies the triumph of sinuous curves, expertly structured in keeping with Christian Dior's legacy.

For the fiftieth anniversary of the house, the Spring-Summer 1997 Haute Couture show paid tribute to one of the muses of the couturier and founder, his mother Madeleine, and to a period, that of the early 1900s. "I thank heaven I lived in Paris in the last years of the Belle Époque. They marked me for life. My mind retains the picture of a time full of happiness, exuberance, and peace, in which everything was directed towards the art of living," confided Christian Dior in his memoirs.[1]

This collection therefore illustrated a bold dialogue between the past and the present, to capture the seduction of the future. John Galliano reinterpreted the corsets and lace of Madeleine Dior, by incorporating the multicolored ornaments of Maasai warriors. Thousands of multicolored beads slide and dance over the silk of the *Kusudi* dress, nearly in rhythm with the model's steps, embracing and subtly accentuating her waist, highlighting without over-emphasizing it, while the Maasai-style choker contributes to her stately demeanor.

Deliberately overlapping this exotic mystery is a fascination for the beauty of the female body, wrapped in a form-fitting black silk mermaid dress inspired by the works of Italian painter Giovanni Boldini, a popular portraitist of elegant society women during the Belle Époque. John Galliano was also able to place his models in contradictory poses that combined arched curves, tension and freedom. In them, we discern the fluid, vigorous brushstrokes of a great society painter.

MORGANE PAULISSEN

1. Christian Dior, *Dior by Dior: The Autobiography of Christian Dior*, London, V&A Publishing, 2nd ed., 2007, p. 171.

Following double page, left: Peter Lindbergh, *Kusudi* and *Kitu* dresses, Spring-Summer 1997 Haute Couture collection, models Kiara Kabukuru and Debra Shaw. Right: Patrick Demarchelier, *Princesse Gwallior* suit, Fall-Winter 1997 Haute Couture collection, model Danielle Zinaich.

The detailed program presenting John Galliano's 1998 Haute
Couture collection for Christian Dior was "a poetic tribute to the
Marquesa Casati." Held in the Napoleon III-style main staircase of
the Paris Opera, the show was organized like a Belle Époque
high-society party, full of spectacular silhouettes and choreographed
for the sumptuous décor designed by the architect Charles Garnier.

The *Shéhérazade* evening ensemble, consisting of a long satin
sheath dress flaring in the back and a silk velvet kimono jacket
embroidered by the Lanel house with Swarowski crystal gems, is
worn by a model whose dramatic pose and sophisticated makeup are
reminiscent of portraits of Luisa Casati painted and drawn by many
artists, including Léon Bakst, the decorator and costume designer
for the Ballets Russes, and Giovanni Boldini.

During the costumed balls she organized in Venice in 1913, where
she hosted leading lights of the literary and artistic world, Luisa
Casati created a sensation with her original, sophisticated appearances, dressed in Oriental outfits designed by Léon Bakst or created
by the couturier Paul Poiret. Impressed by the creative vitality of the
choreography of *Shéhérazade*, performed by the Ballets Russes
in 1910 at the Palais Garnier in Paris, and by the vibrant colors of
Léon Bakst's Oriental costumes and sets, Paul Poiret was captivated
by this fairy-tale world. He showcased it by orchestrating memorable
parties, including one he christened "La Mille et Deuxième Nuit"
(The Thousand and Second Night), attended by Paris high society
dressed up as characters from the famous tales of the Arabian
Nights. He also drew on this theme for his couture designs.

Christian Dior summed up Poiret's innovative role with this
statement: "With the coming of Poiret all this was altered."[1] In his
memoirs, he analyzed the revival of fashion in the years preceding
the war of 1914: "The figure of the elegant woman was no longer
corseted, but gracefully, and cunningly, shackled. The fashionable
ideal of the odalisque, or hieratic princess of Oriental legends, was
given its supreme expression by Ida Rubinstein, dressed by Bakst."[2]

For the Spring-Summer 1998 collection, John Galliano, a keen
connoisseur of costume history, paid a brilliant triple homage,
to Casati's theatrical eccentricity, to the aesthetic influence of the
Ballets Russes via Léon Bakst, and to the decisive role of Paul Poiret,
who popularized Orientalism. Overlapping the Belle Époque references that forged Christian Dior's taste, Galliano modeled the
brightly colored evening jacket of the *Shéhérazade* ensemble after a
gouache by Georges Lepape illustrating a "Persian fête at Poiret's."[3]

MARIE-SOPHIE CARRON DE LA CARRIÈRE

1. Christian Dior, *Dior by Dior: The Autobiography of Christian Dior*,
    London, V&A Publishing, 2nd ed., 2007, p. 15.
2. Ibid.
3. *Femina*, December 15, 1912.

Léon Bakst, design for the set of the ballet *Shéhérazade*, 1910,
gouache, gold highlights, watercolor and pencil on paper.
Paris, Musée des Arts Décoratifs, Département des Arts
Graphiques, dépôt du FNAC.

Left: Michael Thompson, *Shéhérazade* ensemble, Spring-
Summer 1998 Haute Couture collection, model Esther de Jong.

John Galliano for Christian Dior.
Haute Couture, Spring-Summer 1999.
Long mermaid-line crêpe sheath dress
with draped shoulder straps and
black glove motif at the hips.
Paris, Dior Héritage. Inv. 1999.52

John Galliano created this bias-cut sheath from ivory crêpe satin, consisting of eight trumpet-flared panels with no bustier. The color, line, material and technique were borrowed straight from the fashion of the 1930s. The complexity of the draped fabric forming the cowl neck, featuring asymmetrical, crossed shoulder straps, as well as the line of twenty-five round buttons concealing the zipper, create an experimental and perfectly finished look to this dress—one that Madeleine Vionnet herself would have been pleased with. The black glove motif on the hips adds an enigmatic touch that suggests the illusions of Elsa Schiaparelli's dresses. She was influenced by both Dalí and Cocteau; in 1937, the latter designed a bolero embroidered with a face and a woman's hand for Schiaparelli.[1]

In this collection, where "everything is not always what it seems,"[2] it is hard to distinguish what is from what is represented. The three black gloves on this ivory-colored dress are an illusion. They cannot be worn, but the seams have been delicately sewn and the round buttons are no less real than those covering the zipper. Depending on the viewer's position, this black glove motif could be mistaken for the model's gloved hands as she strikes a glamorous contrapposto. This motif is perpetuated through movement, as when the model places her hands elsewhere, mysteriously multiplying the hands. During the show, this design was presented in front of a torn panel of white paper, after Philippe Halsman's famous photograph of Cocteau and his illusionary effect. "As you may have gathered, the mood is surrealistic, in the way that Dalí and Cocteau understood it—witty and startling at times, but always romantic."[3]

This dress recreates the vision Christian Dior may have had of fashion around 1935, a style he then left behind. "Couture was weary of only catering for painters and poets, and wanted to revert to its true function, of clothing women," wrote Dior.[4] Reinforcing the link between Dior's inspiration and surrealism, Galliano repositioned the couturier's work within the continuity of the fashion and art that preceded it. Dior continued: "Dominating every avant-garde effort, the beacon of Jean Cocteau illuminated and revealed all."[5] "This prince of light knew and respected the princes of darkness," responded Cocteau in turn.[6]

ÉRIC PUJALET-PLAÀ

1. Paris, Musée des Arts Décoratifs, Elsa Schiaparelli donation 1973, inv. UFD 73-21-1711.
2. Program for the Spring-Summer 1999 collection.
3. Ibid.
4. Christian Dior, *Dior by Dior: The Autobiography of Christian Dior*, London, V&A Publishing, 2nd ed., 2007, p. 27.
5. Ibid, p. 174.
6. Jean Cocteau, "Adieu à Christian Dior," *Arts-Spectacles*, no. 642, October 30, 1957.

Man Ray, views of the exhibition *Exposition surréaliste, Sculptures, objets, peintures, dessins*, Galerie Pierre Colle, June 1933. The images include works by Dalí, *Buste rétrospectif d'une femme* (1933) and *La Chaise atmosphérique* (1933); by Giacometti, *Table* (1933), *Palais* (1932) and *Mannequin* (1932–1933); by Joan Miró, *Tête humaine* (1931); and by Max Ernst, *L'Europe après la pluie* (1933).

Right: Michael Thompson, dress from the Spring-Summer 1998 Ready-to-Wear collection, model Olga Pantushenkova.

John Galliano for Christian Dior. Haute Couture,
Spring-Summer 2000. Newspaper print
silk taffeta salopette. Silk moiré waistcoat.
Paris, Dior Héritage. Inv. 2000.44

Combining the words Dior and scandal in the same sentence sounds like a contradiction in terms, given just how much the house has always been a bastion of French Haute Couture, tradition and classicism. Yet John Galliano's Spring-Summer 2000 collection was by far the most controversial show the fashion world had seen in recent decades. Galliano drew his inspiration for this collection, nicknamed "Clochard" (Hobo), by observing homeless people during his morning jog along the banks of the Seine in Paris. The models wore torn, unraveled, unstructured garments strung with various objects, including small bottles of alcohol, toothless combs and so on. In the trade press, the show was described as "exhilarating, "unsettling," "maddening,"[1] "all-out," and a "mix of luxury and tatters."[2] In France, the general press, usually less focused on fashion shows, nevertheless covered it widely and aggressively. Critics wrote about "luxury hobos with a sordid aftertaste," saying that Galliano "had transported Dior to the Cour des Miracles,"[3] and noting that it was tone-deaf to "launch the 'hobo' style when there are 6 million people unemployed."[4] Other journalists protested that "the House of Dior is not what it used to be," and that since Galliano arrived, "the very haute couture traditional suits had been definitively [...] relegated to a 'museum' status."[5]

Yet this overlooks the fact that Christian Dior, and especially his iconic New Look dresses in 1947, had in their time triggered huge scandals, with their "fantastic yardage of material," "enormous spreading skirts," as Dior described them himself.[6] During a trip to the United States, he talked about "a shower of anonymous letters, written by the enemies of the 'liberated bosom,' of rounded hips, of long skirts," which made a woman look like "a stuffed doll of the time of the Civil War."[7] The primary criticism of these skirts was about their length, as these women viewed this as a step backward in their efforts for more freedom. In France and England in 1947, when ration cards were still required to purchase fabric, it was the huge yardage of material required to make the New Look *Corolle* skirts that shocked people—up to twenty meters—given that during the Occupation, an entire dress had to be made from three meters of fabric, no more.

Life magazine, in its October 27, 1947 issue, published photographs depicting poorly dressed Parisian women assaulting a model wearing a New Look dress. A genuine story or a staged event? Regardless, these images illustrate just how the new fashion was received and the sense of uneasiness toward the poverty of the era, which Haute Couture seemed to disdain. Christian Dior was well aware of this "poverty-stricken, parsimonious era, obsessed with ration books and clothes coupons: it was only natural," he said, "that my creations should take the form of a reaction against this dearth of imagination."[8]

DENIS BRUNA

1. Suzy Menkes, "Deconstructing Dior,"
   International Herald Tribune, January 18, 2000.
2. *Women's Wear Daily*, January 18, 2000.
3. *Le Journal de la Haute-Marne*, January 18, 2000.
4. *Le Figaro*, January 27, 2000.
5. *Le Meilleur*, January 29, 2000.
6. Christian Dior, *Dior by Dior: The Autobiography
   of Christian Dior*, London, V&A Publishing, 2nd ed.,
   2007, pp. 23, 34.
7. Ibid., pp. 45, 144.
8. Ibid., p. 22.

Walter Carone, a young woman wearing
a New Look dress is set upon by a group
of housewives outraged by the yardage of the fabric,
Rue Lepic in Paris, October 1947.

Right: Inez van Lamsweerde & Vinoodh
Matadin, ensemble from the Spring-Summer 2000
Haute Couture collection, model Amber Valletta.

Following double page: Nick Knight,
ensemble from the Spring-Summer 2000 Haute
Couture collection, model Jacquetta Wheeler.

John Galliano for Christian Dior.
Haute Couture. Fall-Winter 2003.
Embroidered gray pin-striped jacket.
Polka dot silk and crin.
Paris. Dior Héritage. Inv. 2004.6

This is a hybrid silhouette, an elegant suit that has been hiked up to dance a wild flamenco. The gray jacket expresses all the rigor of a suit—of a pin-striped Savile Row English suit, restyled by John Galliano in a feminine spirit. In opposition to this strict suit is a brilliantly colored tulle skirt with sparkling sequins, extravagant in the meters of fabric used and the length of the train, dancing and swaying with each step.

John Galliano expressed his own identity in this twofold silhouette, that of a child who, at the age of six, left his native Gibraltar for London. "We came from this sunny clime, blue sky, a mix of cultures and religion and flamenco and spices and smells," he explained. "We moved into a very poor South London suburb. […] Gray thunderous clouds, wet chalk. I felt like an alien."[1] With this dress, the artistic director reconnected with a well-established source of inspiration that has existed since Christian Dior. Where the founding couturier dreamed up summer outfits and flounced dresses with names like *Madrid*, *Barcelone*, *Tolède* and *Andalousie*, and where his successor, Yves Saint Laurent, drew inspiration from the more severe and dark world of Velázquez and Goya with models like *Rosita* and *Lola*, John Galliano celebrated Spain, which became even more colorful in contrast to the British rigor of a gray suit. It offers a joyous vision: the Spain of flamenco, of course, whose popular imagery is part of the iconography of great Spanish painting. John Galliano also paid it a vibrant tribute in the Fall-Winter 2007 collection, in the form of designs inspired by Picasso, Velázquez, El Greco, Zurbarán and Ignacio Zuloaga.

In addition, this outfit by Galliano is not unlike *El Jaleo* by American painter John Singer Sargent, depicting a Spanish dancer. Indeed, the entire Fall-Winter 2003 collection is all about dance. The idea was to create "an abstract and conceptual interpretation of dance; to create clothes that come to life."[2] John Galliano, who had learned from his mother how to dance the flamenco on tables to make more noise, dreamed up a dancer who was exhausted from spinning so frenetically; it was this fatigue that gave such unexpected spontaneity to the dresses. The sleeves are rolled up, and on closer examination, the jacket looks like a layering of a T-shirt, a bra and a vest, reminiscent of the unique style of professional dancers in rehearsals, as they throw on different clothes, adjusting them quickly as they move. For John Galliano, this overlap of England and Spain was the story of two different worlds that came together in a genuine creative alchemy: Haute Couture and dance, rigor and spontaneity, the expertise of the tailoring atelier along with that of the dressmaking atelier.

ALIX D'HAUTEFEUILLE

1. Ingrid Sischy. "Galliano in the Wilderness." *Vanity Fair*, July 2013.
2. Press kit for the Fall-Winter 2003 collection.

Irving Penn, dress from the Fall-Winter 2003
Haute Couture collection, model Élise Brombez.

John Galliano for Christian Dior.
Haute Couture. Spring-Summer 2004.
Embroidered jacket and skirt.
Paris, Dior Héritage. Inv. 2004.50

At the start of this show, a shade, a shadow, slowly appeared at the back of the catwalk, plunged into near total darkness. It was hieratic in posture, with unique volumes, atop which guests could just make out a headdress and ceremonial beard inspired by Ancient Egypt. A real-life Haute Couture hieroglyph. The model swept forward, wearing a jacket and skirt entirely embroidered in gold. Her body, clad in a corset underneath this mosaic of gold strips, seemed to be sculpted. The bust was flattened, legs clad in a sheath; over this long, narrow shape, with exaggerated bell sleeves, oversized drapery was arranged below the waist. In the words of the press kit, it was "a collection mixing references to the wonders of ancient Egypt of the Pharaohs with reminiscences from the 1950s, with Christian Dior's 'H' line, and photographs by Richard Avedon and Irving Penn."

John Galliano, who drew his inspiration from all over the globe, had just returned from a trip to Egypt, visiting Cairo, Luxor and Aswan. The first dress in the show conjured up the excessive use of gold by the Pharoahs and the sensuality of Cleopatra. There is a touch of ancient fashion history in the draping, inspired by Egyptian belts, as well as a nod to architectural heritage in the breastplate, which resembles a pyramid—not to mention an archaeological influence as well, in the crown and false beard, divine and royal attributes with which the artistic director adorned his woman-as-idol.

In this celebration of a new type of Egyptian woman, he returned to a source of inspiration that marked the earliest years of the house. Christian Dior produced designs named *Égypte*, *Cléopâtre*, *Suez* and *Ramsès*—such as the long straight coat from the *H* line of the Fall-Winter 1954 collection, a line that put an end to the New Look and was nearly as scandalous. The *Mazette* dress, which the American magazines found so shocking in 1954, is an example of this line, "based on the lengthening and reduction of the bust." "The parallel lines that form the elongated letter H provide the structure for dresses, suits and coats,"[1] as explained at the time. John Galliano adopted this way of stylizing the body as a clean line, by flattening the bust. By replacing the draping that Christian Dior used with a Cleopatra-style belt, he took this encounter between 1950s femininity and Egyptian inspiration to the limit. And, a true perfectionist, the artistic director pursued this blend of references beyond the garments, to include the poses. John Galliano, fascinated by the work of Richard Avedon and Irving Penn, noted a resemblance between the models' poses in their photographs and those of women depicted on Egyptian frescos. Halfway down the catwalk, the Haute Couture woman-Pharaoh of the Spring-Summer 2004 collection stopped for an instant, arched backward, and let herself be photographed in profile as in these iconic ancient images, to reveal the full extent of the sculptural volume of the dress she was wearing.

ALIX D'HAUTEFEUILLE

1. Program from the Fall-Winter collection. 1954.

Following double page, right:
Paolo Roversi, dress from the
Spring-Summer 2004
Haute Couture collection.
model Gemma Ward.

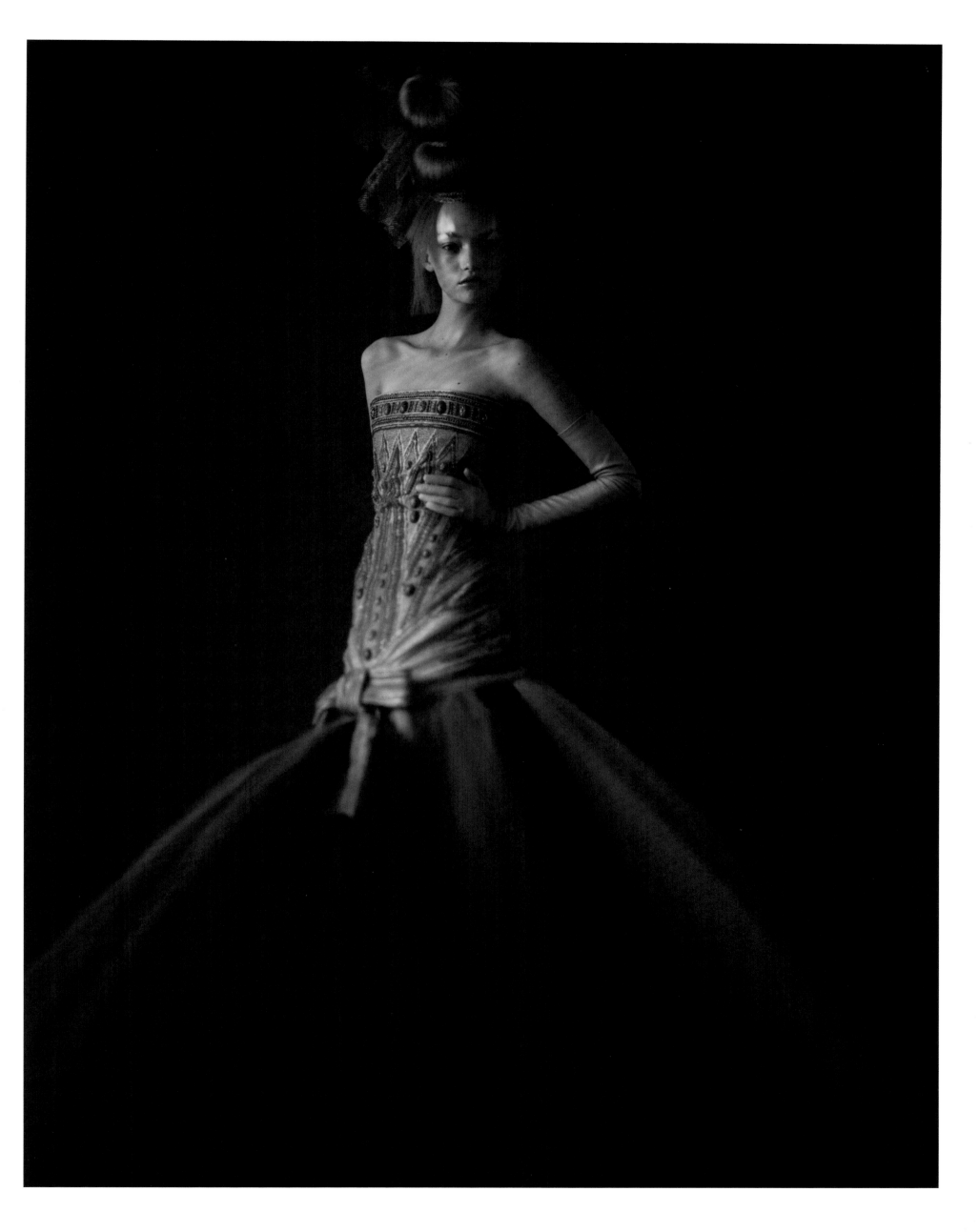

John Galliano for Christian Dior. Haute Couture. Fall-Winter 2004. Moiré bustier gown with gold embroidery. Paris. Dior Héritage. Inv. 2005.25

This dress is an eloquent example of the historicism in John Galliano's creative work and in the history of the Dior house. The moiré bustier, with its cinched waist and push-up bust, is reminiscent of courtesans from the 1890s to the 1900s. The full skirt with drapery ascending around the body seems to reveal Galliano's fondness for Giovanni Boldini's portraits of society women. Yet the blue-gray and white colors, as well as the colored silk and gold embroidery, are even more suggestive of the eighteenth century. The collection's press kit describes the "Wedgwood blue" and "embroidery reminiscent of hand-painted eighteenth-century motifs inspired by Sèvres porcelain."

For Galliano, as for most of the designers inspired by the long story of historic costumes, it was not about borrowing from an era or any particular style, but more about combinations, superimpositions, a "mix and match," as he called it himself. Indeed, the descriptions of the dresses in the show speak of a "very free vision of a collection blending nineteenth-century references steeped in romanticism" and "eighteenth-century motifs," dotting the precious fabrics. The historicist themes, particularly those of the eighteenth century, are leitmotifs with Galliano, who had his first major success at Saint Martin's School of Art, in 1984, with a collection inspired by the Incroyables, a set of eccentric young Parisians who challenged fashion codes with their extravagant style during the Directoire.

The eighteenth century was also a recurring theme for Christian Dior, something of an autobiographical echo. In his memoirs, he wrote that "from 1900 to 1914, decoration à la Louis Seize was all the rage in the 'new' houses in Passy,"[1] where he grew up. This fascination is also clear in his boutiques, decorated in shades of Trianon gray and white, as well as in his homes, like the Château de La Colle Noire, where the bedrooms were lined with toile de Jouy, and his last house, in Passy, Boulevard Jules-Sandeau, where he designed the décor and defined the style as decidedly "1956 Louis Seize."[2]

These elements, freely borrowed from the eighteenth century, permeated Christian Dior's dresses and the Dior house. In 1947, "these long skirts, emphasized waists, and tremendously feminine fashions were instantly baptized the New Look,"[3] as he wrote in his memoirs, all references the fashion from the last decades of the eighteenth century.

Press releases from the Dior house from 1952 to the present mention "Richelieu heels" and "buttons sculpted from eighteenth-century bronzes" and cite Marie-Antoinette, Rose Bertin, Versailles and the Trianon, illustrating a profound and recurring attachment to this century that was so exceptional in terms of the decorative arts.

DENIS BRUNA

1. Christian Dior, *Dior by Dior: The Autobiography of Christian Dior*, London, V&A Publishing, 2nd ed., 2007, p. 20.
2. Ibid., p. 192.
3. Ibid., p. 143.

Élisabeth Louise Vigée Le Brun, *Gabrielle Yolande
Claude Martine de Polastron, duchesse de Polignac*, 1782,
oil on canvas. Versailles, Musée National des Châteaux
de Versailles et de Trianon.

Willy Maywald, *Eugénie* dress, Fall-Winter
1948 Haute Couture collection (*Ailée* line).

Laurent Van der Stockt, John Galliano
preparing his first Haute Couture
collection for Dior, Spring-Summer 1997,
model Karen Mulder. This dress was
inspired by the 1948 *Eugénie* design.

For Christian Dior, fashion was the last refuge of magic, a sanctuary filled with effects and illusions created by the successive artistic directors for the Christian Dior house since February 12, 1947. The Fall-Winter 2005 Haute Couture collection ushered in a new world of designs based on flesh-colored corsets. These corsets hugged the natural curves of the model and perfectly imitated the color of skin. According to John Galliano, they formed the perfect base on which to start designing.

As with the *Dolly* model, the dress disappears into the skin, revealing the embroidered lace motifs on the black tulle. The body seems to be wearing this embroidery alone, in this way revealing, as was John Galliano's intention, "the work of the ateliers [...] and the techniques of the *petites mains*, which are usually hidden."[1] This new concept, which he called "Nude," involved re-assessing the structure of a dress itself. He had to start with a blank slate, the better to highlight the line of the design. It was a pictorial, even literary approach to fashion. With this collection, John Galliano wanted the interplay of transparencies to reveal the ephemeral nature of a charcoal drawing, the wash of a watercolor and the confidence of a brushstroke.

Dolly perfectly expresses this new approach, which underscored the refinement of embroidery or the perfect makeup. As Christian Dior said in his *Little Dictionary of Fashion*, published in 1954, "the best makeup is the most natural, it should remain invisible."[2]

The trompe-l'œil corsets in the Fall-Winter 2005 collection marked a stylistic turning point that creative and image directors for Dior makeup have incorporated into their work in color. Drawing on natural skin tones, the makeup line *Diorskin Nude*, for example, created by Tyen in 2009, enhances the skin by creating the illusion of luminous nudity; he says that "it is a colorless color, in which nudity is bared."[3]

Putting on makeup to create the impression of no makeup and dressing in flesh-colored mousseline to efface the dress are both trends toward a more natural, truthful effect. This quest continues today with the same diligence. Peter Philips, current creative and image director for Dior makeup, is particularly sensitive to this aesthetic, based notably on the quality of foundations, which can conceal or highlight a nude finish. Like the trompe-l'œil corset of the *Dolly* dress, Nude is a wonderful tool for creating new illusions in fabrics and cosmetics.

VINCENT LERET

1. Program for the Fall-Winter 2005 collection.
2. Christian Dior, *Christian Dior's Little Dictionary of Fashion*, London, Cassel and Company Ltd., 1954.
3. Jerry Stafford, *Dior, l'art de la couleur*, Rizzoli International Publications, 2016.

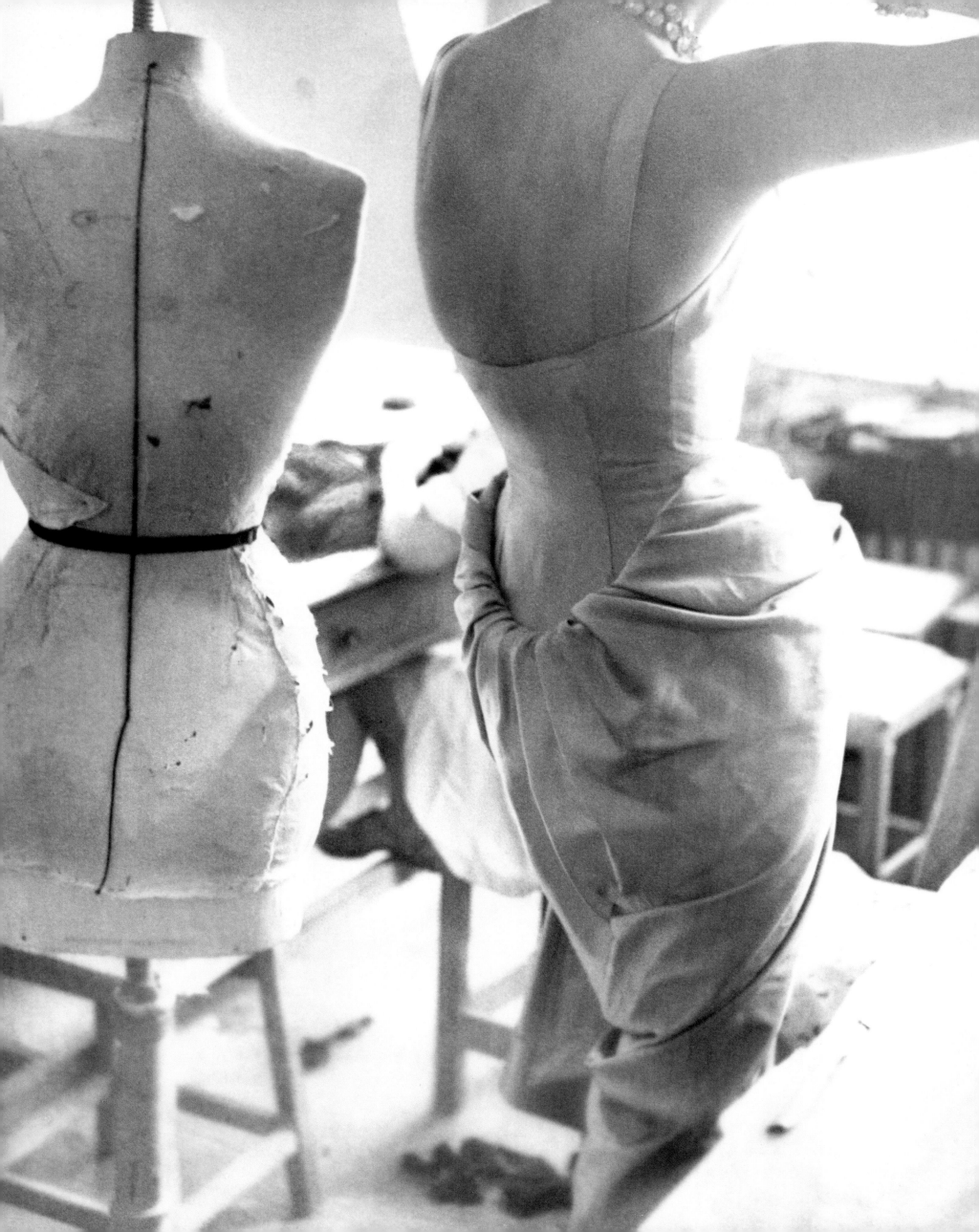

Richard Avedon, *Workroom*, House of Dior, August 1947.
Fall-Winter 1947 Haute Couture collection, *Corolle* line.

John Galliano for Christian Dior.
Praline evening gown. Haute Couture,
Fall-Winter 2005. Taffeta and flesh tulle dress,
worn with a trompe-l'œil corset.
Paris, Dior Héritage. Inv. 2006.5

Praline? It's a kind of small pink candy that was first created in the seventeenth century. It is also the name of a star model Christian Dior met when he worked with Lucien Lelong. In his memoirs, he described her as having "the quality of being a mannequin turned into a woman, rather than a woman turned mannequin."[1] It is also a flamingo-pink afternoon dress from the Spring-Summer 1948 collection. And finally, it is this dress in shaded green taffeta and flesh-colored tulle, worn with a trompe-l'œil corset resembling a dressmaker's dummy, which John Galliano presented at his Fall-Winter 2005 Haute Couture show. It was a unique event: Christian Dior would have been one hundred that year, and his successor as the house's artistic director was paying tribute to the couturier and to his work. Various scenes retraced the creative trajectory, illustrating how the original image became an ultimate fantasy. This one was called "Constructing a Dress," and featured a series of four silhouettes, *Lucky*, *Praline*, *France* and *Victoire*, named for models who worked with the founder. This *tableau vivant* included a profusion of references. "I was inspired by the representations of Monsieur Dior's work," explained John Galliano in the press kit. Indeed, these silhouettes offer a glimpse into a moment of a collection's evolution, captured by the photographer Bellini: the fittings. They showed Christian Dior draping silk taffeta around his model Sylvie, in front of tangled lengths of fabric and boxes. What this image shows, as do John Galliano's four silhouettes, is the creative gesture, the flashes of inspiration that sculpt the fabric on the body of a women, so that each best expresses the beauty of the other. This is the birth of a dress.

But what was merely suggested in Bellini's photograph, and what is fully revealed in this *tableau vivant*, is the very essence of the creative act: the dialogue between the couturier and his ateliers. The first atelier is the *tailleur*, or tailoring atelier, which made the corset that redesigned the curves and hips of our *Praline* dress. The second is the *flou*, or dressmaking atelier, to which we owe the draped tulle and taffeta that seem to wrap weightlessly around the body. It is as if the dress were frozen in the moment of its creation, at the very instant that best illustrates the symbiosis between the designer and the workshops.

JÉRÔME HANOVER

1. Christian Dior, *Dior by Dior: The Autobiography of Christian Dior*, London, V&A Publishing, 2nd ed., 2007, p. 129.

Following double page, left: Tim Walker,
France dress, Fall-Winter 2005 Haute Couture
collection, model Imogen Morris Clark.
Right: Tim Walker, *Praline* dress, Fall-Winter
2005 Haute Couture collection, models Imogen
Morris Clarke and Stella Tennant.

Sixty years after Christian Dior's New Look collection, John Galliano pursued the same dreams of textile construction in his Spring-Summer 2007 collection, with a ballet of Japanese-inspired designs underpinned by origami techniques. The *Lu-Lee-San* cocktail dress is quite simply a marvel, full of the signature surprises of the Christian Dior house. This bustier gown echoes the poetic science of paper folding, here given an Haute Couture interpretation through broad gazar pleats.

The technique chosen to make this dress evokes the phantasmagorical world of Christian Dior's childhood, spent between Granville and Paris. In his memoirs, the couturier details every object, as if each one of them were a secret confidant: the roofs of the bamboo and straw pagodas above the doors, the outsized fans, all the "*Japonaiseries* one sees on screens,"[1] which were a constant source of wonder to him. This decorative historicism was considered good taste at the time in cultivated circles, as reflected in Victor Hugo's house in Guernsey, located close to Granville. These elements illuminate a long-lost environment for which Christian Dior maintained a certain degree of nostalgia. In this list, the couturier did not forget to mention the large panels painted from Japanese prints that surrounded the staircase in the Villa Les Rhumbs, which he used to gaze at "for hours."[2]

The *Lu-Lee-San* dress offers a trip back in time, to the founder's childhood years. Its colors are reminiscent of those of the Villa Les Rhumbs and its natural environment: the blue-gray of the landscaped rockeries, the silver-gray of the maritime vegetation, the gray-green of the tides, the yellow-gray of the cliffs overgrown with gorse bushes.

Gray was certainly the couturier's favorite color, and it was omnipresent in the décors of the Louis XV-style interiors that the young Christian Dior rediscovered in Paris after vacationing in Normandy. For his couture house, Christian Dior naturally chose this same gray, which he liked to compare to that of the Trianon, in Versailles, a prestigious reference that was well suited to the style the couturier wanted to emulate in the interiors of 30 Avenue Montaigne.

The couturier wanted a small couture house, reserved for a select clientele who would find a warm and intimate environment, a calm setting in which to discover his creations. For Dior, there was a salon perspective just as there was a theater perspective. The Dior gray became a backdrop against which the couturier would project the future of fashion.

VINCENT LERET

John Galliano for Christian Dior. *Lu-Lee-San* dress. Haute Couture, Spring-Summer 2007. Silk gazar cocktail dress. Paris, Dior Héritage. Inv. 2007.73

1. Christian Dior, *Dior by Dior: The Autobiography of Christian Dior*, London, V&A Publishing, 2nd ed., 2007, p. 169.
2. Ibid.

Steven Meisel, *Lu-Lee-San* dress, Spring-Summer 2007
Haute Couture collection, model Natalia Vodianova.
Right: Steven Meisel, *Lu-Lee-San* dress, Spring-Summer
2007 Haute Couture collection, model Missy Rayder.

John Galliano for Christian Dior.
Mariya Markina inspired by Bérard dress.
Haute Couture, Fall-Winter 2007,
Le Bal des Artistes collection. Long gown
in triple organza by Taroni, hand-painted
by Genève Cotté, embroidered tulle veil.
Paris, Dior Héritage. Inv. 2008.15

An impressive assembly of famous photographers, illustrators and painters inspired
this collection; each dress is linked to a guardian spirit—from Irving Penn to René
Gruau, Giovanni Boldini, Joshua Reynolds, Édouard Manet and Antoine Watteau.
Among all these geniuses, the painter Christian Bérard is probably the person
who was the closest to Christian Dior. "His drawings taught one to transform daily
life into a magic world of passion and nostalgia. I bought as many of his sketches
as I could, and covered the walls of my room with his inspired paintings," wrote
the couturier, describing their meeting around 1928 among a small group of friends
gathered around Max Jacob.[1]

As an active participant in exhibitions held in galleries run by Jacques Bonjean,
and later Pierre Colle (a partner of Christian Dior's), Bérard was described by
art critic Waldemar-George, editor of the magazine *Formes*, as belonging to the
neo-humanist (or neo-romantic) group. These artists were characterized by a
desire to highlight the importance of the human figure, in opposition to Cubism.
Christian Bérard, who worked in set design and as an illustrator for *Vogue* and
Harper's Bazaar, had a decisive influence on the career of the couturier, who was
three years younger. He brought together painting, theater, fashion, the press and
society events, and revived figurative work, notably through his contribution in 1945
to the success of the "Petit théâtre de la mode" at the Musée des Arts Décoratifs.

This fascinating evening gown replicates specific images from Christian
Bérard's watercolors highlighted with ink. The fifteen meters of off-white triple
organza by Taroni were painted specially by Genève Cotté as part of a project in
which Steven Robinson also played a large role. An assistant to John Galliano, he
died a few weeks before this collection, which was dedicated to him, was presented.

Using a number of Christian Bérard's sketches provided by John Galliano,
Genève Cotté first made several trials on pieces of fabric, reproducing motifs
such as flowers, silhouettes and faces. John Galliano designed this dress, which
has large areas of color on the skirt and draped panels, with a few touches of
bright colors, like a bouquet, on the right shoulder. These motifs were painted
with acrylic paint on the organza, which was stretched on a frame, and
positioned according to instructions from the tailoring atelier. The painted
fabric was then covered with tulle. This lightweight veil blurs the edges of the
underlying patches of color and dulls the shine of the silk, thereby suggesting
the matt aspect of watercolor paper. The lines of black ink with which Bérard
underscored his sketches are also reproduced via embroidered black sequins
sewn to the tulle. These black lines create outlines over the pleated dress
underneath. Shiny, precise, clean and distinct, these sequined outlines float atop
the organza, illustrating the lightness of Bérard's drawings, whose beauty
conveys more of a glimpse of the world, rather than a clear depiction.

This tribute to Christian Bérard, known to his friends as "Bébé," seems to
be sculpted and draped from one of his drawings, right up to the edges.

ÉRIC PUJALET-PLAÀ

1. Christian Dior, *Dior by Dior: The Autobiography of Christian Dior*, London,
    V&A Publishing, 2nd ed., 2007, p. 177.

Christian Bérard, *Hommage à Christian Dior*, 1947.
Note the façade of 30 Avenue Montaigne.

Right: Eugene Kammerman, Christian Bérard
and the model Marie-Thérèse in the *cabine*,
during Christian Dior's first show, February 12, 1947.

John Galliano for Christian Dior. *Michaela Kocianova*
Inspired by Picasso ensemble. Haute Couture,
Fall-Winter 2007, *Le Bal des Artistes* collection.
Duchess satin ensemble. Paris, Dior Héritage. Inv. 2008.16

"To celebrate the sixtieth anniversary of the house of Christian Dior, we explored
Christian Dior's first collection, not of fashion, but of his favorite artists," says the
program for the collection. The models formed *tableaux vivants* on the podium, as if a
number of famous portraits had suddenly come together, without immediately indicating
the connection to a Renoir, a Gainsborough or a Toulouse-Lautrec. The show was something
like a *bal masqué* at which historical figures were freely interpreted. Mary Stuart, the Princess
of Cleves, Diana the Huntress, the Queen of the Night, geishas and shepherdesses
pranced and posed, as they watched others—courtesans, blue fairies, archduchesses
and mantilla-clad women of Seville—step on stage.

Amid all these silhouettes used as pretexts to display a proliferation of fabric, this
slender, Picasso-inspired harlequin looks extremely simple. The costume consists of a
hundred gray and mauve diamond-shaped pieces of fabric. These colors were inspired
by the artist's melancholy paintings of performers from his blue and pink periods.
The harlequin is a recurring theme in Picasso's work—examples include the stage
curtain for *Parade* in 1917, the harlequins in 1923 and the portrait of Paul, the artist's
son, in 1924. In addition, the painter also drew from the Commedia dell'arte when he
set out to design the sets and costumes for Sergei Diaghilev's ballet *Pulcinella* (1920).
John Galliano overlapped Picasso's multiple images of the harlequin in this ensemble.
The designer assimilated all the classical and contemporary iconography of this
costume. He in turn provided a vision enriched by the approaches of Watteau, Cézanne,
Severini and Derain, who had each handled this matter brilliantly. It combines
subdued colors with luxurious aspects (the sheen of satin and lines of sequins).
The composition is traditional—the peplums on the jackets were borrowed from the
Pulcinella costume; the ruff and hat are authentic—but the finishing deliberately leaves
certain aspects incomplete (some diamond shapes are offset or only partially outlined).

Christian Dior partnered with Jacques Bonjean to run a gallery from 1928 to 1931 at
34 Rue la Boétie (Picasso's studio was nearby, on the same street at no. 23). The young
gallery owner acquired his artistic background by spending time with certain key
figures who had contributed to the success of the Spanish painter: "We were just a
simple gathering of painters, writers, musicians and designers, under the aegis of
Jean Cocteau and Max Jacob," he wrote.[1] The idea of Dior and his friends was to bring
together the great masters of contemporary art—Braque, de Chirico, Dufy, Matisse
and Picasso—alongside up-and-coming artists from the next generation. Dior, who had
become a couturier, dedicated the *Picasso* dress to the painter during the Fall-Winter
1949 collection, and described in his memoirs his intense adolescent admiration for the
brilliant artist: "It seems odd that in 1967 people tax with avant-garde ideas and futuristic
tastes the self-same works and masters that we were admiring between the ages of fifteen
and twenty and who, for ten years, had already been famous among our more enlightened
elders, led by Guillaume Apollinaire."[2]

ÉRIC PUJALET-PLAÀ

1. Christian Dior, *Dior by Dior: The Autobiography of Christian Dior*,
   London, V&A Publishing, 2nd ed., 2007, p. 176.
2. Ibid., p. 174.

André Derain, *Arlequin à la guitare*, 1924, oil on canvas, Paris,
Musée de l'Orangerie, Jean Walter and Paul Guillaume collection.

Right: Phil Poynter, *Michaela Kocianova Inspired by Picasso*
ensemble, Spring–Summer 2007 Haute Couture collection,
model Mariacarla Boscono.

John Galliano for Christian Dior. Haute Couture,
Fall-Winter 2008. Embroidered silk and wool.
Paris, Dior Héritage. Inv. 2009.28

Designed by John Galliano, this embroidered caramel silk and wool *degradé* dress was livened up by a panther print belt and matching 1930s cloche hat.

Throughout the history of Dior, the panther motif has been a recognized Dior signature along with the houndstooth and Prince of Wales check. Originally referred to as the *Jungle* print, it was introduced at Christian Dior's first show and appeared on wool crêpe and chiffon.

Viewed as giving chic allure to his otherwise pretty and feminine styles, the *Jungle* print was inspired by Mitzah Bricard, Dior's mysterious muse. "Her high standards are inflexible," he wrote in his memoir *Dior by Dior*.[1] The designer also relished how she was "completely cosmopolitan in her elegance," wore colors inspired by Boldini and transformed her Slavic-style beauty into movie-star drama when wearing one of her trademark cocktail hats or turbans pinned with an Indian miniature.

Mitzah Bricard was a notorious femme fatale, noted for declaring "Cartier is my florist" when admirers wanted to send her flowers.[2] She was also the only one of Christian Dior's women—christened the three fates by Cecil Beaton[3]—whose taste and judgment made her irreplaceable. Allowed to trash a dress, a thumbs-down from Bricard usually meant that the outfit was quickly removed from the collection.

Born in Paris on November 12, 1900, Bricard was almost five years older than Christian Dior. However, it was unlikely that the feline-natured Bricard revealed such information or that she was half-Austrian, half-English and her original name was Germaine Louise Neustadt. Instead, she let Dior bask in the knowledge that she had worked at the esteemed fashion houses of Doucet, Molyneux and Balenciaga and that she shared his loathing of vulgarity.[4]

In charge of hats, Bricard had countless ideas and performed magic when using her beautiful hands. Her talent suited Christian Dior, who insisted, "a woman without a hat is not completely dressed."[5] Bricard also possessed a commercial sense and had no problem hoodwinking a client and saying, "What a coincidence; I was just thinking of you, because I have a brand new hat here which would suit you to a tee." With her innate style, she was also the perfect poster girl for Dior's panther print, effortlessly wearing it head-to-toe.[6]

Recognizing the commercial power of the *Jungle* pattern, Dior arranged an exclusivity deal with Bianchini-Férier, the Lyon-based silk manufacturer, and allowed it to infiltrate most of his collections until 1954. He also scored with leopard when using it for muffs, scarves, tops, silk raincoats, jackets and winter coats. John Galliano renewed the Mitzah mania for the leopard print right from his first Haute Couture collection in Spring-Summer 1997.

NATASHA FRASER-CAVASSONI

1. Christian Dior, *Dior by Dior: The Autobiography of Christian Dior*, London, V&A Publishing, 2nd ed., p. 13.
2. Natasha Fraser-Cavassoni, *Monsieur Dior: Once Upon A Time*, New York, Pointed Leaf Press, 2014, p. 87.
3. Mitzah Bricard, Raymonde Zehnacker and Marguerite Carré.
4. Natasha Fraser-Cavassoni, op. cit., p. 88.
5. Ibid., p. 79.
6. Ibid., p. 82.

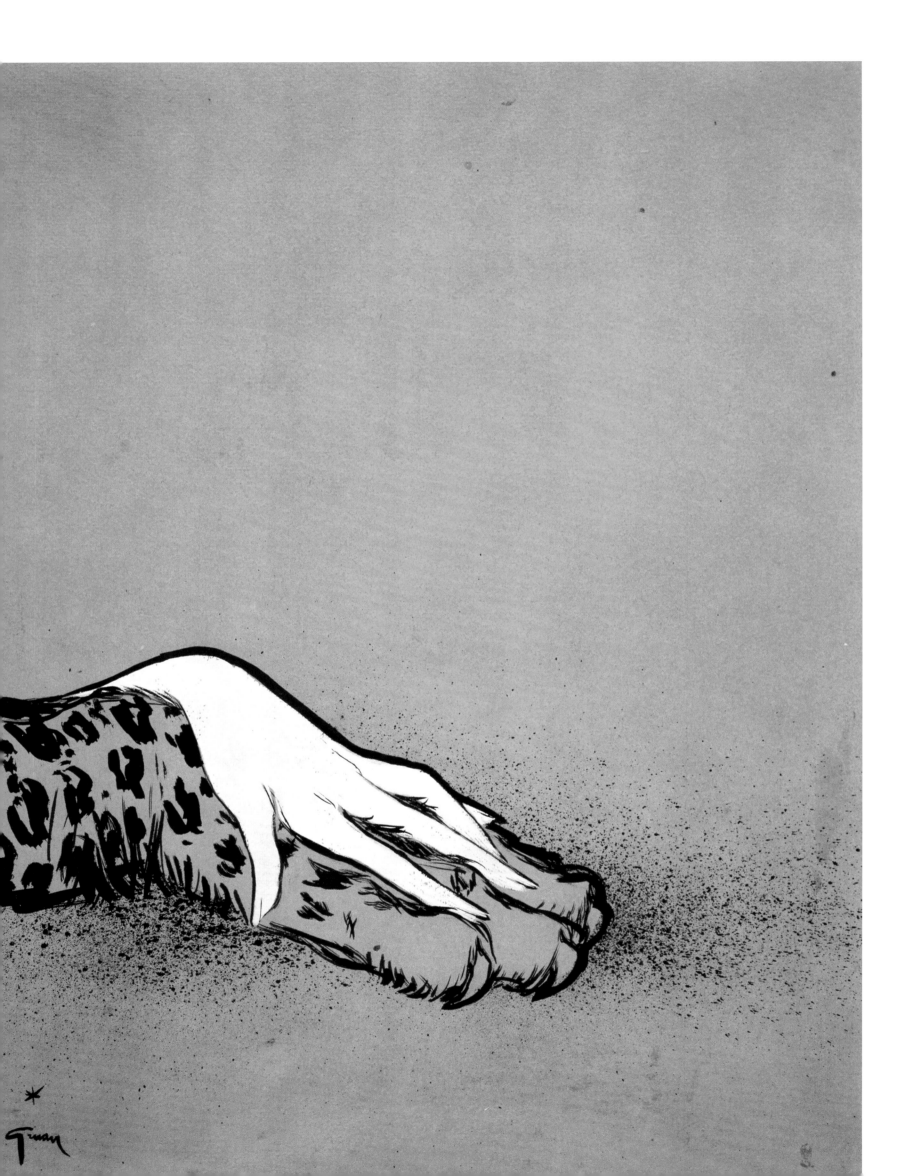

John Galliano for Christian Dior.
Haute Couture, Fall-Winter 2009.
Evening dress. Lingerie corset,
tulle skirt, black silk faille and black lace.
Paris, Dior Héritage. Inv. 2010.50

Having proved that he could put on a fashion show as a piece of theater, John Galliano returned to the calmer setting of the salon at 30 Avenue Montaigne, to present the Fall-Winter 2009 collection. It was a quite literal, even subdued reflection of Christian Dior's work; the models wore day suits, cocktail dresses and evening gowns that seem to have come straight out of a show from the 1950s, with one important difference: certain underpinnings, like garter belts, slips, bustiers and bras, were in full view, worn as clothes in their own right.

"*C'est la fièvre de la cabine!* Inspired by the iconic photographs of Monsieur Dior with his favorite models in the Maison Dior dressing room (or *cabine*), this Haute Couture presentation recreates the energy, excitement and anticipation that surround a Dior salon presentation," reads the collection program. During the couturier's life, and according to his wishes, the Dior dressing room had exactly thirteen young women on whose bodies he physically constructed the collections. Each prototype for a show corresponded to the name of a model and to her measurements. Marie-Thérèse, Lucky, Alla and Victoire—to name just the most famous—would sometimes pose for studio photographs, but their primary role was to stand for fittings of the dresses they would wear during the launch of the collection, then at fashion shows organized for customers throughout the season. The daily presence of these models, who shared this collective dressing room, made the *cabine* something of a women-only zone.

It was when John Galliano first saw a photo feature story of Christian Dior surrounded by his models that the idea of an arsenal of undergarments came to him as the primary theme of the collection. What may appear to be an intrusion into a feminine intimacy, a well-worn game of flipping items inside out, was also, in this case, a reference to one of the iconic products of the Dior house. "Hats are the creations of our fashion department. Christian Dior jewelry. Christian Dior gloves. Christian Dior girdles and bras. Christian Dior stockings. Christian Dior shoes," were the words written on the back of photographs of dresses taken by Willy Maywald in the 1950s for the press. These quasi-ritualistic descriptions seemed to put accessories and undergarments on the same plane, as artful additions to the overall effect, but also as exercises in creation. Through a highly innovative licensing policy, very early on Christian Dior became committed to surrounding the female body with multiple forms that bore his logo and his brands. "I wanted a woman to be able to leave the boutique dressed by it from head to foot, even carrying a present for her husband in her hand."[1]

This evening dress, number 34 in the show, consists of a wide tulle and lace skirt that seems to just barely cover a bustier. The dated look of the voluminous skirt and the wide panels of black faille, harking back to the dress *1951* from Spring-Summer 1951, bring to life a backstage scene from the era of Christian Dior.

ÉRIC PUJALET-PLAÀ

1. Christian Dior, *Dior by Dior: The Autobiography of Christian Dior*, London, V&A Publishing, 2nd ed., 2007, p. 150.

John Galliano for Christian Dior.
Haute Couture, Spring-Summer 2010. Wool dress.
Paris, Dior Héritage. Inv. 2010.58

This wool dress with exaggerated hips demonstrated John Galliano's way with cut and the British designer's talent at marrying tradition with contemporary flair. Such features were evident throughout his Spring-Summer 2010 Haute Couture collection, which evoked Dior's New Look, the elegance of the British riding habit, sparkling evening outfits of British eccentrics and a Cecil Beaton-type décor. Galliano's decision to present the show in the illustrious and much-fabled Dior salon gave intimacy to the occasion. It also brought to mind *The Golden Age of Couture*—an exhibition shown at London's V&A museum—and shed light on Christian Dior's self-confessed anglomania.

In Cecil Beaton's well-versed opinion, the love affair between Britain and the couturier was mutual. "Dior found the key to English society, turned it in the lock and was welcomed as one of its own," he wrote.[1] In many ways, it made sense. The designer, who first went to London in 1926 and made frequent trips to the Channel Islands, associated England with "happiness and personal liberty." "There is no other country in the world, besides my own, whose way of life I like so much," Christian Dior enthused in his memoir *Dior by Dior*. In the 1930s, he began to dress like a British gent in his grey flannel suit, bowler hat and brogues.[2] He was also an admirer of "English traditions, English politeness, English architecture" and even "English cooking."[3]

Growing up in Granville, a sophisticated seaside resort on the Channel, the British influence was all the rage. Christian Dior's family home was an Anglo-Norman villa, built with a view of the Chausey islands, while his childhood wardrobe was spruced up with English knickerbockers, Eton jackets and sailor suits, a British royal family tradition.

Monsieur Dior's history began with early clients like Margot Fonteyn, Vivien Leigh, Nancy Mitford and Princess Margaret. This led to Dior attending the Red Cross charity extravaganza at Blenheim Palace in 1954, organized by the Duchess of Marlborough. The event was repeated in 1958, then in 2016 with Dior's Cruise show.

NATASHA FRASER-CAVASSONI

1. Cecil Beaton, *The Glass of Fashion*, New York, Doubleday, 1954.
2. Christian Dior, *Dior by Dior: The Autobiography of Christian Dior*, London, V&A Publishing, 2nd ed., p. 39.
3. Ibid.

Since 1999, the fragrance *J'Adore* has been dressing and undressing the brand's ambassadors. Nudity revealed or concealed is the gold thread that links together every new ad campaign. In 2004, for the first time, Charlize Theron lent her luminous image to the iconic women's fragrance by the house of Christian Dior. The film displays the sculptural body of the young South African actress under a diaphanous golden veil.

It would be two more years, in 2006, before Charlize Theron would once again appear, this time in a dress inspired by the latest Christian Dior collection. Research by John Galliano into the flesh-colored corsets of the *Nude* line were in perfect sync with the relationship that *J'Adore* had always maintained with nudity. In the 2006 film by Jean-Baptiste Mondino, Charlize Theron walks through the rooms of a Parisian apartment, challenging viewers by shedding her jewels one by one and then unzipping her dress in an unforgettable tracking shot.

For the new film, directed by Jean-Jacques Annaud in 2011, Parfums Christian Dior opted for the prestigious backdrop of the Château de Versailles, set in an imaginary fashion show featuring the most beautiful women who have at one time been the face of 30 Avenue Montaigne. Charlize Theron opens the show under the noble limelight of the Galerie des Glaces in this evening gown made from layers of silk chiffon entirely embroidered with gilded, translucent sequins. Specially made for the film, the dress is accessorized with a long Belle Époque necklace made of gold beads, echoing the striated neck of the *J'Adore* perfume bottle.

The film highlights Christian Dior's devotion to the Age of Enlightenment, when gold embodied both divine and earthly glory. The *J'Adore* dress is the expression of this passion for the history of luxury, French style. It illustrates the opulence of Rose Bertin's designs, as well as the fragrances concocted by Jean-Louis Fargeon, both of whom worked for Queen Marie-Antoinette, as couturiere and perfumer/glover, respectively.

After the *Trianon*, *Vie de château*, *Pompadour*, *Duchesse* and *Nuit de Versailles* models created by Christian Dior in the 1950s, in 2011 the *J'Adore* dress joined the list of couture designs inspired by the aristocratic prestige of eighteenth-century France.

VINCENT LERET

Right: *J'Adore*. Baccarat crystal exclusive edition.
Dior Joaillerie headdress, 2012.

Below: Patrick Demarchelier. Charlize Theron
photographed in the Galerie des Glaces
at Versailles for the perfume *J'Adore*, 2011.

Insert: Sketch of the dress worn by Charlize Theron
in the *J'Adore* film, 2014.

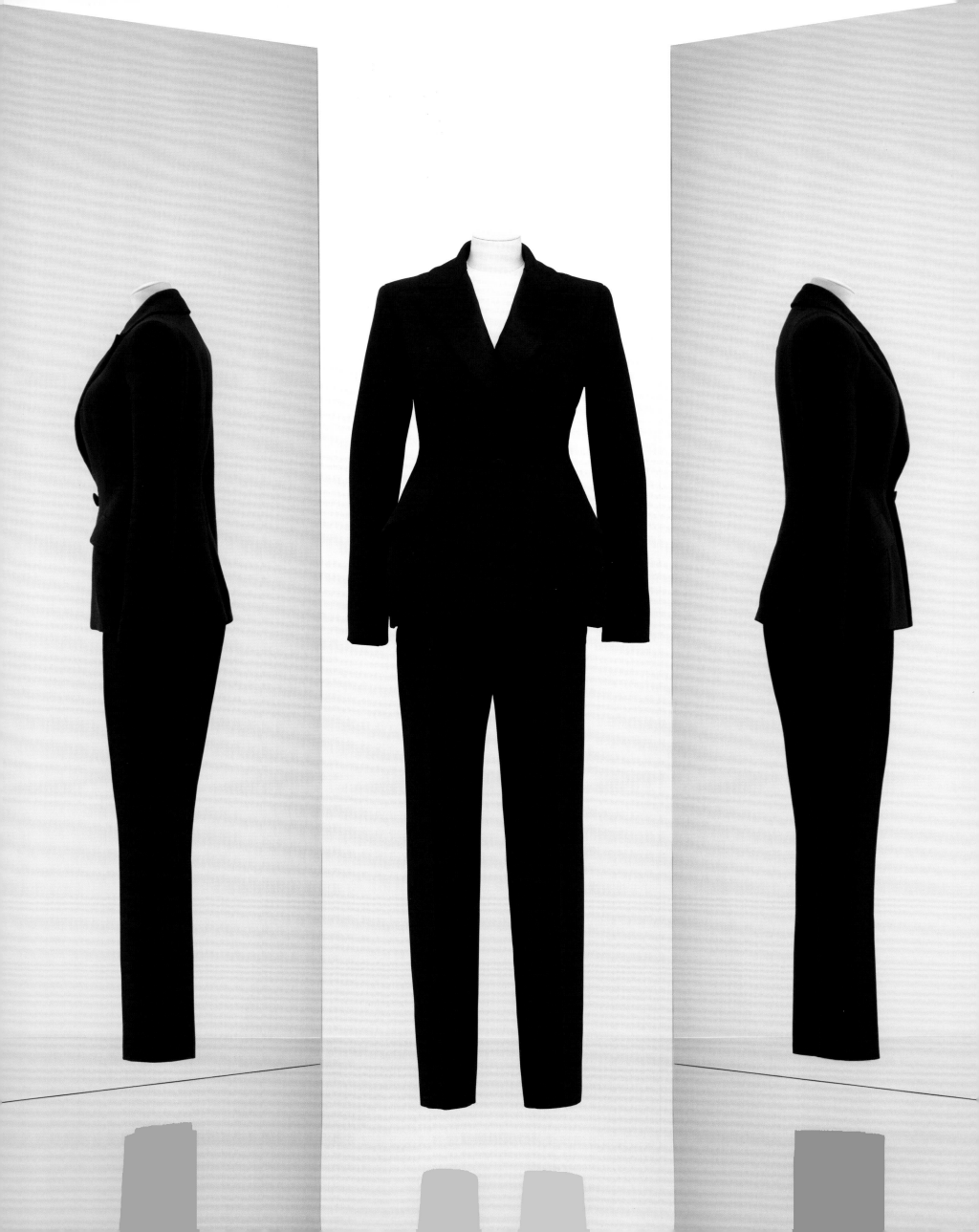

Raf Simons for Christian Dior. Haute Couture,
Fall-Winter 2012. Outfit. *Bar* tuxedo jacket with wool
cigarette pants. Paris, Dior Héritage. Inv. 2013.27

Following double page, left:
Mats Gustafson, illustration
of a tuxedo from the Spring-Summer
2013 Ready-to-Wear collection.

Right: Patrick Demarchelier,
ensemble from the Fall-Winter
2012 Haute Couture collection,
model Kinga Rajzak.

This outfit played an important role in Raf Simons's inaugural show for Dior, as it was the first item on the program. Traditionally, the first design is the one that sends a strong message about the intent and the new ideas embodied in a collection. Here, Raf Simons wanted to pay tribute to the famous *Bar* jacket, the iconic model of the New Look, a highly anticipated formal exercise as the baton was passed from one artistic director to another. Raf Simons's interpretation of the *Bar* was a leitmotif for the entire collection.

Instead of treating the concept of the flower woman as a decorative idea, he transposed it into pure shapes that showcased the body, although without constraining it. What interested him most was the construction of this historic design, an essential aspect for Christian Dior. A former furniture designer, Raf Simons found himself designing for the house of Christian Dior, who had dreamed of becoming an architect. He decided not to show the *Bar* as a jacket and skirt outfit. Quite the opposite: he transformed it to fit a contemporary world where most women were wearing pants and where a tuxedo could be worn equally well for everyday wear as in the evening. The outfit, which could be worn on any occasion, was very much in the spirit of the clothing fashions of the day, with no separation between evening and day wear, and with codes that had become more flexible since Christian Dior's time.

Raf Simons pursued a resolutely modern vision of Haute Couture: "It is a well-established industry, in which the expertise of the artisans is unrivaled by any measure, but today, it is no longer about achieving perfection with a particular duchess satin, silk or tulle. We have to go farther, by working with them on new production techniques and a new type of couture to go with it."[1] In a world where fashion has reached every continent, Haute Couture is the only sector that can express the concept of rarity and uniqueness.

FLORENCE MÜLLER

1. Program for the Fall-Winter 2012 collection.

Raf Simons for Christian Dior. Haute Couture,
Fall-Winter 2012. Organza evening dress
embroidered with pointillist motif chiffon.
Paris, Dior Héritage. Inv. 2013.74

Nearly one million flowers awaited guests attending Raf Simons's
first show for Dior, on July 2, 2012. Cascades of roses, orchids
and delphiniums embellished the walls of the townhouse on
Avenue d'Iéna. Christian Dior himself had made headlines
during the bitterly cold winter of 1947 by including gigantic
bouquets of fresh flowers in his first collection. The flowers
worked the same incredible magic in 2012, especially when they
spilled over onto the Haute Couture dresses themselves.

Raf Simons embraced this association enthusiastically, presenting
a contemporary interpretation of the floral motif. For this white
organza evening dress, 5,000 handmade and individually colored
chiffon squares created an extremely well-designed pointillist
composition on the dress. The effect is entirely pictorial. Like
paintings by Georges Seurat and Paul Signac, the illusion created
by colors placed side by side confers an ephemeral and fleecy
effect on the embroidery. The dress transcends pure technical
expertise, creating instead an immediate sense of wonder.

Sofia Coppola selected this dress in 2013 for the second *Miss
Dior* film she made. Natalie Portman embodies the fragrance in
this dress with thousands of spots of color, symbolizing the
ephemeral nature of the scent. The flashy light of the Hesperides,
the white of the musks, the gentleness of the Grasse rose seem to
be in perfect harmony with the Haute Couture dress. Raf Simons
was no longer aiming to achieve perfection with the fabric, but went
even further, conceiving new production techniques. Researching
materials is essential both for Haute Couture and for fragrances.

Since 2008, Parfums Christian Dior has been working
exclusively with flower producers in the Grasse region.
The cultivation of the prestigious *grandiflorum* jasmine and the
centifolia rose is a return to the legacy of expertise that is
unique and specific to Grasse. *Miss Dior* was also created in
this sun-drenched region, not far from the Château de La
Colle Noire that Christian Dior acquired in 1950. He planted
several hectares of jasmine, rose and lavender for use in
fragrances. He could study at leisure the colors, shapes and
scents of the flowers. It is through Dior's ever-present
research that the house's designers have been able to extract
from nature her sweetest secrets.

VINCENT LERET

Andrew Durham, Natalie Portman during
the film shoot for the *Miss Dior* perfume
advertisement, directed by Sofia Coppola, in 2012.

Right: Patrick Demarchelier, dress from the Fall-Winter
2012 Haute Couture collection, model Esther Heesch.

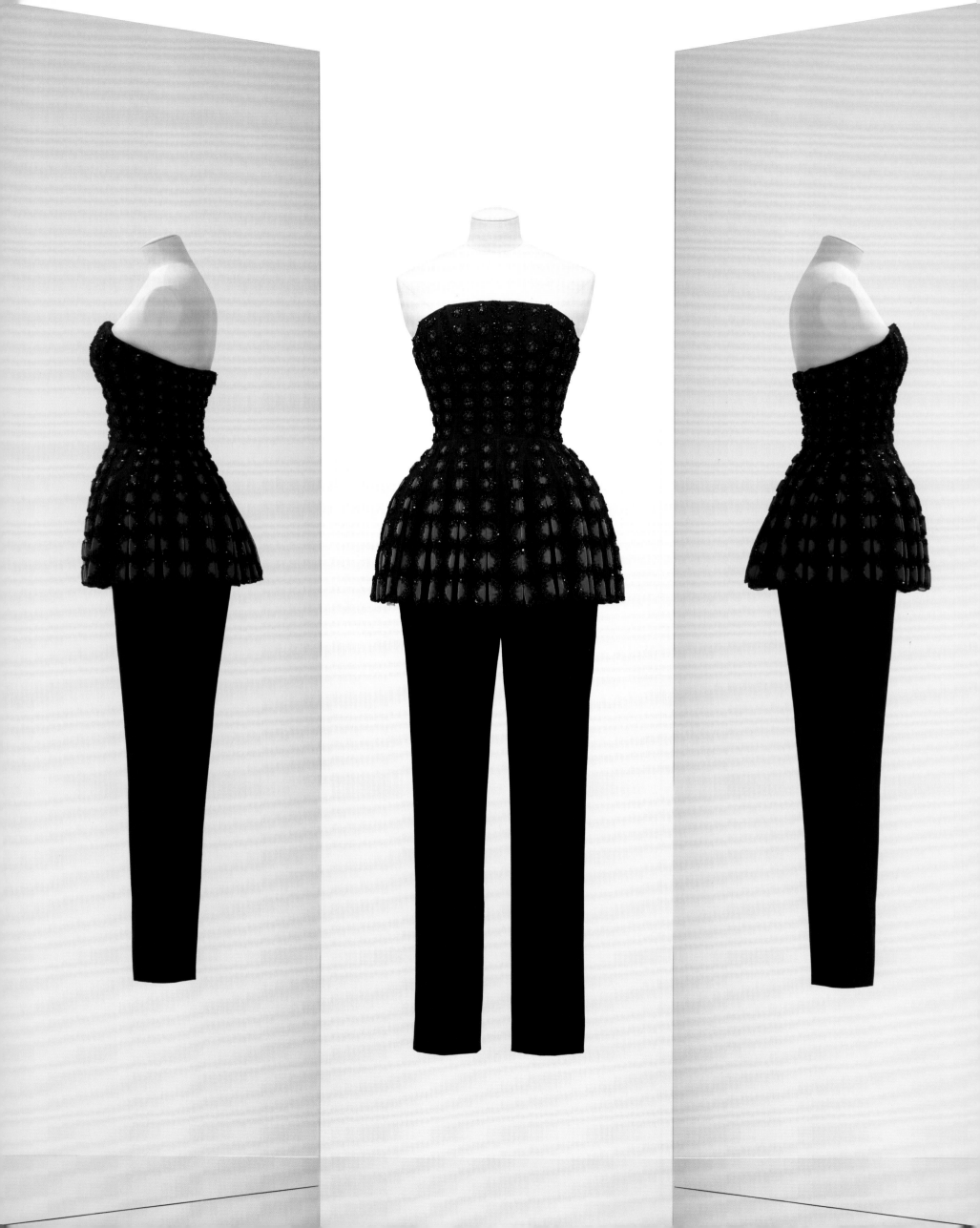

Raf Simons for Christian Dior. Haute
Couture, Fall-Winter 2012. Ball gown.
Fuchsia embroidered cut-off bustier ball gown,
inspired by the *Esther* dress from the
Fall-Winter 1952 Haute Couture collection.
Navy blue wool cigarette pants.
Paris, Dior Héritage. Inv. 2013.49

Raf Simons returned to the theme of the evening gown with the goal of
breathing new life into the expression of Haute Couture. He referenced
one of the house's archive designs, the *Esther* evening gown from Winter
1952, which he transposed into a seemingly similar dress, but one that
has been literally cut off at the hips and shortened to become a basque
bustier. Raf said of Dior that the couturier "could construct something
so perfect and yet he would often throw in a detail on purpose to break
that perfection. He would make what he did human for the wearer."[1]

This new version of the *Esther* dress demonstrates Raf Simons's ability
to link the history of the house with a highly contemporary vision of the
formal dress, by associating an embroidered bustier with cigarette pants.
The Belgian couturier, known for his minimalism and spare use of effects,
says he is fond of "the radical, of confronting two different ideas; in this
respect, the collection presents a juxtaposition of Haute Couture styles
inspired by several periods."[2] Other designs in this collection also include
apparently contradictory ornaments. These are the so-called two-sided
dresses, in which the front features a futuristic embroidery, while the back
repeats the emblematic embroidery themes of the house. These "all-over"
embroideries look more like textures than a scattered motif, as was the
custom during Christian Dior's time.

Raf Simons's priority when he joined Dior was to change the way materials
were selected by looking for new suppliers and asking them to develop new
and unusual fabrics. "A lot of modernity can come from materials, even
if I also use very traditional embroideries," he said when discussing the
new textiles he brought to Dior.[3] His modern approach to Haute Couture
also stems from his removal of the corsetry elements from the bustiers,
in order never to interfere with the natural movement of the body.
The evening dresses are worn nonchalantly, hands in pockets, an
important detail that steers clear of the formalism of evening wear.

FLORENCE MÜLLER

1. Program for the Fall-Winter 2012 collection.
2. Sylvia Jorif, "Haute couture, Que vive Dior!," *Elle*, July 13, 2012.
3. Loïc Prigent, "L'envol de Raf," *Vogue Paris*, September 2012.

Still from the film *Dior and I* directed by Frédéric Tcheng in 2012 and released in 2015. Raf Simons studying the *Esther* dress, Fall-Winter 1952 Haute Couture collection (*Profilée* line), which inspired several designs in his first collection for Dior.

Right: Willy Vanderperre, ensemble from the Fall-Winter 2012 Haute Couture collection, model Daria Strokous. This dress was designed as a shortened evening gown. The flared shape and embroidery recall styles from the eighteenth century.

Raf Simons for Christian Dior. Haute Couture,
Fall-Winter 2012. Three-quarter-length yellow duchess satin
evening dress with Sterling Ruby SP178 shadow print.
Paris, Dior Héritage. Inv. 2013.56

This dress is the physical manifestation of Raf Simons's encounter with
Californian Sterling Ruby, an artist who is equally talented in the media
of painting, ceramics, video, collage and textiles. More specifically, it was
inspired by his SP (Spray Painting) series, consisting of fields of gradated
color from deep black to fluorescent green on large canvases. Raf Simons
drew on the street and graffiti aspect of spray paint, a strong part of the
urban artistic tradition of Los Angeles. In addition, Sterling Ruby often
includes in his exhibitions garments that have been recycled, dyed, bleached
and splattered with pigments, as an extension of his abstract pictorial
vocabulary. This collaboration was deeply inspiring to Raf Simons:
"I take in art every day, I can't explain it; it's a part of me and it's only
natural to include it in my work," he explained in the documentary *Dior
and I*, filmed as he was preparing his first collection in 2012.

The colors on this bustier dress with a wide duchess satin skirt range
from dark to flashy, and in places seem to blend together subtly to form a
new shade. To adapt an abstract painting by Sterling Ruby to fabric—in
other words, to transform a contemporary work of art into an Haute
Couture design—requires a warp-printing technique in which the motif is
created by dyeing the warp threads in graduated colors. The motif only
appears once the various threads have been woven into the fabric.
This process, called shadow printing, creates a fascinating sense of
movement, depth and relief on the fabric. The result is similar to the flame-
like patterns produced by the "chiné à la branche" technique popular in
the eighteenth century; silk manufacturers in Lyon, for example, used it in
the 1950s to create the softly blurred effects that Christian Dior often used.

This Haute Couture dress reflects Raf Simons's constant research into
new fabrics, new designs and new techniques, while respecting and
showcasing ancestral expertise: "I think that Haute Couture is vibrant
and perfectly in sync with our modern society. There will always be
women who want something unique," he explained.[1] This creative
process is inherent in the history of the house, as Christian Dior also
loved to design and select fabrics for their quality and originality.

Raf Simons selected this dress to symbolize his new vision of couture
and his passion for contemporary art, revealed during his first Dior
Haute Couture show.

MORGANE PAULISSEN

1. *Dior* magazine, no. 1, Autumn 2012, p. 42.

Following double page, left: Sterling Ruby, *SP198*,
2012, spray paint on canvas. Courtesy Sterling Ruby/
Galerie Gagosian. Right: Willy Vanderperre,
three-quarter-length evening gown, inspired by the
work of Sterling Ruby *SP28*, Fall-Winter 2012
Haute Couture collection, model Nicole Pollard.

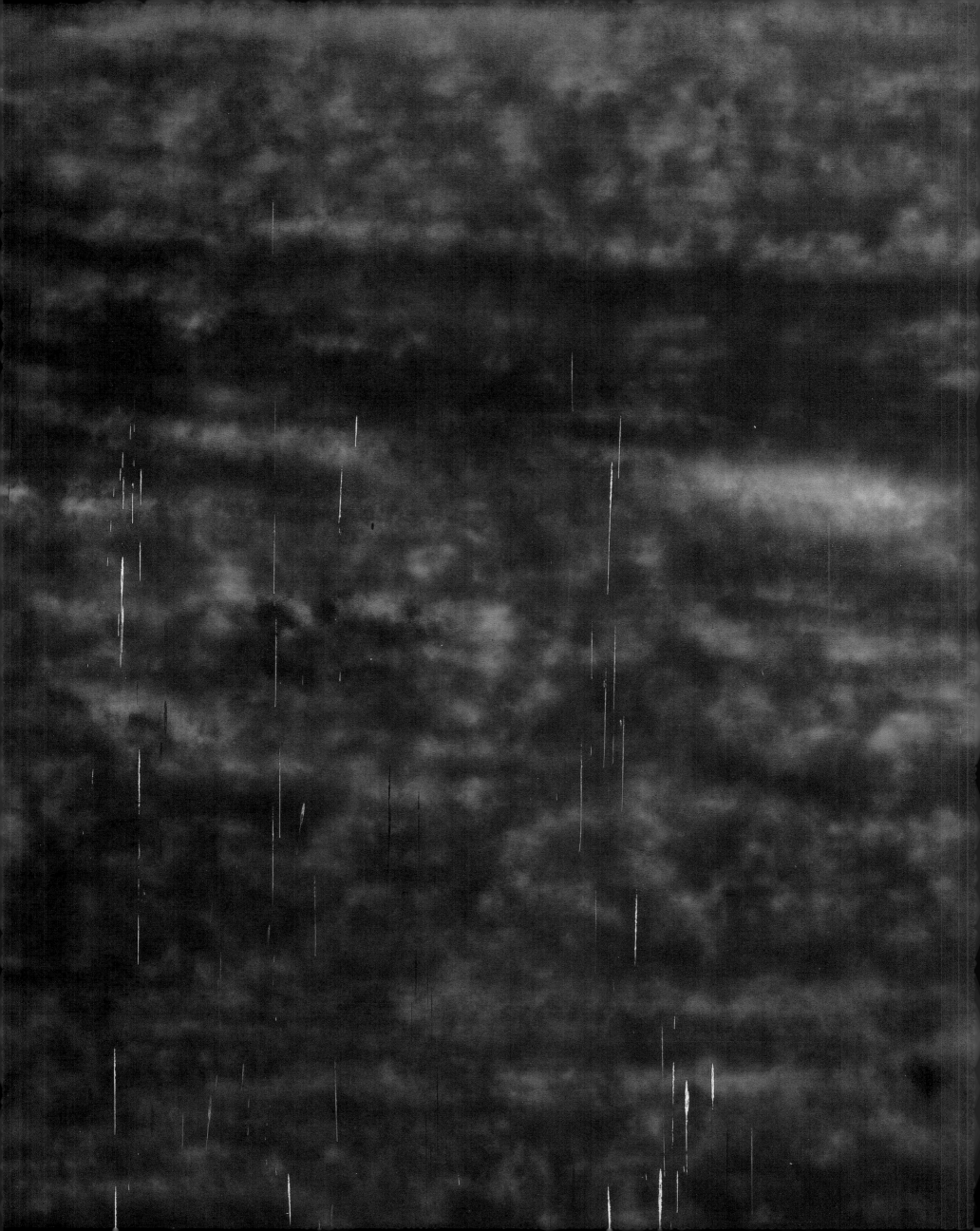

This bustier ball gown is part of a collection that Raf Simons designed "to be about the very idea of spring."[1] The models literally emerged from boxwood hedges like flowers in full bloom. Porcelain pink is the dominant color of these dresses, tributes to the freshness of spring and the beauty of youth.

Jennifer Lawrence chose to wear this dress for the Oscars at the last minute, the morning of the event itself: "I just woke up and tried on the dress, and it fit, thank God!"[2] The star from Kentucky rose to fame in 2010 for her role in *Winter's Bone*. She discovered the House of Dior during Raf Simons's first collection for Winter 2012. "His designs are breathtaking; that was my first fashion show, and I was speechless. I thought that Raf was extremely talented and I wanted to be part of his adventure," related the young actor.[3] Jennifer Lawrence, who became a Dior ambassador for many of its beauty and accessory campaigns, went on: "I felt that fashion in general was a huge scary monster, but I think that I understand this world better now. I had never had anything so beautiful to put on before I wore these clothes. It all started with a red coat from the Dior show; when I saw it, I was stunned. [...] I never let anyone take it from me. I even slept with it!"[4]

The powder pink shade of this dress was also one of Christian Dior's favorite colors, because it reminded him of the color of his childhood home in Granville. He felt that pink was "the sweetest of all the colors," and that "every woman should have something pink in her wardrobe. [...] It is the color of happiness and of femininity."[5] Pink appears in all of the collections, and Dior's favorite shade was a porcelain pink, popular in the eighteenth century. Pink also shows up for every occasion, in day dresses like *Bonbon* and *Bagatelle*, and in evening gowns like *Fête* and *Amadis*. Yves Saint Laurent and Marc Bohan perpetuated this fondness for pink in multiple designs. And John Galliano incorporated any number of shades of pink in tributes to Monsieur Dior's magnificent ball gowns; in the traditional lingerie line for Winter 2009; and in a nod to Degas's dancers with tulle tutus for Winter 2003. Raf Simons, famous for his sense of color, also incorporated Christian Dior's beloved powder pink, starting with his first show, Winter 2012.

FLORENCE MÜLLER

Raf Simons for Christian Dior.
Haute Couture, Spring-Summer 2013.
Silk bustier evening gown.
Paris, Dior Héritage. Inv. 2013.125

1. Dior press kit, Haute Couture Spring-Summer 2013.
2. Sarah Karmali, "Jennifer Lawrence's Last-Minute Oscar Dress Fitting," *Vogue.co.uk*, February 26, 2013.
3. Lynn Hirschberg, *Dior* magazine, Autumn 2013, no. 3, p. 42.
4. Ibid.
5. *Christian Dior's Little Dictionary of Fashion: A Guide to Dress Sense for Every Woman*, London, Cassell and Company Ltd., 1954, text on "Pink."

Christopher Polk, Jennifer Lawrence
receiving the Academy Award for Best Actress,
for her role in *Silver Linings Playbook*, 2013.

At first sight, the *Tarot* dress, with lines of perfect simplicity, is an enigmatic masterpiece which, in its intricate details, combines artisanal expertise with iconographic mystery. Drawing on a vocabulary that favors a unique stylistic approach above all, the ecru silk taffeta with charming dusty pink reflections is enhanced with complex embroidery and hand-painted sections which required 1,400 hours of work. Depictions of the natural world are combined with imaginary tarot motifs in a fascinating and whimsical ensemble.

The inventive freedom with which the various elements are arranged on the bustier and the skirt avoid any predictable symmetry or impression of depth: the fabric has become a canvas where the subject is constantly pushed aside by other objects that catch the eye. There are multiple centers of interest, blurring an understanding of the story.

The tarot cards, which were part of the symbolism that Monsieur Dior so loved, become an "incoherent tribute" in the hands of Maria Grazia Chiuri. The motifs, simply designed but magnificently painted or sewn, are inspired by symbols of a fairy-tale vocabulary; they illustrate a highly personal interpretation of the Dior myth and its transposition to our time.

For the superstitious among us, the symbols are like keys that can open doors to secret rooms or lead to foreign lands, so it is essential to know how to decipher them to predict and shape the future. Christian Dior, who could not do without the prophecies of his trusted fortune-teller, Madame Delahaye, liked the magical, dreamlike, mysterious and divinatory nature of tarot cards. Superstition thrives on symbols, and this aspect was so important to Christian Dior that he adorned some of his dresses with a sprig of lily-of-the-valley, his lucky flower. But symbols also link us to a mythical, timeless place, and reproducing them on garments seems almost to be a challenge: to premonition, to clairvoyance, to the future. Tarot cards are like the letters of an imaginary alphabet, with which it becomes possible to embellish mythical stories full of hidden meaning. They become the elements of a game, bringing them more in sync with our current mindset. The dreamlike power of Maria Grazia Chiuri's designs lets us view them from an alternate angle, demonstrating that nothing is sacrosanct, that everything can change.

Tarot cards—by definition obscure, incomprehensible, remote—are nonetheless used with a light touch in this new Dior narrative. The world presented by the couture house is represented by an iconography filled with lucky charms: stars, animals, cupids, flower, shrubs and clouds. A large tree of life appears on the bustier, a fusion of three different characteristics: a respect for tradition, an effort at renewal and a push for innovation. Flourishing on the front of the dress, this tree becomes a torch, ultimately a symbol of fashion itself, which emerges at the junction of these three directions.

MARIA LUISA FRISA

III
L'Impératrice

IV
L'Empereur

Christian Dior in the atelier of Christiane,
who is disguised as a fortune-teller,
during the Fête de la Sainte-Catherine.

Above: Christian Dior's lucky star.
Granville, Musée Christian Dior.

Maria Grazia Chiuri for Christian Dior.
Jardin fleuri dress. Haute Couture,
Spring-Summer 2017. Sage green tulle
bustier dress with feather embroidery.
Paris, Dior Héritage

The *Jardin fleuri*, with its feather embroidery creating the effect of an Impressionist painting, recalls the importance of the flora and fauna theme to the Dior house. This theme is often explored in the creation of costume jewelry, which has played a major role since the inception of the house. The greatest *paruriers* have worked with Christian Dior, from Francis Winter to Roger Jean-Pierre, Roger Scemama, Gripoix, Mitchel Maer, Maryse Blanchard, Marie Vidal and the Maison Rousselet. After Dior's death, the jewelry department continued to be a major concern under the direction of Michèle Thebaut, Frédérique Dauphin-Meunier, Isabel Canovas and Françoise Leroy-Beaulieu. For the first New Look collection in 1947, "most of the costume jewelry [was] designed to add color to the costume and avoid[ed] the setting of massive metal so much seen in ordinary costume gadgets."[1] For the following summer, Comte Étienne de Beaumont, a famous member of the café society and the gentleman *parurier* for Chanel and Elsa Schiaparelli in the 1920s and 1930s, created pieces of jewelry for Dior featuring "strands of colored gem stones with pearls, suggestive of the jewels of Indian Rajahs."[2] Starting in 1948, the House of Dior signed an agreement with the New York firm of Louis Kramer to produce costume jewelry for the American market that would be sophisticated enough to compete with fine jewelry. The designs were launched on May 15, 1951, under the name "Christian Dior Creations by Kramer." Starting in 1955 in Europe, Christian Dior became the first couturier to sign a jewelry licensing agreement, with jewelry maker Arthur Grosse.

The quivering bee created around 1955 was one of the most successful pieces made by the Henkel & Grosse firm, based in Pforzheim. The bee motif then appeared often in Christian Dior's embroidery designs and jewelry, as he saw his firm as the beehive of Avenue Montaigne. The bee showed up in jewelry during Gianfranco Ferré's era, as a layette motif for Baby Dior starting in 1996, in dark embroidery in the rock-inspired accessories from Dior Homme by Hedi Slimane in 2001 and in the fine jewelry collections by Victoire de Castellane, including "Milly-La-Forêt" and "Pré Catelan." In 2017 Maria Grazia Chiuri adopted this motif as the symbol of teamwork and combined expertise, working together toward a shared goal of excellence.

The snake-shaped necklace worn with this dress was designed by the artist Claude Lalanne, who, with her husband François-Xavier Lalanne, formed one of the most prominent artist couples in the postwar period; they were hugely popular for their whimsical worlds filled with a magical bestiary. Claude and François-Xavier Lalanne began working together in 1956 and created multiple outdoor sculptures, notably for Central Park in New York and for the Santa Monica fountains in California. Claude Lalanne created several breathtaking window displays for Christian Dior in the 1950s, before contributing to Maria Grazia Chiuri's design for the Dior garden several decades later. The "herbaceous fontange in silk flowers"[3] headpiece that completes this garden was made by the famous milliner Stephen Jones, known for his ethereal and imaginative designs.

FLORENCE MÜLLER

1. "Christian Dior Shows Second Empire Neck Ribbons,"
   Women's Wear Daily, April 4, 1947, p. 13.
2. "Paris Couture Openings at Peak," *Women's Wear Daily*, February 9, 1948.
3. Press kit, Summer 2017, Dior Héritage.

Walter Carone, preparations for the Spring-Summer
1954 Haute Couture collection (*Muguet* line).

Right: Tierney Gearon, *Brise de mémoires*
dress, Spring-Summer 2017 Haute Couture
collection, model Blanca Padilla.

Insert: Sketch of the *Jardin fleuri* dress,
Spring-Summer 2017 Haute Couture collection.

Maria Grazia Chiuri for Christian Dior. *Essence d'herbier*
cocktail dress. Haute Couture, Spring-Summer 2017.
Ecru fringe cocktail dress, floral raffia and thread
embroidery, studded with Swarovski crystals, derived
from a Christian Dior original. Paris, Dior Héritage.

Maria Grazia Chiuri's first fashion show for Dior took place in an enchanted
forest that appeared as if by magic in the middle of the gardens of the
Musée Rodin. A maze led to a magical clearing sectioned off by boxwood
cut into benches for guests. Maria Grazia Chiuri offered up her vision of
femininity, so dear to the couturier. This tribute to the founder inspired her
to explore the house's library, with its carefully conserved drawings by
Christian Dior himself, the style guides and illustrations of the collections,
and fashion photographs from 1947 to 2017. In the archives, featuring
hundreds of dresses, the designer closely examined the models and
accessories packed in archival boxes or suspended on anatomical hangers.

For *Essence d'herbier*, Maria Grazia Chiuri, who wanted to use
embroidery as a contemporary décor, took her inspiration from an
embroidery sample created especially for Christian Dior and now housed
in the Granville museum. This embroidery was made by a master
embroiderer, René Bégué, known as Rébé, who in 1974 donated a part
of his archives to the Musée des Arts Décoratifs.

With its light motif of seeds, it echoes the very signature of this famous
Haute Couture supplier. At the time, great embroiderers like Rébé would
visit the couture houses some five months prior to the collections to get
an idea of what the couturiers might want in terms of embroidery. After
returning to his house in Rabastens-sur-Tarn, René Bégué and his wife
would spend two months creating nearly 200 drawings "colored entirely
in pastel." In Rébé's words: "They were cleaned up by my technicians once
we returned to Paris, transferred to the fabric, embroidered and shown to
the couturiers who could then create their models from them."[1] He also
said that his profession was "the most complicated in the world," as
everything was done by hand "as in the eighteenth century,"[2] and he
found inspiration "everywhere in daily life" and in museums, explaining
that "the great painters were an endless source of ideas, shapes, colors,
wealth."[3] René Bégué had a special relationship with Christian Dior, who
called him "the artist," and many years after the death of the couturier,
he shared his memories, with a touch of nostalgia: "He used to come to
our house in Rabastens every year, and we worked together for a few days.
He was a friend. I wanted to leave the profession when he died."[4]

The idea of an armful of wildflowers scattered on a dress perfectly
expresses Christian Dior's fondness for the unpretentious meadow flowers
and gardens depicted by Impressionist artists. By exploring this theme of
raffia embroidery, Maria Grazia Chiuri gave it a new dimension. Craftspeople
today innovate, while incorporating a traditional approach to embroidery.
For another ball gown in this collection, the designer wanted to create an
effect of faded flowers. Delicately handmade silk flowers were literally crushed
in a book to create the impression that they came from an herbarium.

FLORENCE MÜLLER

1. Claude Le Roux, "La haute couture obéit à un magicien," *Paris-Presse,
   L'Intransigeant,* February 18, 1961, p. 6.
2. *Rébé l'artiste, illusions brodées,* exhibition guide, Rabastens,
   Musée du Pays rabastinois, July 1-September 24, 2000.
3. Claude Le Roux, op. cit., p. 6.
4. Ibid.

Sophie Carre, embroidery for the
Essence d'herbier dress, Spring-Summer
2017 Haute Couture collection.

Right: Paolo Roversi, *Essence d'herbier*
dress, Spring-Summer 2017 Haute
Couture collection, model Jean Campbell.

Maria Grazia Chiuri for Christian Dior. *Esprit de changement* suit. Haute Couture. Spring-Summer 2017. Satin and wool tuxedo-style trouser suit. Hooded *Bar* jacket. Paris. Dior Héritage.

Maria Grazia Chiuri opened her first Haute Couture show with a series of different takes on the tuxedo look, which she views as being synonymous with contemporary femininity. She started this theme with the *Bar* jacket, which she reinterpreted in several different outfits that appeared at a rapid clip, all while retaining its original legendary power—aware that "in every aspect, repetition is transgression," as Gilles Deleuze wrote in 1968 in *Différence et Répétition*. The *Esprit de changement* ensemble tells a story of multiple voices via a single color: black, the color of ink. The austere and rigorous intensity of this tone and the interplay of shimmering materials have been part of the Dior house—and its myth—from the start.

Several of the most iconic Dior codes appear in this suit: the jacket evokes the proportions of the *Bar* jacket, fitting tightly over the bust, emphasizing the waistline and widening at the hips over roomy culottes that fall to the ankles, creating a line similar to the mythical design of the 1947 *Corolle* collection. But in this garment, the references are revitalized by the contemporary sensibility of Maria Grazia Chiuri, who decided to focus on the purity of the line and work with the concept of full and empty spaces, drawing on all the various possibilities offered by black, a color that holds a special meaning in the Dior palette: "The most popular and the most convenient and the most elegant of all colors."[1] These variations are created by placing different types of material side by side to compose a choreography of shifting surfaces and multiple sensations: a piece of opaque black wool, which absorbs light, with deep black pleated satin that covers the model and is so lightweight that it moves with every step. The cleanly defined hem lengths hark back to the early years of the house. They also illustrate Chiuri's longstanding reflection on the theme of femininity. Her convictions are on clear display on the white T-shirt bearing the words of Nigerian author Chimamanda Ngozi Adichie, "We Should All Be Feminists," which Chiuri wanted to display on the podium of her first ready-to-wear show, demonstrating that harmony and a sense of proportion go perfectly well with feminist advocacy.

The hood is revealing of Chiuri's approach to the Dior legacy: the designer introduced a certain number of elements that belong with contemporary codes, which in addition could push the magnificence of Haute Couture toward a more fashion trend, closer to sports attire, yet without sacrificing the link to the immense and magnificent hoods of evening capes.

MARIA LUISA FRISA

1. Christian Dior. *The Little Dictionary of Fashion*. London. Cassel & Company. 1954.

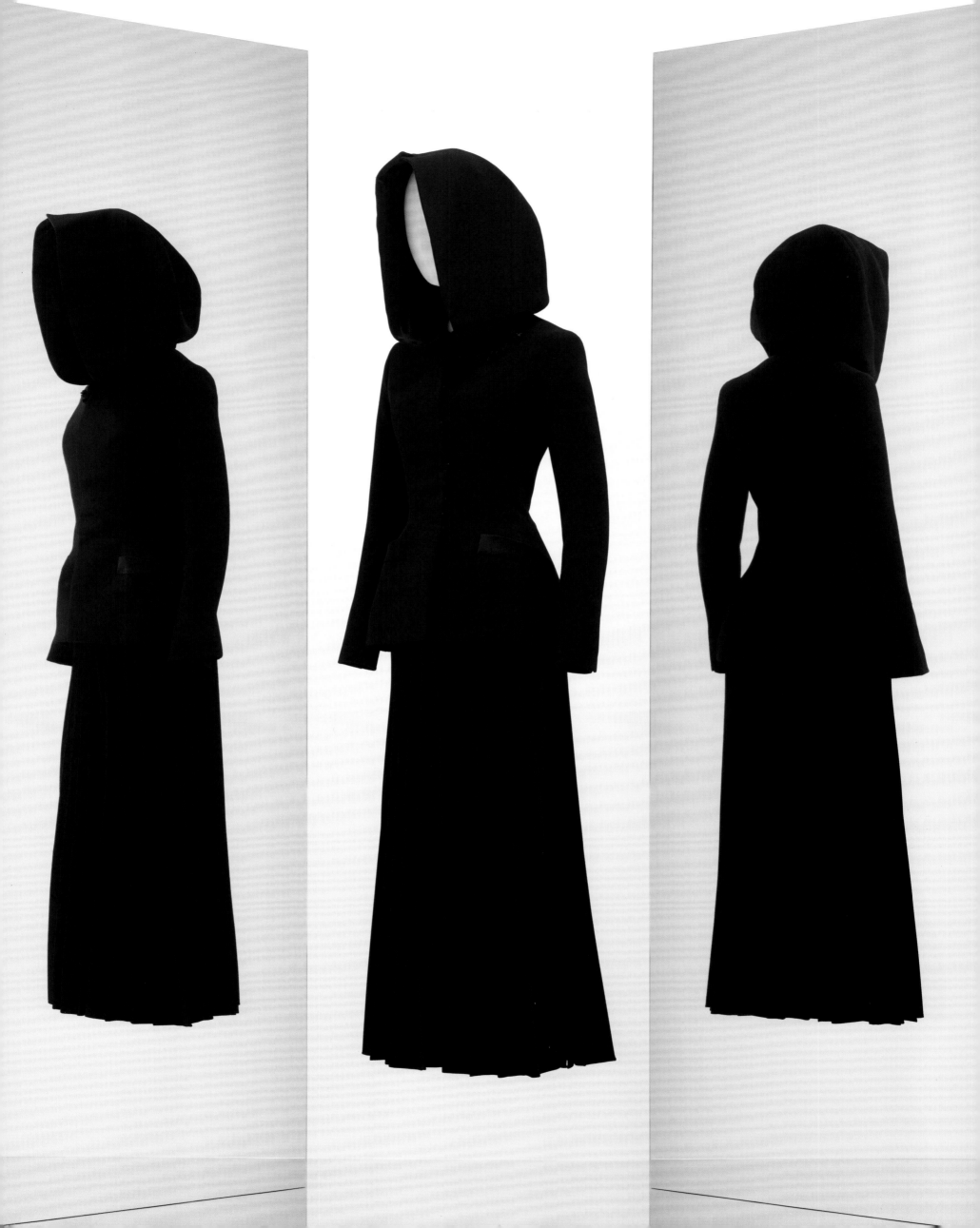

Above: Sophie Carre, Maria Grazia Chiuri
during a work session at Dior, 2017.

Left: Brigitte Lacombe, *Esprit de changement*
trouser suit, Spring-Summer 2017
Haute Couture collection, model Ruth Bell.

Insert: Sketch of the *Esprit de changement* suit,
Spring-Summer 2017 Haute Couture collection.

Following double page: Michal Pudelka,
Brise de mémoires, *Tyche* and *New Junon* dresses,
Spring-Summer 2017 Haute Couture collection.

Maria Grazia Chiuri for Christian Dior.
Rêve infini suit. Haute Couture, Spring-Summer 2017.
Double peplum pleated *Bar* jacket.
Sunray-pleated pants. Paris, Dior Héritage

The *Rêve infini* outfit is the fascinating result of Maria Grazia Chiuri's approach, which saw her return to the style codes of the Dior house without fetishism or nostalgia. This is clearly a Dior suit in length and proportion, yet it is the textures of the materials—both lightweight and meticulously structured—that draw the eye. She made an unusual choice of incorporating transparency to visually distinguish between the various sections forming the silhouette. Each garment seems to be metamorphic: the design of the bodice reflects the purity of a *Bar* jacket, an effect then entirely contradicted through the use of diaphanous, translucent silk that flares out in multiple small pleats ending in gadroons along the hem. The pleats then become softer and more open over black pants through which shorts are visible, a motif that recurs, a mark of recognition.

The silk fabrics differ in feel; they are sometimes crisp, sometimes fluid. The sensations they create, in direct contact with the body, transform the act of being clothed into an intimate, sensitive experience that has always been an integral part of the emotions and dreams that are inspired by fashion—whereby dressing oneself is a personal pleasure, an opportunity to compose or redefine one's image and, through it, one's own identity.

Clothes lead us to think about the countless variations created by fashion design. By its nature, its very existence, it is a poetic gesture, imbued with dreams and culture. It is almost like watching an endless repetition, energized by the particular vision of each artistic director as they reinterpret Dior's syntax. Through their sensibilities, each one makes a priority of the dreams and desires of women of their era. Reassessing femininity in the light of day-to-day experience is one of the characteristics of Maria Grazia Chiuri's approach to her appropriation of Dior's work. She creates a new definition of femininity when the legacy of the house overlaps with her interpretation, which she compares to the timeless image of the Dior woman, updated in form and content. The stratifications and transparencies confer a metaphorical aspect to femininity: it is no longer about an outfit that can be immediately understood, but a journey of discovery, whose multiple facets are alternately revealed and concealed. The eye of the Dior house, which captures and embodies the woman of today, is now, for the first time, that of a woman, reflected by the sensitivity and intelligence of Chiuri.

MARIA LUISA FRISA

Page 360: Maria Grazia Chiuri
for Christian Dior, *New Junon* dress,
Spring-Summer 2017 Haute Couture collection.

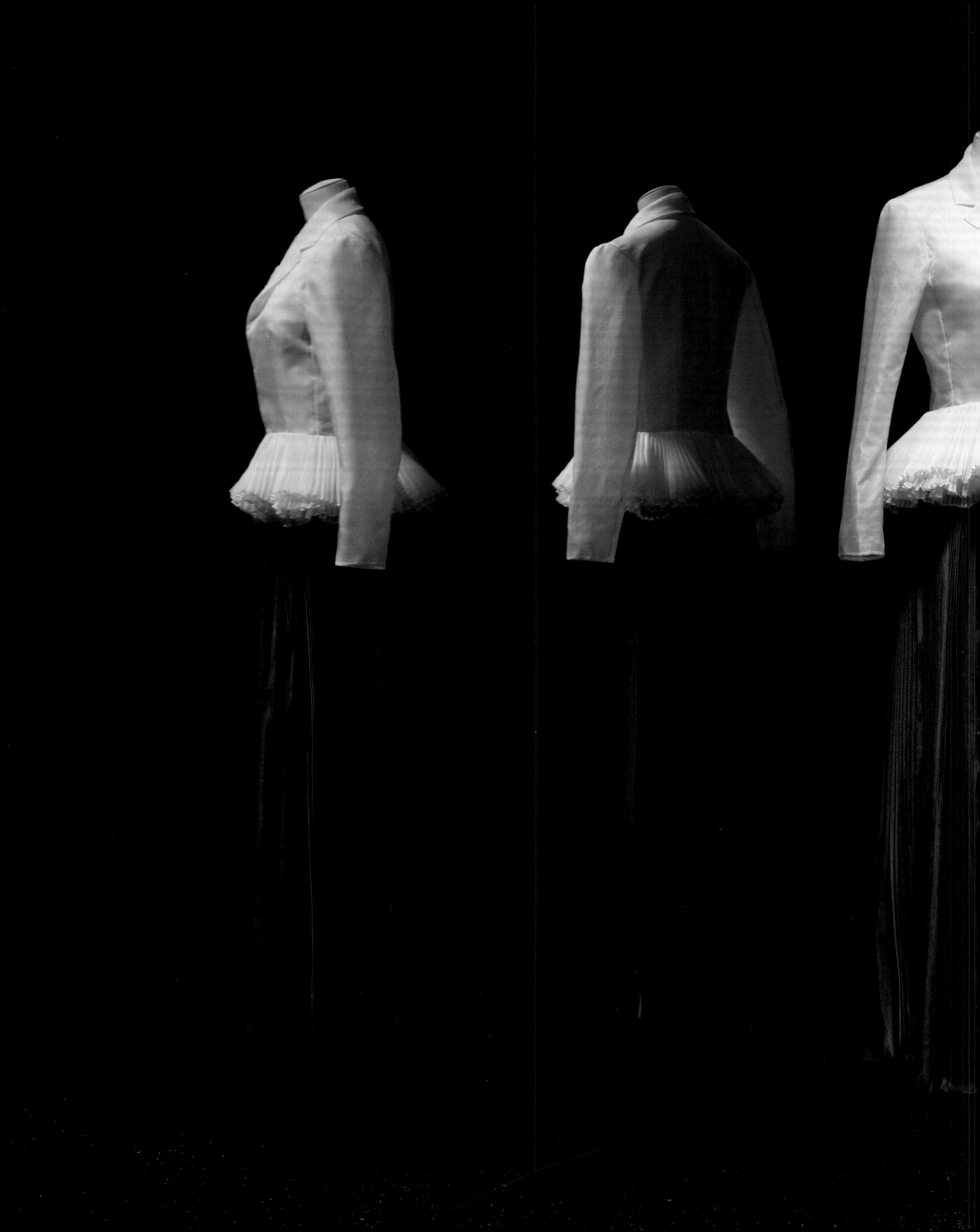

TIMELINE 1947 – 2017

1905
Christian Dior is born in Granville on January 21 to Alexandre Louis
Maurice Dior (a wealthy industrialist in the fertilizer and detergent
business), and Marie-Madeleine Dior, née Martin. Christian has an older
brother, Raymond, and will have three younger siblings: Jacqueline,
Bernard and Catherine.

1906
The Dior family moves into the Villa Les Rhumbs on the heights
of Granville overlooking the sea.

1910
The Diors move to Rue Richard-Wagner (now Rue Albéric-Magnard)
in the 16th arrondissement of Paris, keeping the Villa Les Rhumbs
as their holiday home.

1919
A Granville fortune-teller tells the fourteen-year-old Christian,
"You will suffer poverty, but women are lucky for you, and through
them you will achieve success."

1923
Christian Dior completes his secondary education at the
Lycée Gerson, a private high school, and goes on to study at
the Institut d'Études Politiques in Paris.

1928-1931
Christian and his friend Jacques Bonjean open an art gallery
on Rue La Boétie.

1931
Dior's mother dies, and his father goes bankrupt.

1932-1934
Dior and Pierre Colle open a gallery on Rue Cambacérès. In 1933,
they present an exhibition on Surrealism featuring works by artists
including Salvador Dalí, Marcel Duchamp, Max Ernst, Alberto
Giacometti, Pablo Picasso and Man Ray.

1934
Dior has tuberculosis and goes to convalesce in Font-Romeu
in the Pyrenees. During this period, he decides to turn to fashion
and begins to draw.

1935
Encouraged by his friends Jean Ozenne and Max Kenna, Dior
sells drawings to milliners and couture houses including Jean Patou,
Schiaparelli, Nina Ricci, Maggy Rouff, Worth, Balenciaga, Molyneux
and Paquin. He also works as an illustrator for *Le Figaro* newspaper
and *Le Jardin des Modes* fashion magazine.

1938
Robert Piguet hires Christian Dior as a designer. While working for Piguet,
he designs the *Café Anglais* dress that establishes his reputation.

1939-1940
Dior is called up for military service. When he is demobilized, he joins
his father in Callian, in the south of France, where he grows vegetables
and draws for *Le Figaro*.

1941-1946
Dior joins the house of Lucien Lelong as a designer. He innovates
with pencil skirts and rounded pleats, and designs the *Welcome* suit
that heralds the New Look.

1946
In the spring, Christian Dior and the industrialist Marcel Boussac
decide to join forces and create the Christian Dior couture house.
The company is founded on October 8. On December 16, the couture
house opens at 30 Avenue Montaigne, with two dressmaking ateliers,
one tailoring atelier and a staff of eighty-five people.

1947
The first Spring-Summer collection is presented on February 12.
The *Corolle* and *En 8* lines are an instant hit. Carmel Snow, editor-in-chief
of *Harper's Bazaar*, declares, "My dear Christian, your dresses have such
a New Look!" – a New Look symbolized by the *Bar* suit.
The Dior perfume company, Parfums Christian Dior, is founded on March 4.
Its director is Dior's childhood friend Serge Heftler-Louiche.
The first *Miss Dior* perfume is launched in December.
Neiman Marcus awards Christian Dior the "fashion Oscar" in Dallas
on September 9. Dior visits Los Angeles, San Francisco, Chicago
and New York to study his American clients' tastes and expectations.

1948
Christian Dior-New York opens on Fifth Avenue to design and sell exclusive
luxury ready-to-wear and accessories. Christian Dior Perfumes
New York Inc. is launched the same year. In Paris, a millinery department
is entrusted to Dior's muse Mitzah Bricard, and a fur department is created.
Christian Dior buys a property called the Moulin du Coudret
in Milly-la-Forêt, where he goes to unwind between collections.

1949
Christian Dior Hosiery is created in the United States,
and the *Diorama* perfume is launched.

1950
Christian Dior is awarded the French Legion of Honor for his
contribution to the fashion and textile industry.
On April 26, he presents his collection to Queen Elizabeth and
her daughter Princess Margaret at the French Embassy in London.
Marlene Dietrich insists on a Dior wardrobe for her role in
Hitchcock's *Stage Fright*.

1951
The Dior company now has a staff of some 900 people. It creates
several costumes for Charles de Beistegui's "Ball of the Century"
at the Palazzo Labia in Venice.
Christian Dior publishes his first book, *Je Suis Couturier*
(*Talking about Fashion*).

1952
Christian Dior Models Ltd. is created in London.

1953
The first Christian Dior boutique (in partnership with Cartier) opens
in Caracas, selling replicas of Haute Couture designs. After
attending the inauguration, Dior travels in South and Central America.
The Christian Dior-Delman company is founded. It manufactures
made-to-measure shoes designed by Roger Vivier.
Frédéric Castet is appointed head of the tailoring atelier.
Christian Dior moves to a townhouse on Boulevard Jules-Sandeau
in the 16th arrondissement of Paris.

1954
Christian Dior's Little Dictionary of Fashion is published in the United States.
The Duchess of Marlborough organizes a Dior fashion show at Blenheim
Palace on November 3. Two thousand people attend this charity event
in aid of the British Red Cross, at which Princess Margaret is the
guest of honor.

1955
A large boutique decorated by Victor Grandpierre is inaugurated
on the corner of Avenue Montaigne and Rue François-1ᵉʳ in Paris,
and the Dior perfume company launches its first box sets of lipsticks
in twenty-two different shades.
Yves Saint Laurent becomes Dior's design assistant.
On August 3, Christian Dior gives a lecture, followed by a fashion show,
for over 4,000 students in the Grand Amphithéâtre of the Sorbonne.
Christian Dior is nominated for an Oscar for best costume design for
Vittorio De Sica's *Terminal Station*.

1956
Dior publishes his autobiography, *Christian Dior et Moi* (*Dior by Dior*).
The *Diorissimo* perfume is launched. Its dominant note is lily-of-the-valley,
Christian Dior's lucky flower.

1957
Christian Dior appears on the cover of the March 4 issue of *Time* magazine.
Marc Bohan is hired to design and manufacture the fashions for
Christian Dior Models Ltd. in London.
On the night of October 24, Christian Dior dies of a heart attack
in Montecatini (Italy). In accordance with his wishes, Yves Saint Laurent
is appointed creative director of the fashion house.

1958
Yves Saint Laurent presents his first collection on January 30. It features
the innovative *Trapèze* line, which marks a turning point in the history
of the House of Dior.
The Fall-Winter collection is presented in November at Blenheim Palace
in the presence of Princess Margaret.
Roger Vivier launches his shoe brand under the Dior label.

1959
The 1959 Spring-Summer collection, presented over four days in Moscow's
Red Square, draws 11,000 visitors.

1960
Marc Bohan becomes creative director at Christian Dior in November.

1961
The first Christian Dior boutique opens in London.
Marc Bohan presents his first collection, characterized by the *Slim Look*.

1966
The first Dior eau de toilette for men is launched. *Eau Sauvage*, created
by Edmond Roudnitska, revolutionizes men's fragrances in terms of both
scent and aesthetics.

1967
Serge Lutens is appointed creative director of makeup at Dior,
where he will stay for twelve years.
Philippe Guibourgé creates the *Miss Dior* ready-to-wear line,
and a Miss Dior boutique opens on Rue François-1er.
Princess Grace of Monaco inaugurates the Baby Dior boutique
at 28 Avenue Montaigne in September.

1968
Frédéric Castet becomes creative director of the Fashion Furs department.
Parfums Christian Dior is sold to Moët-Hennessy.

1970
Marc Bohan creates the Christian Dior Monsieur line, later managed
by Christian Benais, then Gérard Penneroux.

1980
Tyen becomes creative director of makeup.

1983
Marc Bohan is awarded the Golden Thimble for his Spring-Summer
Haute Couture collection.
Dominique Morlotti is appointed creative director of
Christian Dior Monsieur.
Bernard Arnault buys the Financière Agache group, owner of
Christian Dior Couture.

1985
Bernard Arnault becomes CEO of Christian Dior Couture.
Isabelle Adjani is guest of honor at the ball held at the Château
de Vaux-le-Vicomte to celebrate the launch of the *Poison* perfume.

1987
A major retrospective exhibition, inaugurated by François Mitterrand,
is held at the Musée des Arts Décoratifs to celebrate the fortieth
anniversary of the House of Dior.

1988
Marc Bohan is awarded a second Golden Thimble for his Fall-Winter
Haute Couture collection.

1989
Marc Bohan is succeeded by Italian couturier Gianfranco Ferré,
who is awarded the Golden Thimble for his first Fall-Winter
Haute Couture collection.
Bernard Arnault takes over the LVMH group, owner of Parfums Christian
Dior. The couture and perfumery segments are brought together again.

1992
Patrick Lavoix is appointed creative director of Christian Dior Monsieur.

1995
Bernadette Chirac presents Diana, Princess of Wales, with a brand
new Dior bag during her official visit to Paris. The bag will be named
Lady Dior in her honor.

1996
John Galliano succeeds Gianfranco Ferré on October 14.
A major exhibition is held at the Metropolitan Museum of Art in New York
to celebrate the fiftieth anniversary of the House of Dior. At the Met Gala,
Lady Diana wears the first Dior dress designed by John Galliano.

1997
John Galliano presents his first Haute Couture collection for Dior. Nicole
Kidman wears a dress from his collection at the Oscar awards ceremony.
The Musée Christian Dior opens in the Villa Les Rhumbs in Granville.

1998
Dior Joaillerie is founded, with Victoire de Castellane as creative director.

1999
The *J'Adore* perfume is launched.

2000
Hedi Slimane becomes creative director of Christian Dior Monsieur
and changes its name to Dior Homme.

2005
The Musée Christian Dior in Granville celebrates the centenary
of the designer's birth with *Christian Dior homme du siècle*, an exhibition
tracing his life.

2007
Kris Van Assche succeeds Hedi Slimane as creative director at Dior Homme.
To celebrate its sixtieth anniversary, the House of Dior stages the
Fall-Winter Haute Couture show, followed by a ball, at the Orangerie
of the Château de Versailles.

2008
The *Christian Dior and Chinese Artists* exhibition at the Ullens Center
for Contemporary Art (UCCA) in Beijing features twenty-five works
by contemporary artists alongside eighty Haute Couture dresses.

2011
John Galliano leaves Dior and is replaced by assistant designer Bill Gaytten.
The *Inspiration Dior* exhibition featuring the couture house's iconic designs
and a selection of artworks opens at the Pushkin Museum in Moscow.
On October 15 and 16, the public is invited to discover the behind-the-scenes
craftsmanship at 30 Avenue Montaigne during the House of Dior open
days (*Journées Particulières*) initiated by the LVMH group.

2012
On April 9, Raf Simons is appointed creative director of women's wear.
He presents his first Haute Couture collection in July.

2013
The *Journées Particulières* event is held for the second time, in June.
The *Esprit Dior* exhibition opens in September at the Museum of Contemporary
Art (MOCA) in Shanghai. It features over a hundred pieces from 1947 to 2013,
alongside a selection of contemporary artworks.
In December, the *Miss Dior* exhibition at the Grand Palais in Paris presents
works by fifteen female artists from around the world, freely inspired
by the *Miss Dior* perfume.

2014
Peter Philips becomes creative director of makeup.

2015
Raf Simons leaves Dior in October. He is replaced by Serge Ruffieux and Lucie
Meier.

2016
In July, Maria Grazia Chiuri becomes Dior's first female creative director.
She launches her debut ready-to-wear collection in September.

2017
Maria Grazia Chiuri presents her debut Haute Couture collection in January.
A masked ball is held after the show, in the sculpture garden of the Musée Rodin.
Three major exhibitions celebrate the seventieth anniversary of the House of
Dior: *Christian Dior et Granville, aux sources de la légende* (Musée Christian
Dior, Granville), *The House of Dior, Seventy Years of Haute Couture* (National
Gallery of Victoria, Melbourne) and *Christian Dior, Designer of Dreams* (Musée
des Arts Décoratifs, Paris).

This book was published in conjunction with the exhibition *Christian Dior: Designer of Dreams*, at the Musée des Art Décoratifs, Paris, July 5, 2017 to January 7, 2018.

The exhibition was organized by Les Arts Décoratifs, with the support of the house of Christian Dior.

We would like to thank Swarovski for its generous patronage.

LES ARTS DÉCORATIFS

President
Pierre-Alexis Dumas

Managing Director
David Caméo

Director of the Museums
Olivier Gabet

Director of Communication
Pascale de Seze

EXHIBITION

Curators
Olivier Gabet
Director of the Musées des Arts Décoratifs

Florence Müller
Curator of Textile Arts and Fashion, Avenir Foundation, Denver Art Museum

With the assistance of
Anna Frera
Exhibition Assistant

Éric Pujalet-Plaà
Assistant Curator at the Musée des Arts Décoratifs, Fashion and Textile

Head of Exhibitions Department
Jérôme Recours

Assisted by
Anaïs David
Stéphane Perl
deputies

Sarah Ben Hamida
Julia Gerbault
Malina Hervieu
Kevin Lebouvier
project managers

Exhibition design
Nathalie Crinière, Anne Lebas, Hélène Lecarpentier

Signage
Anamorphée

CATALOG

Scientific coordinator
Florence Müller

Editorial coordination and production
Publishing Department of Les Arts Décoratifs

Translation from French
Lisa Davidson, Sally Laruelle

Copyediting
Joe Nankivell
Karolina Gallufo, mot.tiff inside

Iconography
Lola Carsault
Cécile Niesseron

Art direction
Fabien Baron, Baron & Baron

Photographs
Nicholas Alan Cope

Production of photographs
Kitten

Photographic alterations
Digital Giant

Photoengraving
Les artisans du Regard

We would like to extend our thanks to

Bernard Arnault, Chairman and Chief Executive Officer of LVMH / Moët Hennessy-Louis Vuitton,
Sidney Toledano, President and CEO of Christian Dior Couture,
Claude Martinez, President and CEO of Christian Dior Parfums

At Christian Dior Couture, we would like to thank
Olivier Bialobos, Senior Vice President Global Communications
Gérald Chevalier, International Events Director
Jérôme Gautier, Head of Publishing
Soizic Pfaff, Dior Heritage Director
Hélène Starkman, Cultural Projects Coordinator
Daphné Catroux, Exhibition Coordinator
Perrine Scherrer, Iconographer

As well as Mathilde Favier, Jérôme Hanover, Alix d'Hautefeuille, Philippe Le Moult, Morgane Paulissen, Stéphanie Pélian, Hélène Poirier, Julie Voisin, and at Dior Héritage Solène Auréal, Camille Bidouze, Séverine Breton, Amélie Bossard, Sylvain Carré, Cécile Chamouard-Aykanat, Justine Lasgi, Alexander Lopez, Joana Tosta, Jennifer Walheim.

At Christian Dior Parfums, we would like to thank
Jérôme Pulis, International Communication Director
Frédéric Bourdelier, Brand Culture & Heritage
Vincent Leret, Patrimony Project Manager and Responsible for the Collection
Sandrine Damay-Bleu, Patrimony Project Manager

At Swarovski, we would like to thank Nadja Swarovski

We would also like to express our gratitude to the many institutions and individuals who agreed to loan works for the duration of this exhibition, a major factor in its broad scope:

Antwerp
Dries Van Noten
Dries Van Noten, Patrick Scallon, Thomas Klein

Figueres
Gala-Salvador Dalí Foundation
Montse Aguer, Laura Bartolomé

Granville
Musée Christian Dior
Brigitte Richart, Barbara Jeauffroy-Mairet, Gwenola Fouilleul

Grasse
Musée international de la Parfumerie
Olivier Quiquempois, Grégory Coudere, Cindy Levinspuhl

London
Museum of London
Sharon Ament, Flora Fyles, Stephanie Kirkness, Melina Plottu
Victoria and Albert Museum
Tristram Hunt, Claire Wilcox, Liz Wilkinson
Thom Browne
Thom Browne, Matthew Foley, Kelly Connor
Alexander McQueen
Marc Quinn Studio, courtesy galerie Thaddaeus Ropac, Paris
Damian Simpson, Kristina Tencic
Condé Nast UK – Vogue UK
Carole Dumoulin, Brett Croft

Los Angeles
Sterling Ruby, courtesy galerie Gagosian, Paris
Maria Martinelli

New York
The Richard Avedon Foundation
Katrina Dumas
Museum of Modern Art
Glenn D. Lowry, Ann Temkin, Lily Goldberg
The Metropolitan Museum of Art
Thomas Campbell, Andrew Bolton, Bethany Matia, Cassandra Gero
Condé Nast US – Vogue US
Becky Mickel

Paris
Christian Dior Parfums
Collection Lucile Audouy
Madame Danièle Louis, private collection
Alexandre Percy, private collection
Madame Michèle Thourenin, private collection
Dior Héritage
Fondation Pierre Bergé – Yves Saint Laurent
Pierre Bergé, Aurélie Samuel, Valérie Mulattieri, Leslie Veyrat, Tiphanie Van Duyse
Fondation Giacometti
Catherine Grenier, Alban Chaine
Galerie 1900-2000
Marcel Fleiss, Rodica Sibleyras
Malingue Gallery
Daniel Malingue, Perrine Le Blan

Galerie-musée Baccarat
Thaddaeus-Ropac Gallery
Katrina Dumas
Jean Paul Gaultier
Jean Paul Gaultier, Jelka Music, Morgane Raterron
Givenchy
Guillemette Duzan, Lauriane Mazollier
Louis Vuitton
Marie Wurry, Bleue-Marine Massard
Musée d'Orsay and Musée de l'Orangerie
Laurence des Cars, Claire Bernardi, Sylphide de Daranyi, Élise Dubreuil
Musée du Louvre
Jean-Luc Martinez, Sébastien Allard, Vincent Rondot, Marc Etienne,
Olivier Laville, Mélanie Dézier
Musée du Quai Branly – Jacques Chirac
Stéphane Martin, Yves Le Fur, Hélène Joubert, Laurence Dubaut
Musée national d'Art moderne – Centre Georges Pompidou
Bernard Blistène, Brigitte Léal, Rania Moussa Morin
Musée Picasso
Laurent Le Bon
Palais Galliera
Olivier Saillard, Véronique Belloir
Petit Palais, musée des Beaux-Arts de la Ville de Paris
Christophe Leribault, Isabelle Collet
Rochas
Philippe Bénacin, Nathalie Prevoteau, Aurélie Garcia
Condé Nast France – Vogue Paris
Vanessa Bernard, Laure Fournis

San Francisco
De Young, Fine Arts Museum of San Francisco
Max Hollein, Jill d'Alessandro, Anne Getts, Julian Drake, Christina Stone
Versailles
Musée national des Châteaux de Versailles et de Trianon
Catherine Pégard, Laurent Salomé, Fréderic Lacaille

We are very grateful to the many photographers who contributed their
visions of Dior's designs to the exhibition:
Patrick Demarchelier (Thomas Bonnouvrier)
Tierney Gearon (Khai Le)
Jean-Paul Goude (Virginie Laguens)
Frank Horvat (Léna Futel)
International Center of Photography (Claartje van Dijk, James Kopp)
Dominique Issermann
William Klein (Pierre-Louis Denis)
Nick Knight (Charlotte Knight, Carrie Scott, Fiona Gourlay)
David LaChapelle (Ghretta Hynd)
Brigitte Lacombe (Janet Johnson)
Annie Leibovitz (Leon Wong)
Peter Lindbergh (Benjamin Lindbergh)
Galerie Louise Alexander (Frederic Arnal)
Serge Lutens
Steven Meisel (Michael Van Horne)
Sarah Moon (Guillaume Fabiani)
Norman Parkinson Archive (Aris Kourkoumelis)
Michal Pudelka (Sarah Mahini)
Paolo Roversi (Silvia Sini, Filippo Roversi)
Indivision Sieff (Barbara Rix-Sieff, Aude Raimbault Amiot)
Mario Sorrenti (Gregory Spencer)
Emma Summerton
Juergen Teller (Rozi Rexhepi, Sally Waterman, Josselin Merazguia)
Mario Testino
Willy Vanderperre
Tim Walker (Alex Pasley-Tyler)
Bruce Weber (Nathaniel Kilcer)

The entire fashion and textile collection at the Musée des Arts Décoratifs
is supported by the DEFI.

We are grateful to all those who contributed to the exhibition and its
companion book:

Sophie Annoepel-Cabrignac, Giovanna Bertazzoni, Christine Besson, Andrea
Boscardin, Emmanuelle Boucher, Rachel Boyle, Laura Caruso, Carles Cervós
Pujol, Hélène Chancerelle, Lorraine Châteaux, Camille Constanty, Genève
Cotté, Sylphide de Daranyi, Anne-Gaëlle Dufour, Anne-Gaëlle Duriez,
Patrizia Facci, François Fabre, Katherine Field, Arne Glimcher, Jean-Pierre
Grosselin, Dominique Hascoet-Brunet, Jean-Marc Heftler-Louiche, Lori Iliff,
Zoé Imbert, Greg McKay, Sandra de Laszlo, Pascale Leautay, Isaure Lecœur,
Mathilde Lecorre, Sylvia Lorant, Sophie Mathieu, Gilles Neau, Georgiana
Necualescu, Ghislaine Noël, Maryse Pagerie, Laurent Papillault des
Charbonneries, Francesco Pastore, Jean-Louis Quémar, Daniel Regard,
Anne Robbins, Emilie Ryan, Béatrice Saalburg, Tony Sandro,
Dominique Sauvegrain, Marie-Christine de Sayn-Wittgenstein, Damian
Simpson, Arlette Souhami, Camille Spear-Gabel, Laurent Této, Marjan Tharin,
Lila Thibault, Jean Tholance, Aurore Tomasi, Dominique de Urresti de la Sota
and Sacha Vichnevski.

At Baron & Baron, we would like to thank Fabien Baron, as well as Lisa Atkin,
Adélaïde François-Poncet, Fatti Laleh, Tomie Peaslee, Boqin Peng, Margot
Populaire, Jordan Quimby, Tyler Stevens and Ailsa Wong.

At Walterschupfer, we would like to thank Férid Ouertani.

At Kitten, we would like to thank Arnaud and Anaïs.

We also extend our thanks to Will Bunce, Sylvain Cabouat, Bertrand
D'Amiens, Gaëtan Donnars, Jacques Evomo, Laurent Harbulot,
Kim Harding and Clément Mahjoub for their assistance during the photo
shoots with Nick Alan Cope.

Finally, at the Musée des Arts Décoratifs, we extend our warmest thanks
to all those who provided their unwavering support for this project:

Quitterie de Poncins, Secretary General
Sponsorship Department, particularly Juliette Sirinelli
Communications Department, particularly Isabelle Mendoza, Marie-Laure
Moreau and Fabien Escalona
Museum Administration, particularly Sophie Malville and Alexandra Popescu
Conservation department, particularly Hélène Andrieux, Véronique Ayroles,
Réjane Bargiel, Monique Blanc, Dominique Forest, Anne Forray-Carlier,
Audrey Gay-Mazuel, Pamela Golbin, Véronique de La Hougue, Romain Lebel,
Sophie Motsch, Marion Neveu, Jean-Luc Olivié, Marie-Hélène Poix,
Évelyne Possémé, Béatrice Quette and Julie Ruffet-Troussard
Publications and images, particularly Carol Chabert and Pauline Juppin
Preventive conservation and management, particularly Joséphine Pellas
and Myriam Teissier
Library and documentary resources, particularly Élise Barzun,
Emmanuelle Beuvin and Laure Haberschill
Visitor services, particularly Sébastien Quéquet

Creative direction & Design :
Fabien Baron, Baron & Baron

Cover:
Christian Dior, *Bar* suit, Spring-Summer 1947 Haute Couture collection.
John Galliano for Christian Dior, Spring-Summer 2000 Haute Couture collection.
Maria Grazia Chiuri for Christian Dior, *New Junon* dress, Spring-Summer 2017
Haute Couture collection.

First published in the United Kingdom in 2017 by Thames & Hudson Ltd.
181A High Holborn, London WC1V 7QX
www.thamesandhudson.com

First published in the United States of America in 2018 by Thames & Hudson Inc.,
500 Fifth Avenue, New York, New York 10110
www.thamesandhudsonusa.com

Reprinted 2017, 2018

Original edition © Les Arts Décoratifs, Paris 2017

British Library Cataloguing-in-Publication Data
A catalogue record for this book is available from the British Library

Library of Congress Control Number: 2017941614

ISBN 978-0-500-02154-5

Printed and bound in Italy